# Better Neighbors

# Better Neighbors

## *Toward a Renewal of Economic Integration in Latin America*

Chad P. Bown, Daniel Lederman,
Samuel Pienknagura, and
Raymond Robertson

 **WORLD BANK GROUP**

# Contents

**Boxes**

**Figures**

# Foreword

In recent years, Latin America and the Caribbean (LAC) slipped off the high growth path of the 2000s, a boom period that brought with it large reductions in poverty and inequality. Not surprisingly, regional leaders are now putting a high premium on gaining the footing necessary for stable and more sustainable growth and for the preservation of the significant social gains of the recent past.

Few in LAC doubt that a deeper and more robust integration into international markets is crucial for lifting the region's long-term growth rate going forward. Paradoxically, just as citizens and policy makers in the region appear ready to embrace outwardly oriented growth strategies, the world is not helping. The current sluggishness of global trade may be prolonged, and antiglobalization attitudes have been stiffening in advanced economies. Still, regional integration has moved to the forefront of the policy debate in LAC, as it seems to offer a viable intermediate solution.

Whether such a response will deliver the expected growth dividends is not a given. It will depend on the underlying vision of regional integration and the extent and quality of complementary domestic policies and reforms. The chances of success will certainly improve if LAC avoids the key mistake of "old regionalism," namely, pursuing inward-looking regional integration at the expense of, or as a substitute for, global integration. There is growing consensus that such an approach typically leads to uncompetitive and inefficient firms. Sustained efforts will be needed to push toward an intelligent renewal of "open regionalism" (OR), whereby an improved and more integrated region decidedly promotes deeper integration with the world, and vice versa. This is the core message of *Better Neighbors: Toward a Renewal of Economic Integration in Latin America*, the latest regional flagship report of the World Bank's Chief Economist Office for Latin America and the Caribbean.

It is important to acknowledge that the implementation of the open regionalism agenda outlined in this report could be complex, in part due to the comprehensive nature of the proposal. Indeed, the proposed renewal of open regionalism goes beyond tariff liberalization and regional preferences, touching areas as diverse as infrastructure, labor mobility, and the harmonization of regulatory standards. Implementing these efforts can require a large degree of technical and political coordination among countries within the region to be successful. Issues related to migration policy, which constitute an important pillar of the proposal, are often met with resistance by the general public, for instance. Nevertheless, we are delighted that the team has brought these ambitious issues to the forefront. This will likely spark a fruitful regional policy debate at a time when sweeping and purposeful reforms seem unavoidable if we are to keep the region and its people moving forward.

Augusto de la Torre, Chief Economist
Jorge Familiar, Vice President
Latin America and the Caribbean Region
The World Bank Group

# Acknowledgments

This report was prepared by a team led by Chad P. Bown, Daniel Lederman, Samuel Pienknagura, and Raymond Robertson. Important additional contributions were made by Erhan Artuc, Simone Bertoli, Emily Blanchard, Juan José Bravo, Tatiana Didier, Enrique Fanta, Michael Ferrantino, Rebecca Freeman, Constantino Hevia, Russell Hillberry, Ruth Llovet Montanes, Anna Maria Mayda, Caglar Ozden, Gabriela Schmidt, Sergio Schmukler, Luis Servén, and Patricia Tovar. Federico Bennett, Rebecca Freeman, and Justin Lesniak provided outstanding research assistance. The work was conducted under the general guidance of Augusto de la Torre, Chief Economist for the Latin America and Caribbean Region of the World Bank.

The team was fortunate to receive superb advice and guidance from the following peer reviewers: Caroline Freund, Paolo Giordano, Mauricio Mesquita Moreira, Marcelo Olarreaga, Jose Guilherme Reis, and Pablo Sanguinetti. We are also grateful for valuable comments and insights received from Anabel González, David Michael Gould, Jesko Hentschel, Dante Mossi, Ha Nguyen, José Daniel Reyes, Sebastián Sáez, Peter Siegenthaler, Joana Silva, and participants at the authors' workshop that took place on October 27–28, 2015. While we benefited and are grateful for the guidance and comments received, the core team is responsible for all remaining errors, omissions, and interpretations.

Book design, editing, and production were coordinated by Aziz Gökdemir, Susan Graham, and Mark Ingebretsen, under the supervision of Patricia Katayama. We are extremely grateful for their help. We also appreciate the assistance provided by Marcela Sanchez-Bender and Alejandra Viveros on the report's publication and dissemination activities. Finally, we thank Ruth Delgado Flynn and Jacqueline Larrabure for unfailing administrative support.

# Abbreviations

| | |
|---|---|
| APEC | Asia-Pacific Economic Cooperation |
| BEC | Broad Economic Categories of the UN Statistical Division |
| BIS | Bank for International Settlements |
| BIT | bilateral investment treaty |
| CAFTA–DR | Dominican Republic–Central America Free Trade Agreement |
| CGE | computable general equilibrium |
| CIRP | covered interest rate parity |
| CMI | capital market integration |
| CPIS | Coordinated Portfolio Investment Survey (IMF) |
| DOTS | Direction of Trade Statistics (IMF) |
| DVA | domestic value added |
| EAP | East Asia and Pacific region |
| ECA | Europe and Central Asia region |
| ECLAC | Economic Commission for Latin America and the Caribbean |
| EFTA | European Free Trade Association |
| EU | European Union |
| EU15+ | European Union 15 extended |
| FDI | foreign direct investment |
| FE | fixed effects |
| FTA | free trade agreement |
| GATT | General Agreement on Tariffs and Trade |
| GSTP | Global System of Trade Preferences |
| GVC | global value chain |
| ICT | information and communication technology |
| IDB | Inter-American Development Bank |
| IIDE | Institute for International and Development Economics |
| IIP | international investment positions |
| IMF | International Monetary Fund |

| | |
|---|---|
| IRS | increasing returns to scale |
| IS | import substitution |
| LAC | Latin America and the Caribbean region |
| LSCI | Liner Shipping Connectivity Index |
| M&A | mergers and acquisitions |
| MENA | Middle East and North Africa region |
| MFN | most favored nation |
| MNC | multinational corporation |
| MPT | modern portfolio theory |
| NAFTA | North American Free Trade Agreement |
| NBER | National Bureau of Economic Research |
| OECD | Organisation for Economic Co-operation and Development |
| OLS | ordinary least squares |
| OR | open regionalism |
| PIIE | Peterson Institute for International Economics |
| PPML | Poisson–Pseudo Maximum Likelihood |
| PPP | purchasing power parity |
| PTA | preferential trade agreement |
| R&D | research and development |
| RCA | revealed comparative advantage |
| RoOs | rules of origin |
| RTAs | regional trade agreements |
| SAR | South Asia region |
| SEDLAC | Socio-Economic Dataset for Latin America and the Caribbean |
| SITC | Standard International Trade Classification |
| SMEs | small and medium enterprises |
| SOE | state-owned enterprise |
| SSA | Sub-Saharan Africa region |
| TFP | total factor productivity |
| TPP | Trans-Pacific Partnership |
| TSD | trade-in-services data |
| TTB | temporary trade barrier |
| UN COMTRADE | UN Commodity Trade Statistics database |
| UNCTAD | United Nations Conference on Trade and Development |
| UNIDO | United Nations Industrial Development Organization |
| USITC | U.S. International Trade Commission |
| WTO | World Trade Organization |

# Introduction and Summary of Results

In a clear break from its past, Latin America and the Caribbean (LAC), particularly South America, experienced a growth spurt with equity during the first decade of the 21st century.[1] In fact, LAC's gross domestic product (GDP) growth rate over the past decade stood at about 4 percent, well above the region's historic average of 2 percent. Moreover, the incomes of the poorest households in many countries in the region grew at a faster pace than those of high-income households. Unfortunately, the latest period of prosperity seems to have waned; and, with a few exceptions in Central America and the Caribbean, countries in the region confront once more a reality of low growth.

As the good times have faded, there is now a clear understanding that such impressive performance was the result of a demand boom fueled by an increase in the price of LAC's exports relative to the price of the region's imports (a terms-of-trade improvement) (de la Torre, Filippini, and Ize 2016). Moreover, the slowdown has brought back fears of economic instability. To be sure, there is no evidence to date suggesting that LAC is returning to the volatile days of the 1980s, partly because of improvements in its macrofinancial framework. Yet it is undeniable that

such fears exist, especially in the context of expected increases in global interest rates. Against this backdrop, policy makers in LAC are now in search of sources of long-term growth and stability.

One policy area that has moved back to center stage is regional integration. Indeed, since at least the 1960s, LAC has experimented with various forms of regional integration with the hope that fostering regional economic ties can yield the type of economic success that the region has long sought. The current push toward regional integration has been influenced by the success of the East Asia and Pacific region (EAP), where intraregional trade, exports to the rest of the world, and incomes have risen together as the region continues to catch up to the income levels of the United States (de la Torre, Lederman, and Pienknagura 2015). Whether this coincidence of trade and growth outcomes is the result of regional commercial or other policies—or whether regional growth itself caused the rise of intraregional trade and global exports—remains an open question. Still, EAP continues to be a source of inspiration for Latin Americans.

Hence, underlying the push in favor of deeper integration at the regional level is the belief that part of LAC's low growth problem is its low level of intraregional economic integration. In fact, LAC has levels of regional integration that pale in comparison to those of the European Union (EU), EAP, and Eastern Europe and Central Asia (ECA). Taken at face value, this suggests that pursuing formal policy arrangements with the potential of strengthening economic links within the region might boost growth in LAC.

The goal of leveraging formal trade arrangements to accelerate growth is evident in many of the trade agreements that are in place in the region. For example, an objective of the Pacific Alliance—the 2012 integration agreement between Chile, Colombia, Mexico, and Peru—is "driving further growth, development, and competitiveness of the economies of its members."[2] Similarly, the Dominican Republic–Central America Free Trade Agreement (CAFTA-DR) lists the creation of "new opportunities for economic and social development" and "new employment opportunities and improved working conditions and living standards in their respective territories" as some of its resolutions.[3] And, although not explicitly stated in the agreement, many view Mercosur—the customs union comprising Argentina, Brazil, Paraguay, Uruguay, and República Bolivariana de Venezuela—as a useful vehicle to achieve higher growth for the countries in the Southern cone (Fanelli 2007).

The objective of taking advantage of regional integration to boost growth is not new to LAC. In fact, the region has explored several models of integration to achieve this goal—from the "old" regionalism that prevailed until the late 1980s, which emphasized the role of regional integration and import substitution as integral parts of industrialization strategies, to the "new" regionalism that emerged amid the wave of reforms that the region implemented in the 1990s (see IDB 2002). Importantly, the latter form of regional integration views regionalism as a stepping-stone toward the goal of global integration, hence earning the label of "open regionalism" (hereafter OR).[4]

This report revisits the concept of OR and presents evidence supporting the idea that a revitalized OR strategy can contribute to growth with stability by exploiting the complementarities between regional and global economic integration. It proposes a five-pronged strategy, including (i) reducing external most-favored-nation (MFN) tariffs; (ii) deepening economic integration between South America and Central and North America; (iii) harmonizing rules and procedures governing the exchange of goods, services, and factors of production; (iv) stepping up efforts to reduce LAC's high trade costs; and (v) integrating labor and capital markets in the Americas. This agenda is nothing short of a wholesale renewal of the notion of OR.

Since the 1990s, OR in LAC focused primarily on preferential trade agreements and their relationship with trade policies affecting trade with extraregional partners (Bergsten 1997). The ultimate goal of the renewal of the OR strategy is to enhance the region's competitiveness with respect to the rest of the world, which depends on smart (yet complex) policies that enhance intraregional economic integration while also lowering barriers to international trade with the rest of the world. Because the magnitude of bilateral trade and migration flows is dependent on the geographic distance between economic partners, a key analytical challenge is to assess the potential of region-wide efficiency gains that can be attained through regional integration efforts (beyond the pull of geography), combined with domestic structural reforms and further liberalization of trade with the rest of the world. The preponderance of the evidence compiled for this study suggests that how the Americas become integrated can affect the region's long-term growth prospects and stability, precisely because the forces of geography imply that pro-growth global integration cannot be achieved without strengthening our own neighborhood. A key implication is that the renewal of OR embraces domestic structural reforms that can raise the economic efficiency of the Americas as whole.

To be clear, the analysis presented in the report does not quantify the impact that OR has had on LAC economies in the past. Nor does it quantify the potential gains of the proposed renewal of the OR strategy. Rather, it relies on the economics literature to identify accepted channels through which different forms of international economic integration can stimulate growth and stability, which in turn can be quantified as an indirect way of assessing the priorities for the renewal of OR in the Americas. The report draws upon two prominent strands of economic theory. The first is the idea that the gains from trade depend on differences between countries. In these "neoclassical" models, these differences are usually modeled as arising either from factor supplies (for example, being "labor abundant" or "capital abundant") or from technology. The second is the idea that trade facilitates learning, either through the experience of exporting or from the exposure to new products and ideas that are embodied in imports. Although these are not the only theories that explain trade and the gains from trade, these are two that have perhaps the longest and most established history in international economics.[5] The intuition from these models can, in certain ways, also apply to factor market integration.

To keep the discussion focused, the report leaves aside two important aspects of regional integration. First, it does not discuss the effects of economic integration on inequality and poverty, a subject that has been widely discussed in the existing literature.[6] The potential effects of international integration on inequality and poverty are important to consider but go beyond the scope of this report. For now, it suffices to say that there is evidence that global integration in LAC has probably helped reduce inequality. Following the extensive trade liberalization of the 1990s, wage inequality eventually fell throughout Latin America (Lopez Calva and Lustig 2010; Silva and Messina, forthcoming). Falling inequality could be linked to trade, as predicted by neoclassical trade theory (Robertson 2004). Perhaps more important, concerns about poverty and inequality are generally considered to be less effectively addressed through trade policies than through alternatives, such as expanding the coverage of public education, improving

the quality of education in poor neighborhoods, or conditional cash transfers, among other policies that would not hamper growth and economic efficiency. The second limitation of this study is that it does not discuss noneconomic objectives and consequences of regional integration.[7]

The rest of this introduction briefly discusses some of the key findings of the report. It first discusses the importance of geography in shaping both economic performance and integration patterns around the world. Having discussed the role of geography, the overview analyzes observed regional integration patterns. Then it assesses the benefits of integration through two separate theories—one that argues that potential efficiency gains depend on how much countries can complement each other, and another one that argues that benefits depend on how much countries can learn from each other. With this evidence in hand, the introduction lays out the five-pronged strategy for renewing OR in the Americas. In discussing each area of the strategy, the introduction presents the current state of policies in the region as well as the challenges that lie ahead.

## Even in the age of globalization, geography matters for trade, factor flows, and economic performance

In recent decades the world has experienced significant technological and economic changes that have transformed international economic relations. These changes have led many to claim that "distance is dead" or that "the world is flat."[8] In short, one expects that in a "flat world" a country's economic performance should not be affected by its geographic location. The Internet and improvements in transportation have certainly affected trade patterns and facilitated new trade relationships

As significant as these changes are, however, the effect of distance does not seem to have disappeared. As discussed in chapters 1 and 2, geographic forces are also important drivers of economic integration. That is, even in the absence of policies favoring regional integration, proximity facilitates economic integration. This bias is the by-product of costs associated with the movement of goods, people, and, to a lesser extent, capital across borders. The literature has found that such costs increase with distance.

The incidence of geography on trade and factor flows (capital and labor) has important implications for the patterns of regional integration observed across regions. Countries that are geographically closer to their regional partners are expected to have higher levels of regional integration compared to those that are more distant.

Chapter 1 shows that economic performance around the globe is also geographically clustered. In particular, a country's economic performance in both the long run and the short run is highly correlated with that of its neighbors. The likelihood that two countries will simultaneously experience prolonged episodes of either high growth or low growth falls with geographic distance. Similarly, the probability of two countries going through the same phase of a business cycle decreases with geographic distance. Moreover, the geographic forces that shape economic performance haven't diminished over time. On the contrary, they have increased. Regional forces affecting a country's GDP growth have gained prominence in the recent past, to the point that, for the average country in the world, they have surpassed country-specific and global factors as key determinants of macroeconomic fluctuations.

Regional forces have become increasingly important over time for Latin American countries as well. By the 1995–2011 period they were as important as country-specific factors. To be sure, the lion's share of this increase is due to the rising prominence of forces that similarly affect many countries in the region but are linked to developments in other corners of the world. This finding is likely explained by China's rise in the global economy and the impact it has had across LAC (see de la Torre et al. 2015).

There are at least two hypotheses for the geographic clustering of economic performance. One is that it is a consequence of trade and the integration of capital and labor markets, which themselves are geographically clustered (see Calderón, Chong, and Stein 2007). Another is that endowments, institutions, and other determinants of economic performance are geographically clustered.

Regardless of the explanation, the geographic clustering of economic performance and the way it has evolved over time affect the gains from integration predicted by neoclassical models of trade based on endowment or technological differences and by models of learning through trade. Similarly, the forces of geography are expected to affect the observed levels of regional integration. The rest of this chapter analyzes in more detail these two points. The analysis will then guide the policy discussion that lays the ground for the proposed renewal of OR.

## Regional trade in LAC and in the Americas: International comparison and determinants

Regional trade flows are an integral part of international trade flows. As chapter 2 shows, approximately half of total trade flows occur between regional partners. There are, however, significant differences in the incidence of intraregional trade flows in total flows across regions. At one extreme stand EU15+ (European Union 15 extended) and EAP, regions where intraregional exports accounted for 60 and 50 percent of total trade in 2014, respectively. At the other extreme stand regions such as South Asia (SAR), Sub-Saharan Africa (SSA), and the Middle East and North Africa (MENA), where intraregional exports accounted for a meager 10 to 15 percent of total trade in 2014.

As mentioned above, the remarkable performance of EAP in terms of regional trade integration has caught the attention of other regions, including LAC. However, replicating EAP's experience has proven a difficult challenge for LAC. The region has pursued regional integration efforts through formal trade integration agreements since the 1960s, efforts that have only intensified since the mid-1990s. Indeed, prior to the year 2000 the average country in LAC held a preferential trade agreement with about 4 regional partners; by 2013 this number rose to close to 10. Despite these efforts, the incidence of intraregional exports in LAC's total exports has remained stable at about 20 percent.

The discussion above raises a question: Why is the region not more integrated? Or, more precisely, what are the constraints to boosting regional trade that face policy makers in LAC? To answer these questions, the rest of this section explores a potential explanation that follows the insights of the international trade literature pointing to economic size and trade frictions associated with geographic distance as gravitational forces shaping trade flows.

## Size and geographic distance matter for trade flows

Understanding the determinants of international trade patterns is a research goal that dates back to the early 1800s. One empirical model that appears to fit the trade data particularly well is the so-called gravity model of trade.[9] Its central tenet is that trade flows should be proportional to the GDP of trading partners and inversely proportional to their geographic distance. The positive relationship between bilateral trade flows and the GDP of trading partners captures the idea that large, wealthy countries demand and supply more goods from and to the rest of the world relative to smaller countries, yielding high levels of trade between them.[10] The inverse relationship between trade and distance captures the idea that trade implies moving goods, and that the cost of moving goods is expected to increase with distance.[11] Hence, the prices charged by more distant producers are expected to be higher than those of producers nearby, resulting in lower demand for exports (varieties) from more distant countries. The effects of distance, therefore, may prevent countries from realizing the benefits of trade predicted by neoclassical models.

The relationship predicted by the gravity model has important implications for understanding the regional integration patterns discussed above. First of all, the negative relationship between trade flows and distance predicted by the gravity model and observed in the data implies that, all other things equal, trade flows between nearby partners are expected to be higher than between faraway partners. In other words, even if trade policy around the world were nondiscriminatory, the gravity model predicts that trade should be largely regional because of trade costs that vary systematically with geographic distance.

Another important implication of the gravity model is that differences in the size and distance between countries within regions can play an important role in explaining differences in the incidence of regional trade across regions. In particular, regions comprising countries with large GDP values and with short distances between them are expected to exhibit higher regional trade flows as a share of total trade than others, all else equal.

The insights of the gravity model suggest that, in order to carefully assess LAC's standing in terms of regional integration and to understand the factors underpinning it, one should take into account the impact of geography and size on trade flows. The analysis presented in chapter 2 follows this approach and compares LAC's standing relative to other regions in terms of intraregional trade, after stripping away the impact of these variables.[12]

The results in chapter 2 show that the average pair of countries in LAC, which originally ranked poorly in terms of the incidence of regional trade, has intraregional trade flows that are in line with or exceed what is predicted by gravity variables. In contrast, EAP, a region that ranked second in the original comparison of intraregional trade flows, presents levels of intraregional trade that are statistically lower than those predicted by gravity variables.

Importantly, chapter 2 also highlights that the conclusions of the gravity benchmarking are sensitive to the definition of region because the inclusion or exclusion of countries can change the size and distance of the average pair of countries in the region. This will, in turn, affect intraregional trade patterns because of the role of geography and size in shaping trade flows. For instance, an assessment of integration in the Americas (as opposed to LAC alone) provides substantially different conclusions—intra-Americas trade is statistically larger compared to what gravity variables would predict, suggesting that the inclusion of the United States and Canada boosts trade in the Americas beyond what would be predicted by their economic size and distance to LAC countries.

The results from chapter 2 show that, if one of their objectives is to increase intra-LAC or intra-Americas trade flows, Latin American policy makers have two options. Countries in the region could grow at a rate higher than that of the average country in the world, or they could reduce trade frictions associated with policies and distance. But clearly growth is a policy goal in its own right, and arguably a more important one than regional integration per se. Thus, instead of focusing on policy actions that have the sole objective of boosting regional integration, the rest of this introduction discusses integration strategies that can help LAC achieve high and stable growth.

## The conceptual arguments for a renewal of open regionalism

This study assesses the benefits of different integration strategies through the lens of two prominent strands of economic theory. The first is inspired in neoclassical models, which suggest that the gains from trade and economic integration more broadly crucially depend on how different economies are in terms of their technologies and their endowments. The gains are expected to be larger when partners are more different. Likewise, the gains in terms of stability are also expected to be larger when trade occurs between dissimilar countries because they are exposed to different types of shocks.

The second strand of theory highlights the role of economic integration as a conduit for technological diffusion and learning. According to these theories, countries could, for example, learn from the technological content embodied in the goods they import. This knowledge content depends on the innovation efforts of a country's partners and those of their partner's partners (Coe and Helpman 1995; Lumenga-Neso, Olarreaga, and Schiff 2005). Similarly, economic integration may allow firms in one country to learn about the goods, production processes, and business relationships in third markets of the firms with which they interact in another country. This, in turn, may facilitate productivity improvements and entry and survival in third markets (Morales, Sheu, and Zhaler 2014; Chaney 2011). Importantly, according to these theories the characteristics of a country's partners matter for the benefits stemming from learning. The gains are expected to be larger when a country's partners are knowledge hubs (invest in research and development [R&D]) or when they are open (have more business connections and trade with knowledge hubs)

What do these two strands of the theory imply for the attractiveness of different economic integration strategies for LAC countries? From the point of view of neoclassical models, countries in the region would benefit the most by seeking trading partners that are not near them. In particular, chapter 2 shows that, in all regions, integration with the rest of the world appears to provide larger potential efficiency gains compared to regional integration. In LAC, however, the average pair of countries appears to be much more similar compared to the average pair of countries in developing regions, such as EAP or ECA.

Even so, chapter 2 shows that there are still important differences among LAC countries that could lead to neoclassical-style gains from trade. It shows that there is a positive relationship between the similarity of the revealed comparative advantages (RCAs) of a given pair of countries and that pair's similarity in terms of economic size.

Likewise, there are marked differences in terms of patterns of RCA between countries in South America and those in Central and North America. In fact, the average efficiency gains that LAC countries could obtain from trade with regional partners outside their subregion are comparable to those that could be attained from trade with partners elsewhere in the world. These findings suggest that deeper integration between small and large countries in LAC and between South America and Central and North America could yield efficiency gains if the neoclassical theories are valid.

In addition to limiting the efficiency gains predicted by neoclassical trade models, the similar trade structures observed between LAC countries, especially those that are nearby, also limit the prospects for regional integration to deliver stability. LAC economies are typically exposed to similar shocks (for example, terms-of-trade shocks), thus limiting the scope for regional integration to diversify country-specific risks. This point is supported by chapter 2, which shows that the volatility of LAC's exports would rise if the weight of regional partners on a country's export basket increases. This is due to the volatile and correlated import demands observed in LAC countries.

Learning models do not provide much more support to regional integration. Chapter 2 shows that countries in LAC do not have as many trade connections as do other countries in the world and invest too little in R&D, thus limiting the benefits predicted by these models. To be sure, the desirability of integrating with specific partners depends on how transferable knowledge is between countries. If knowledge is fully transferable, the characteristics of a country's partners become irrelevant because countries can build upon the stock of knowledge of the world. In this case, the stock of knowledge of a country can be appropriated by that country's trading partners, the partners of its partners, and so on. In contrast, if knowledge transfers and learning are not easily diffused across space, the characteristics of a country's trading partners become more important and

countries will differ in their stock of knowledge. The assumption that there are frictions to knowledge diffusion and learning is supported by evidence, suggesting that the identity of partners matters (Keller 2002). Moreover, frictions appear to increase with distance, both geographic distance and distance in levels of development, which means that the potential gains from trade from the point of view of learning models will depend on the characteristics of a country's nearby partners. A country is expected to have more scope for learning when its nearby partners are knowledge hubs or have strong commercial ties with knowledge hubs.

There seems to be tension, therefore, between geographic forces and the policies that facilitate regional integration and the predictions of economic models that drive countries in LAC to look for efficiency gains beyond their immediate neighbors. Indeed, there is a tension between preferential trade arrangements that provide incentives for intraregional trade perhaps at the expense of trade with the rest of the world and the realization that geography naturally favors intraregional trade. Why would LAC pursue an integration strategy that combines global and regional integration? The short answer is that there are important complementarities between regional integration and global integration that make LAC's international competitiveness and its ability to reach extraregional markets dependent on regional integration. Thus, a comprehensive renewal of OR can make LAC more competitive in global markets.

There are several reasons why a balance between regional and global integration efforts can boost LAC's competitiveness. First, the impact of geography is unlikely to disappear any time soon. This implies that trade links with nearby countries will affect the global competitiveness of countries in the region. The link between regional trade and global competitiveness is most clearly illustrated in the case of "regionally traded goods" (see chapter 2). These are goods and services for which the costs associated with distance are so high that they are typically exchanged only by neighboring countries and for which the policy-related barriers to trade are not import tariffs per se, but rather differences in regulatory schemes. For these goods and services, regional integration efforts are equivalent to global integration. Notable examples of these goods and services are electricity and land transportation. Hence, regional efforts to assure the quality and the efficient provision of these types of goods and services will be crucial for the growth and stability prospects of LAC and for the ability of the region to gain international competitiveness in sectors that use these "regionally traded goods" intensively.

Similar arguments can be made in the case of labor markets. Migration decisions are shaped by the costs faced by migrants to move and successfully adapt to the host country. Chapter 4 presents evidence that these costs, which can be monetary and nonmonetary, are expected to increase with distance. Moreover, there is evidence of persistent wage differentials between countries in LAC, which suggests that there is scope for achieving region-wide efficiency improvements by enhancing the intraregional mobility of labor. Expanding the talent pool for employers, and the employment options for workers, may facilitate matching and a more efficient allocation of workers across countries.

Geography also appears to affect the ability of international economic interactions to facilitate the diffusion of knowledge and a country's ability to learn from the experience of its peers. Knowledge diffusion and learning can be larger between nearby countries. The strength with which these channels affect a country's growth and competitiveness, however, will be affected by the stock of knowledge, the level of development, and the degree of global integration of its peers. For example, a country's likelihood to enter into and survive in third markets is larger when its current trading partners are actively exporting to those markets (see chapter 2). This implies that a country's ability to learn from the experiences of its nearby partners depends on how open they are to global trade, which illustrates the complementarities

between regional integration and global integration. Thus, the potential growth and competitiveness benefits that LAC countries can get from interacting with their neighbors will depend on regional efforts to invest in innovation and to integrate globally.

Coordinated regional efforts can also facilitate LAC's competitiveness in relation to the rest of the world, even if these efforts are not directly aimed at strengthening regional trade and factor market links. This point can be easily illustrated in the case of infrastructure and logistics, two areas where the region has a noticeable deficit. Domestic and regional policies that seek to improve the quality of LAC's infrastructure and connectivity can lower the costs associated with distance for all countries in the region, costs that rank among the highest in the world. Moreover, the potential for region-wide competitiveness gains is expected to be greater to the extent that these policies are implemented by a large number of countries in the region.

In a nutshell, the preponderance of the evidence discussed above suggests that, for LAC to reap the benefits of international integration, it has to exploit the complementarities between efforts to integrate at the regional level and those aimed at integrating globally. In the past, the OR strategy of some countries in the region was short on the "O" and long on the "R." Going forward, a rebalancing might be desirable in the renewal of OR as a means to achieve higher growth with stability.

## Toward the renewal of OR in the Americas: Past efforts and current challenges

Since the 1990s, with varying timing and intensities, most countries in the region advanced policies with the central objective of pursuing a global integration agenda (the "O") through strengthened relationships with their immediate neighbors (the "R"). The early momentum toward OR, however, has slowed in some countries and completely stalled in others. This report seeks to illustrate with evidence what could be done going forward in the five areas that constitute the renewal of OR in light of the economic models discussed earlier.

## 1. Tariff liberalization with the rest of the world: An unfinished agenda

Past efforts in the OR agenda are perhaps most clearly seen in the commercial policy front. Since the 1990s, MFN tariffs (external tariffs applied to nonpreferential partners) have significantly diminished in most LAC countries. For some countries, these reductions were the result of the negotiations to join the World Trade Organization (WTO). For others, reductions in MFN tariffs go beyond their WTO commitments and appear related to advances in regional preferential agreements. For instance, Estevadeordal, Freund, and Ornelas (2008) studied regional preferences and MFN tariffs in ten LAC countries for the period 1990–2001 and found that preferential tariff reductions in a given sector led to a reduction in the MFN tariff in that sector. Their evidence supports the idea that regionalism in LAC in the 1990s was in fact a building block toward global trade integration, thus satisfying Bergsten's (1997) definition of OR.

Chapter 3 documents that this OR trade agenda continued well into the 2000s in many Central American countries, in Mexico, and in some South American countries like Chile, Colombia, and Peru. Average MFN tariffs in these countries are noticeably lower today compared to what they were in the mid-1990s. In parallel, preferential agreements with regional and extraregional partners flourished over the past 15 years. In contrast, in other South American countries the building-block effect of regional preferential agreements appears to have stalled.

A proximate cause behind the diverging paths in MFN tariffs observed between certain South American countries, especially those in Mercosur, and the rest of the region is the advent of free trade agreements (FTAs) with high-income economies. MFN tariffs fell sharply during the 2000s in countries that signed preferential agreements with the United States and Europe, and they remained flat in countries that did not (chapter 3). Thus, the positive reinforcement between regional preferences and external liberalization appears to have mutated in the 2000s. Regional preferences alone do not seem related to further MFN liberalization; rather, external liberalizations appear to follow preferential agreements with key players in the global economy. Clearly, the evidence does not establish a causal link between the two because the relation can be spurious or driven by other factors. The evidence does, however, illustrate the diverging paths of applied MFN tariffs of countries that signed preferential agreements with large economies, such as the United States and Europe, and those that did not.

A deeper, and arguably more interesting, cause behind these differences, which is discussed in chapter 3, is the intensity with which countries in LAC participate in global value chains (GVCs). Final goods tariffs are expected to decrease as the domestic content of imports increases (Blanchard, Bown, and Johnson 2016). Thus, participation in GVCs gives countries an incentive to reduce tariffs. This is consistent with the fact that Mexico and countries in Central America, which are deeply immersed in GVCs, have lower tariffs compared to countries in South America with an incipient participation in GVCs.

Importantly, the above differences show that tariff liberalization with the rest of the world is still an unfinished agenda for many countries in the region. Despite significant reductions over the past two decades, many countries in the region, especially those in South America, still have relatively high MFN tariffs (chapter 3). Lowering MFN tariffs could facilitate LAC's ability to connect to countries that offer large potential for efficiency gains and learning opportunities according to the models that constitute the organizing conceptual framework of this study.

Moreover, chapter 3 shows that most countries in the region, even those with relatively low MFN tariffs, display noticeable tariff binding "overhang"—defined as the difference between applied/effective MFN rates and the tariff commitments countries have with the WTO. Tariff binding overhang introduces uncertainty in trade relationships as governments have the option to raise import tariffs without risk of WTO-sanctioned retaliation, thus distorting investment decisions. From this it follows that reducing the tariff binding overhang can lead to welfare improvements (Handley and Limão 2015). Cutting applied and binding MFN tariffs, however, may require difficult political decisions. In the case of custom unions, for example, all member countries should in principle agree to reduce MFN tariffs, and often the benefits of such decisions can take time to materialize.

Pursuing further reductions in MFN tariffs and reducing the tariff binding overhang could help build a more open, globally connected LAC, which could in turn yield dynamic gains for countries in the region. New research prepared for this study shows that entry into, and survival in, new product markets is more likely when a country's trading partners have more trade connections. These findings, together with the forces of geography, imply that a more open LAC can facilitate entry into global export markets for countries in the region. Similarly, reducing tariff binding overhang can reduce policy uncertainty and stimulate local economic activity and attract foreign investment.

## 2. Enhancing the global integration of the Americas with tariff preferences

Preferential trade agreements (PTAs) are an integral part of today's global trade architecture. Moreover, their presence has been on the rise, especially in recent decades. In the early 1980s, the average country in the world granted tariff preferences to approximately 6 partners. In the early 2000s that number doubled, and by 2011 it had reached 28 countries.

LAC countries are no exception to this pattern. In fact, the increasing number of PTAs has been one of the defining traits of LAC's OR agenda. In the early 1980s, the average LAC country granted preferences to about 6 countries; by 2010 that number had increased to 23.

Despite the advances made by the region in terms of preferential agreements, chapter 3 shows there is scope for further improvements as part of the renewal of the OR agenda. On the regional front, there is still room for additional regional preferences, especially between South America and Central and North America, which have notably different patterns of net exports. This would be consistent with neoclassical theories of the gains from trade.

Clearly, achieving the objective of broader tariff preferences between Mercosur and Mexico and Central America is not free of difficulties. It would entail addressing complex political economy constraints that limit the ability of countries to grant preferences in specific sectors. These challenges were manifested in the context of the Brazil–Mexico auto pact, where diverging views between the two countries created difficulties for eliminating the import quotas imposed by the auto agreement.[13] These sectors may be particularly important in shaping value chain–based trade that could strengthen the region. As was highlighted above, however, the potential efficiency gains to be had from integrating the two ends of the Americas appear too large to be ignored.

Chapter 3 also shows that many LAC countries, especially those in Mercosur, could still offer tariff preferences to high-income partners in addition to pursuing broader regional preferences. Doing so can yield at least two potential benefits. First, it could allow countries in LAC to attain unexploited efficiency gains by deepening commercial ties with economies that have trade structures that differ from those in LAC and that offer a large learning potential. Indeed, once factors affecting trade flows, such as geography and economic size, are taken into account, LAC countries overperform in terms of their trade with partners with which they hold PTAs, which suggests that implementing PTAs with high-income partners could boost trade flows between Mercosur and these countries. A second potential benefit is that signing PTAs with high-income countries has been associated with reductions in extraregional tariffs. If such PTAs were to arise with multiple high-income partners, this could serve as a close substitute for MFN tariff liberalization.

Commercial policy in LAC has surely come a long way in facilitating the region's immersion into global markets and in fostering economic integration in the Americas. This was the main focus of the original OR strategy that emerged in the 1990s. The road ahead requires additional efforts to reduce MFN and extend tariff preferences within the Americas. In addition, the renewed OR strategy could focus on some of the adverse effects of the current "spaghetti bowl" of trade agreements that resulted from the initial OR efforts, an area to which we turn next.

## 3. Harmonizing rules of origin and regulatory frameworks in the Americas to achieve global competetiveness

Trade flows are thought to be affected by a number of variables. OR focused heavily on one of these variables, namely tariffs. By doing so, however, it left aside other barriers to international trade flows; and, in some cases discussed below, it aggravated them. Factors like standards, regulations, or local content requirements affect the decisions of firms to enter export markets and the intensity with which countries trade. Going forward, initiatives to minimize the trade distortions imposed by these trade barriers can have a large impact on the region's global competitiveness because they would act as a region-wide positive productivity shock. In some instances, these initiatives will entail country-specific efforts such as streamlining import processes, or even wholesale reforms of customs agencies, which tend to be complex (see chapter 2). In other instances they will entail coordinated efforts between countries, such as the streamlining of quality and sanitary requirements of products or harmonizing rules.

As discussed in chapter 3, the potential benefits of coordinated efforts to reduce nontariff trade costs are evident with rules of origin (RoOs). RoOs are the criteria needed to determine the national source of a product and are used to decide whether imported products receive MFN treatment or preferential treatment. The rules aim to avoid granting preferences to goods that are produced outside countries' signatories to a PTA. RoOs, however, can impose hefty administrative and compliance costs to exporting firms, costs that are aggravated by the fact that there is a growing number of PTAs and each establishes its own RoOs. Some take the form of minimum value-added content from the country in the PTA, some rely on identifying the country of manufacturing and processing, and some apply a "tariff shift" rule (Estevadeordal and Talvi 2016). Hence, efforts to harmonize and allow for RoOs with full accumulation within the Americas would help LAC attain higher dividends from its existing PTAs, by allowing firms to use materials from other countries without losing preferential access.

The region-wide benefits of advancing nontariff reform efforts are expected to be particularly large for regionally traded goods. First, as noted above, trade in regionally traded goods is bound to occur between nearby countries because they cannot be transported by air or sea. As a result, the exchange of these goods between nonbordering countries involves goods and services transiting through other regional partners, thus making region-wide coordination crucial. Second, among regionally traded goods are goods and services, such as electric current and land transportation, which are fundamental inputs in the production and distribution of other exports. In fact, in the specific case of electricity, although important steps toward an integrated energy grid have been taken, countries in the region have been unable to fully capitalize on these efforts, in part because of conflicting regulatory standards (chapter 2).

## 4. Reducing LAC's cost of distance through investments in infrastructure and logistics

As much as policy-induced reductions in trade costs can facilitate international trade integration, chapter 2 shows that LAC faces higher costs associated with distance compared to other regions. Geography together with economic size appear as the preponderant factors underpinning LAC's relatively low levels of trade integration, both within the region and with the rest of the world. In fact, the region's trade flows appear to be more sensitive to geographic distance compared to other regions, which could mean that LAC faces larger trade costs associated with distance.

There are at least two factors explaining LAC's relatively large costs of distance. The first reason behind this may be the poor quality of the region's infrastructure, a key factor known to drive up trade costs. This argument is supported by data on the quality of land transport. For example, whereas the share of unpaved roads in LAC is about 70 percent, it is less than 50 percent in the South Asia region and less than 30 percent in EAP. Arguably, LAC needs even better road transport infrastructure than other regions, given its challenging geography.

A second reason for LAC's higher trade costs is the region's comparatively weaker position in the global network of maritime and air transport. Unfortunately, LAC is largely connected to these networks via branch lines (as opposed to main lines between hubs), putting it at a disadvantage when it comes to international integration. This is partly the result of LAC ranking poorly in port efficiency. There is thus much scope for LAC to improve its position in the global system through investments that seek to improve the efficiency and infrastructure of the region's ports.

## 5. Achieving region-wide efficiency gains in the Americas through factor market integration

Factor market integration is another element in the renewal of the OR agenda that could bring region-wide efficiency gains. Some regional agreements in LAC took notice of the potential benefits of pursuing policies to integrate factor markets, namely labor and capital markets. Nonetheless, even in these cases the emphasis on trade preferences overshadowed the emphasis on factor market integration. Chapter 4 presents evidence

about the potential benefits from bringing factor market integration to the forefront of a renewed OR strategy.

*Labor market integration in the Americas*
Well-functioning labor markets are essential for countries to reap the benefits from economic integration. Integrated labor markets at the national level guarantee the flow of workers from low-productivity sectors and firms to high-productivity sectors and firms. Similarly, labor market integration across borders through migration can help countries materialize efficiency gains not captured through trade integration.[14] Migration can also help boost growth because it can foster cross-border knowledge transfers. Attracting international talent for sectors in which a country specializes is important in many countries, such as the United States, and will become increasingly important in Latin America as it grows and gains competitiveness in human capital–intensive industries.

Labor market integration may also mitigate the consequences of macroeconomic shocks. Cross-border labor market integration allows workers to respond to adverse wage shocks by giving them the chance to seek employment opportunities in other countries. An example of this mechanism at play was seen in the European Union during the debt crisis of countries in the periphery, where workers from Greece, Italy, and Spain migrated toward France, Germany, and the United Kingdom as labor market conditions deteriorated in the former.[15]

Chapter 4 shows that there are large wage differences between workers of similar characteristics across LAC countries, even after controlling for short-term co-movements in wages. More specifically, data suggest that wage differentials of otherwise similar workers (in terms of the age, gender, and education) across LAC economies during the 21st century tend to be more than 100 percent larger than the average wage differential across Mexican states or the wage differentials across the United States. In addition, the speed at which wages move toward those long-run equilibrium differences is much slower in LAC than within Mexico or the United States, although the short-term co-movement of wages across LAC is strikingly similar to the co-movement of wages across Mexican states and across the United States. These results can be interpreted as evidence of persistent differences in labor productivity across countries in LAC and unrealized region-wide efficiency gains that could be attained through migration.

Promoting cross-border migration flows within LAC may require tackling important regional challenges, especially on the side of Latin Americans' preferences for migration. In a nutshell, chapter 4 shows that Latin Americans prefer to migrate to high-income economies outside of the region. In fact, evidence suggests that intra-LAC migrants are below the number predicted by standard determinants of migration. Data imply that, if migration were costless, the number of Latin American migrants living in other LAC countries would be even smaller.

Fortunately, LAC appears to be a region that is open to migration. Citizens of Latin American countries with available data have pro-immigration opinions that fare well compared to other countries in the world. These relatively positive sentiments toward migrants are also reflected in the views expressed by policy makers. The share of government officials from LAC who view migration levels as too low or satisfactory is higher than in any other developing region (see chapter 4).

This relatively pro-immigration sentiment notwithstanding, policy efforts to attract migrants to LAC may still be subject to difficulties if not managed carefully. The views held by Latin Americans about migrants may be a result of the relatively low levels of migration in the region. In fact, countries that have relatively high immigration rates have less positive attitudes toward migrants compared to those with low immigration rates. Hence, policy efforts to foster immigration can end up affecting public opinion such that the pro-immigration attitudes displayed by Latin Americans up to now could be reversed. To be sure, migration attitudes appear to be affected by other policy-related factors—positive attitudes toward migrants are more common among the more educated population. This highlights the fact that the effectiveness of LAC's integration agenda is tightly linked to the effectiveness of structural reforms in areas such as education; as the rate of accumulation of human capital in LAC advances, attitudes toward immigration might soften.[16]

Evidence suggests that there are efficiency gains to be attained through increased regional labor market integration. LAC's ability to reap these gains hinges on implementing policies, especially on the migration front, that may face short-term opposition in certain countries. Nevertheless, the potential region-wide economic payoffs of further liberalizing international migration in the Americas should not be ignored.

*Capital market integration in the Americas*
Capital market integration (CMI) is important for growth and stability for several reasons. On the growth side, it can expand credit to households, allowing them to invest in durable assets and in human capital acquisition. Similarly, it expands credit to firms, allowing them to take on productive investments that were not otherwise possible, thus raising productivity. CMI, especially in the form of foreign direct investment (FDI), can also foster innovation and productivity upgrades through additional channels. It can enhance competition in the local economy by bringing in new products and new varieties of existing products, and it can bring new processes and managerial expertise that can spill over to domestic firms. On the stability side, credit expansions fostered by CMI can allow households to cope with income shocks and smooth consumption. CMI can also lead to diversification opportunities because firms can invest in new projects that do not face the same risks as existing ones. The downside of CMI, however, is the potential transmission of external shocks to the local economy, potentially exacerbating macroeconomic volatility when capital flows themselves are volatile and decoupled from economic fundamentals.

Countries in LAC have acknowledged the benefits and risks of CMI and have taken steps to allow capital flows into the region. LAC embarked on financial liberalization in the 1990s, which resulted in the region's leading other emerging regions as the most financially integrated in the world in terms of de jure policies (Galindo, Izquierdo, and Rojas-Suárez 2010). In the specific area of FDI attraction, countries in the region have used policy tools such as tax and tariff exemptions to attract foreign firms and capital (see UN 2000)

At the regional level, countries in LAC are signatories of investment agreements, either as chapters of FTAs or through bilateral investment treaties (BITs), with a large number of regional partners. More recently, countries in the Pacific Alliance signed an agreement to create an integrated stock exchange (Mercado Integrado Latinoamericano, or MILA). MILA has the objective of unifying the equity trading platforms of the four countries in the Pacific Alliance and in this way concentrating a bigger number of issuers, investors, and intermediaries.

In spite of recent calls for further CMI among LAC economies (IMF 2016), there is no shortage of financial integration within LAC, once factors such as economic size and geography are taken into account (chapter 4). In fact, financial integration within LAC is higher compared to benchmarks after controlling for such fundamentals. Moreover, the arguments in favor of actions to strengthen regional CMI are weak at best. The case in favor of regional CMI could be justified by appealing to the idea that knowledge diffusion appears to decay with distance, thus limiting the positive spillovers from FDI from faraway countries. As with trade, however, the prospects for growth and stability dividends from intra-LAC capital flows appear to be limited. Multinational corporations (MNCs) from the region display lower investments in innovation and worse managerial practices than their peers from other regions, thus limiting the scope for knowledge spillovers to local firms (Lederman et al. 2014). These observations

suggest that the benefits from regional CMI in LAC are tightly linked to the vigor of the region's growth and innovation agenda. In addition to the limited scope for growth and knowledge spillovers from intra-LAC capital flows, the evidence also shows that geography has a weaker pull on financial flows than on trade or labor flows. This implies that, to gain access to foreign capital at a given cost and knowledge content, a country is not as restricted by its geographic location. Hence, it is difficult to see efficiency or dynamic gains from facilitating intraregional capital market integration at the expense of CMI with the rest of the world.

However, regional agreements can yield efficiency gains in other dimensions and, if enacted jointly, can magnify the growth and stability benefits from global capital integration. For example, MILA provides a unified set of norms and reduces transaction costs for investors seeking opportunities in countries of the Pacific Alliance, thus making it a more appealing investment option. Similarly, regional agreements can facilitate coordination in the provision of incentives to foreign capital among countries in the region and prevent a race to the bottom where countries sacrifice revenue as they compete for FDI. As a result, such coordination has the potential to maximize the positive impact of foreign capital across the region. The bottom line is that initiatives such as MILA should be seen as efforts to improve the collective investment climate, rather than as efforts to increase intraregional capital flows at the expense of foreign investment from the rest of the world.

## It takes a competitive region to make a competitive economy

The time is ripe to bring LAC's OR agenda to center stage. The challenge lies in designing an integration agenda that is conducive to region-wide efficiency gains. This does not imply that integration strategies should seek to build regional ties at the expense of those with the rest of the world. Rather, the region could seek integration strategies that exploit the complementarities between regional and global integration to attain higher global competitiveness. The forces of geography imply that pro-growth global integration cannot be achieved without building a strong neighborhood.

This study, therefore, proposes an ambitious agenda aimed at achieving the type of region-wide efficiency gains discussed above. On the trade front, evidence suggests that there is still room for additional preferences at the regional level, especially between Mexico, Central America, and North America on the one hand, and South America on the other. Importantly, there is significant scope for further tariff liberalization with the rest of the world. The latter would help build a more open neighborhood, from which countries in the region can learn about penetrating foreign markets while taking advantage of regional specialization.

The road ahead also presents the challenge of reducing other nontariff trade frictions. Regional efforts to standardize RoOs, to build more efficient customs agencies, to invest in joint infrastructure projects, and to harmonize procedures and standards are some of the key issues in this agenda. The benefits of these efforts appear to be greatest in the case of regionally traded goods (for example, electricity and land transportation), goods for which the cost of distance is so high that trade typically occurs only between regional partners and where their efficient exchange can lead to improvements in global competitiveness.

Factor market integration, especially in labor markets, stands out as an additional important element of the renewal of OR. Policies aimed at facilitating intraregional migration could allow LAC to capture unexploited region-wide efficiency gains reflected in the region's large wage gaps. Regional coordination in policies to attract foreign capital could also produce efficiency gains by reducing transaction costs and help prevent a race to the bottom whereby countries sacrifice revenue as they compete for foreign investment.

In a nutshell, this study argues that the success of global integration strategies is inextricable from the strength of a country's region. In this sense, the old African proverb "it takes a village to raise a child" applies to the OR strategy delineated here. After all, the evidence suggests that it takes a competitive region to make a competitive economy.

The rest of this report is organized as follows. Chapter 1 documents the geographic clustering of economic performance. Chapter 2 benchmarks regional integration in LAC and presents the trade-related arguments in favor of OR. Chapter 3 discusses the state of trade policy in LAC. Chapter 4 presents the potential benefits of factor market integration in LAC.

## Notes

1. Throughout this report countries are grouped in regions according to several definitions of regions. One regional grouping used extensively is a slight modification of the World Bank regional classification. See annex 1A for a detailed explanation of this regional classification.
2. The objectives of the Pacific Alliance can be found at https://alianzapacifico.net/en/que-es-la-alianza/#what-is-the-pacific-alliance.
3. See CAFTA–DR's preamble.
4. The term "open regionalism" was first introduced during the Asia-Pacific Economic Cooperation (APEC) discussions in the early 1990s (Frankel and Wei 1995). For an early discussion of OR in the context of Latin America and the Caribbean see ECLAC (1994). See also Bergsten (1997).
5. Other notable examples are the intraindustry trade models of Helpman and Krugman (1985, 1989) and the heterogeneous firm models that generally reference Melitz (2003).
6. The academic literature on trade, inequality, and poverty is huge. There are at least six broad literature surveys: Winters, McCulloch, and McKay (2004) and Goldberg and Pavcnik (2004) cover trade liberalization and poverty; Goldberg and Pavcnik (2007) and Harrison, McLaren, and McMillan (2011) cover trade and the distribution of income; Lederman (2013) covers trade and inclusive growth; and Lederman and Porto (2014) cover the distributional consequences of commodity-price fluctuations.
7. See IDB (2002) or Schiff and Winters (2003).

8. The terms the "death of distance" and "the world is flat" were introduced in two books, *The Death of Distance: How the Communications Revolution Is Changing our Lives* by Frances Cairncross (1997) and the international best-seller *The World Is Flat: A Brief History of the Twenty-First Century* by Thomas L. Friedman (2007), respectively.

9. The gravity model of trade was first used by Nobel Laureate Jan Tinbergen in 1962. The author proposed an empirical relation between bilateral trade flows, economic size, and distance that follows the logic of Newton's law of gravity, which states that the force of attraction between two bodies is proportional to their mass and inversely proportional to the distance between them. In Tinbergen's model, economic size plays the role of mass and the geographic distance between two countries plays the role of the distance between the two objects. Originally, the gravity model was presented as an empirical relationship that provided a good description of bilateral trade patterns. Recent advances in the field of international trade have provided microeconomic foundations for the gravity model and a better understanding of the implications of the relationship. Early papers using the gravity equation were reduced-form estimations of the relationship that in many cases delivered misleading predictions (see Head and Mayer 2014). This problem has been solved by the introduction of structural gravity equations derived from formal economic models (see Anderson 1979 or Eaton and Kortum 2002, among others). Importantly, structural gravity equations allow for the analysis of counterfactual policy experiments.

10. Although trade flows are larger, trade over GDP may not be.

11. These costs may be linked to freight and insurance costs, or any other economic friction that increases the costs of international commerce, even when not strictly related to geographic distance. The latter are often associated empirically with language differences and cultural differences, as well as with trade taxes and nontariff barriers.

12. See chapter 2 in this report for details on the benchmarking exercise.

13. The agreement was recently extended until March 2019, and Brazil and Mexico are expected to return to a free trade regime after that. The new agreement increases the quota by 3 percent per year.

14. Migration flows and trade flows can be complements or substitutes. In the extreme where trade is frictionless, the two flows should be substitutes—countries can attain the same efficiency gains by integrating through trade or by integrating factor markets. In contrast, when trade is not frictionless, because of tariffs or other trade frictions, differences in returns to factors of production may arise and factor movements may become complementary to trade flows. Moreover, migration flows can mitigate frictions in the transmission of technology and know-how across borders or in the transmission of information about foreign markets. In these cases, migration flows can foster trade flows, thus reinforcing the potential complementarity between the trade and labor flows.

15. The number of Greek, Italian, and Spanish migrants in Germany increased by 154 percent between 2010 and 2013. In contrast, it grew by 5 to 25 percent between 2007 and 2009.

16. Between 2000 and 2014, the tertiary school enrollment rate in LAC increased from 20 to 40 percent. See Ferreyra et al. (forthcoming) for an analysis of the challenges facing university education in the region.

## References

Anderson, J. E. 1979. "A Theoretical Foundation for the Gravity Equation." *American Economic Review* 69 (1): 106–16.

Bergsten, C. F. 1997. "Open Regionalism." *The World Economy* 20 (5): 545–65.

Blanchard, E. J., C. P. Bown, and Robert C. Johnson. 2016. "Global Supply Chains and Trade Policy." NBER Working Paper 21883, National Bureau of Economic Research, Cambridge, MA.

Cairncross, F. 1997. *The Death of Distance: How the Communications Revolution Is Changing our Lives*. Boston: Harvard Business School Press.

Calderón, C., A. Chong, and E. Stein. 2007. "Trade Intensity and Business Cycle Synchronization: Are Developing Countries Any Different?" *Journal of International Economics* 71 (1): 2–21.

Chaney, T. 2011. "The Network Structure of International Trade." NBER Working Paper 16753, National Bureau of Economic Research, Cambridge, MA.

Coe, D. T., and E. Helpman. 1995. "International R&D Spillovers." *European Economic Review* 39 (5): 859–87.

de la Torre, A., T. Didier, A. Ize, D. Lederman, and S. Schmukler. 2015. *Latin America and the Rising South: Changing World, Changing Priorities*. Washington, DC: World Bank.

de la Torre, A., F. Filippini, and A. Ize. 2016. *The Commodity Cycle in Latin America: Mirages and Dilemmas*. Washington, DC: World Bank.

de la Torre, A., D. Lederman, and S. Pienknagura. 2015. "Doing It Right," *Finance & Development* 52 (3): 28–30.

Eaton, J., and S. Kortum. 2002. "Technology, Geography, and Trade." *Econometrica* 70 (5): 1741–79.

ECLAC (Economic Commission for Latin America and the Caribbean). 1994. *Open Regionalism in Latin America and the Caribbean: Economic Integration as a Contribution to Changing Production Patterns with Social Equity*. Santiago, Chile: United Nations, ECLAC.

Estevadeordal, A., C. Freund, and E. Ornelas. 2008. "Does Regionalism Affect Trade Liberalization toward Nonmembers?" *The Quarterly Journal of Economics* 123 (4): 1531–75.

Estevadeordal, A., and E. Talvi. 2016. *Towards a New Trans-American Partnership*. Brookings Global Policy Brief. Washington, DC: Brookings Institution.

Fanelli, J. M. 2007. "Regional Arrangements to Support Growth and Macro-Policy Coordination in Mercosur," G-24 Discussion Paper, United Nations Conference on Trade and Development (UNCTAD).

Ferreyra, M. M., C. Avitale, J. Botero, F. Haimovich Paz, and S. Urzua. Forthcoming. *At a Crossroads: Higher Education in Latin America and the Caribbean*. Washington, DC: World Bank.

Frankel, J., and S. J. Wei. 1995. "Open Regionalism in a World of Continental Trade Blocs." NBER Working Paper 5272, National Bureau of Economic Research, Cambridge, MA.

Friedman, T. L. 2007. *The World Is Flat: A Brief History of the Twenty-First Century*. New York: Picador/Farrar, Strauss and Giroux.

Galindo, A., A. Izquierdo, and L. Rojas-Suárez. 2010. "Financial Integration and Foreign Banks in Latin America: How Do They Impact the Transmission of External Shocks?" IDB Working Paper Series No. IDB-WP-116, Inter-American Development Bank.

Goldberg, P. K., and N. Pavcnik. 2004. "Trade, Inequality, and Poverty: What Do We Know? Evidence from Recent Trade Liberalization Episodes in Developing Countries." NBER Working Paper 10593, National Bureau of Economic Research, Cambridge, MA.

Goldberg, P. K., and N. Pavcnik. 2007. "Distributional Effects of Globalization in Developing Countries." *Journal of Economic Literature* 45 (1): 39–82.

Handley, K., and N. Limão. 2015. "Trade and Investment under Policy Uncertainty: Theory and Firm Evidence." *American Economic Journal: Economic Policy* 7 (4): 189–222.

Harrison, A., J. McLaren, and M. McMillan. 2011. "Recent Perspectives on Trade and Inequality." *Annual Review of Economics* 3 (1): 261–89.

Head, K., and T. Mayer. 2014. "Gravity Equations: Workhorse, Toolkit and Cookbook." In Vol. 4 of *Handbook of International Economics*, edited by Gita Gopinath, Elhanan Helpman, and Kenneth Rogoff. Amsterdam: Elsevier.

Helpman, E., and P. Krugman. 1985. *Market Structure and Foreign Trade*. Cambridge, MA: MIT Press.

Helpman, E., and Krugman, P. 1989. *Trade Policy and Market Structure*. Cambridge, MA: MIT Press.

IDB (Inter-American Development Bank). 2002. *Beyond Borders: The New Regionalism in Latin America*. Economic and Social Progress in Latin America 2002 Report. Washington, DC: IDB.

IMF (International Monetary Fund). 2016. "Financial Integration in Latin America." IMF Staff Report, IMF, Washington, DC. https://www.imf.org/external/np/pp/eng/2016/030416.pdf.

Keller, W. 2002. "Geographic Localization of International Technology Diffusion." *American Economic Review* 92 (1): 120–42.

Lederman, D. 2013. "International Trade and Inclusive Growth: A Primer." *Indian Growth and Development Review* 6 (1): 88–112.

Lederman, D., J. Messina, S. Pienknagura, and J. Rigolini. 2014. *Latin American Entrepreneurs: Many Firms but Little Innovation*. Washington, DC: World Bank.

Lederman, D., and G. Porto. 2014. "The Price Is Not Always Right: On the Impacts of (Commodity) Prices on Households (and

Countries).” Policy Research Working Paper 6858, World Bank, Washington, DC.

Lopez-Calva, L. F., and N. C. Lustig, eds. 2010. *Declining Inequality in Latin America: A Decade of Progress?* Washington, DC: Brookings Institution Press and United Nations Development Programme.

Lumenga-Neso, O., M. Olarreaga, and M. Schiff. 2005. “On ‘Indirect’ Trade-Related R&D Spillovers.” *European Economic Review* 49: 1785–98.

Melitz, M. 2003. “The Impact of Trade on Intra-Industry Reallocations and Aggregate Industry Productivity.” *Econometrica* 71 (6): 1695–1725.

Morales, E., G. Sheu, and A. Zahler. 2014. “Gravity and Extended Gravity: Using Moment Inequalities to Estimate a Model of Export Entry.” NBER Working Paper 19916, National Bureau of Economic Research, Cambridge, MA.

Robertson, R. 2004. “Relative Prices and Wage Inequality: Evidence from Mexico” *Journal of International Economics* 64 (2): 387–409.

Schiff, M., and L. A. Winters. 2003. *Regional Integration and Development.* Washington, DC: World Bank.

Schwab, K., and X. Sala-i-Martin, eds. 2013. *The Global Competitiveness Report 2013–2014.* Geneva: Word Economic Forum.

Messina, J. and J. Silva. Forthcoming. *Wage Inequality in Latin America and the Caribbean: Understanding the Past to Prepare for the Future.* Washington, DC: World Bank.

Tinbergen, J. 1962. *Shaping the World Economy: Suggestions for an International Economic Policy.* New York: The Twentieth Century Fund.

UN (United Nations). 2000. “Tax Incentives and Foreign Direct Investment: A Global Survey.” ASIT Advisory Studies No. 16, United Nations Conference on Trade and Development (UNCTAD).

Winters, L. A., N. McCulloch, and A. McKay. 2004. “Trade Liberalization and Poverty: The Evidence So Far.” *Journal of Economic Literature* 41 (1): 72–115.

# Economic Performance and Geography: Rising and Falling with Our Neighbors

1

## Introduction

Over the past thirty years, the world has witnessed a wave of globalization. The pace of economic integration around the globe has accelerated since the mid-1980s, as evidenced by the sharp increase in the flow of goods, capital, and people between countries (see World Bank 2002).

To be sure, the world has seen previous waves of globalization.[1] The most recent wave presents important differences compared to previous experiences, however. In addition to significant reductions in tariffs and improvements in transportation in terms of cost, timeliness, and reliability, the past thirty years have seen the advent and diffusion of the information and communication technology (ICT) revolution, which significantly reduced the costs of personal interactions over long distances.[2] All these forces have led to radical changes in the organization of production processes and firms, as well as in the patterns of global trade: goods are now produced in stages that take place in different countries, multinational corporations have gained prominence because they can more easily communicate with foreign

subsidiaries, and services have become increasingly tradeable over this period.[3]

Many economic commentators argue that the sharp reductions in transportation and communication costs driven by technological progress have resulted in the "death of distance," and that the "world is flat."[4] According to this hypothesis, cross-border economic interactions between distant countries are more likely today because the costs associated with distance that shape these interactions have fallen significantly.

Beyond its impact on the organization of firms and trade, one could argue that economic performance more broadly is also part of this "flat world." The claim is that technology has allowed economies to face a leveled playing field in terms of having access to the most advanced technologies. For instance, the rise of massive open online courses allows students in developing countries to have access to the best educators and content from developed countries, leading to a democratization of education (see Acemoglu, Laibson, and List 2014). Similarly, firms and researchers in developing countries now have access to a wider stock of knowledge that in principle can allow them to catch up more quickly to the world technological frontier. More broadly, a more integrated global economy can provide opportunities for developing countries to overcome deficits in physical capital (through international capital flows), in human capital (through migration), and in the availability of high-quality inputs and services (through trade).

Taken at face value, today's flat world is expected to lead to a more integrated global economy and a swift process of economic convergence across the developing world. Indeed, to the extent that economic integration and advances in communications foster technological transfers from developed to developing countries, they should also facilitate the process of convergence of developing countries toward the levels of income per capita of developed economies, regardless of their distance from knowledge-producing economies and their location in the world. In a nutshell, in a flat world economic integration and, more importantly, economic performance, should not be bound by geography.

An aggregate look at the data provides some support to the idea that the past thirty years have been conducive to improvements in economic performance in developing countries relative to developed economies. In fact, a number of developing countries have gained prominence in the global economy as they grew at a faster pace than developed countries. The increasing importance of developing countries over the past few decades is documented extensively in de la Torre et al. (2015). The authors show that the "South," defined as all countries other than the Group of Seven (G-7) and Western European economies, have more than doubled their incidence in global gross domestic product (GDP) over the past 30 years—from below 20 percent in 1985 to above 40 percent in 2012. At the same time, a number of developing countries have broken into global markets since the mid-1980s and have become key players in this new wave of globalization. As a result, the South contributed close to 50 percent of global trade in 2012, up from 25 percent in 1985.

As encouraging as this broad analysis seems for the developing world, a more granular look at the data yields more sobering conclusions. On the trade front, the economics literature has shown that geographic distance is still an important determinant of trade flows (more on this in chapter 2). To be sure, the Internet and improvements in transportation have certainly affected trade patterns and facilitated new trade relationships (see box 1.1). As significant as these changes are, however, the effect of distance does not seem to have disappeared.

Moreover, despite increasing interconnectedness, substantial long-run differences in growth rates and levels of development remain between countries in the developing world. There is no evidence of the widespread convergence in per capita income across the world that some had anticipated, and differences in convergence experiences are stark across regions. This can be easily depicted by an analysis of the evolution of the average GDP per capita relative to the United States across different regions defined by the World Bank (figure 1.1).[5]

Figure 1.1 shows on one extreme East Asia and the Pacific (EAP), a region with many well-known examples of so-called growth miracles, whose average country steadily converged during 1986–2010 to the levels of GDP per capita of the United States. The average country in this region had a level of GDP per capita in 1986 that stood at about 30 percent of that of the United States; by 2010 this share had surpassed 45 percent. On the other extreme stands Sub-Saharan Africa (SSA), a region that not only stands far behind EAP's average relative income per capita but also slightly diverged during 1986–2010, from an average GDP per capita of about 6 percent in 1986 to about 5.5 percent in 2010. Latin America and the Caribbean (LAC) lies in between these two extremes. Its average GDP per capita relative to the United States hovered around 20 percent over the past 25 years, even as it experienced a timid process of convergence in the 2000s.

The differences across regions highlighted in figure 1.1 also hold when looking beyond

## BOX 1.1    Is distance dead? Technology and its impact on international integration

The advent of ICTs and the Internet is regarded as perhaps the most disruptive change affecting international economic interactions in the past thirty years. It has led many economic and business commentators to suggest that economic and business interactions are no longer bound by geography (the "death of distance" hypothesis). A literal interpretation of this hypothesis is that, in the extreme, geographic distance should not affect bilateral trade and factor flows. Despite some anecdotal evidence in support of the "death of distance" hypothesis (Friedman 2007), a large number of academic papers suggest that distance is still an important force shaping economic interactions.

How can one reconcile the expectation that technology would facilitate international economic interactions, especially between faraway countries, and the reality that distance still plays an important role in shaping trade flows? The answer is that most of the evidence of the economics literature supports the view that technology has affected trade, especially by reducing the fixed costs associated with exporting (Freund and Weinhold 2004). These are the costs that are *not* associated with the movement of goods and services from one country in the world to another. Rather, these are the costs of establishing a business relation. They range from transactions that exporters have to undergo before exporting a good or service to the costs of acquiring the information needed by buyers and sellers. There is no robust evidence, however, of systematic changes in the costs that are associated with the movement of goods and services over the past thirty years.

To illustrate the impact that technology has on fixed costs, it is useful to focus on online markets, such as Amazon or eBay, and contrast these with traditional "offline" markets. A seller that wants to serve foreign consumers and firms through offline markets would have to establish client and distribution networks in every destination it wants to serve. In contrast, a seller that operates through online markets can avoid these costs by accessing the online platform's networks. In this sense, online markets reduce unnecessary duplications of transaction costs. The role of technology in facilitating

business transactions by reducing information costs can be illustrated by assessing the differences between online and offline markets from the point of view of buyers. Buyers make decisions regarding the goods they acquire based in part on the information they have about the goods and their producers. A business transaction is more likely if the buyer trusts and has better quality information about a good and its producers. In offline markets information is dispersed and costly to acquire, thus reducing the scope for a transaction to materialize. In contrast, in online markets information is easily accessible. An implication of the cost-reducing effects of online markets is that they make it easier for firms that are smaller or from lesser-known countries to export (Lendle et al. 2012).

What does the evidence say about the link between technology and the costs directly linked to the movement of goods and services across borders? The literature has provided two pieces of evidence suggesting that, at least for a broad set of goods, these costs are still affected by distance. Berthelon and Freund (2008), for example, showed that there is a large degree of heterogeneity across goods in terms of the responsiveness of bilateral trade flows to distance. In fact, most goods have large and negative distance elasticities, which capture in part freight and insurance costs. To be sure, it is undeniable that technology (ICTs and the Internet, specifically) has reduced the transportation costs for certain services (Freund and Weinhold 2002). For example, an architect selling his services to a foreign client can deliver his services at the same cost (close to zero), regardless of the location of the client. For a large share of the goods and services constituting world trade, however, freight costs are still large and have not significantly declined over time (Hummels 2007).

In sum, ICTs and the Internet have changed world trade. They have reduced transaction and information costs, allowing more buyers and sellers to participate in global markets. Nevertheless, moving goods across borders is still costly, and these costs increase with distance. In this specific sense, trade and factor flows are still bound by geography.

**FIGURE 1.1   Real GDP per capita relative to the United States, selected regions**

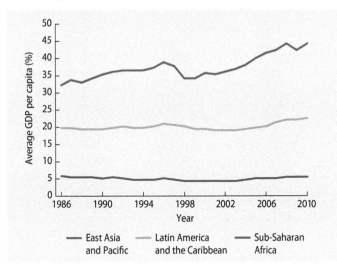

*Source:* World Bank calculations based on data from the Penn World Tables 8.1.
*Note:* Real GDP per capita is measured in 2005 US$ in purchasing power parity (PPP) terms. Real GDP per capita relative to the U.S. for each region is the simple average of all countries in each region with GDP per capita data available for all years from 1970 to 2010. See annex 1A for a description of all countries in each region.

**FIGURE 1.2   Regional distribution of real GDP per capita growth in selected regions, 1970–2010**

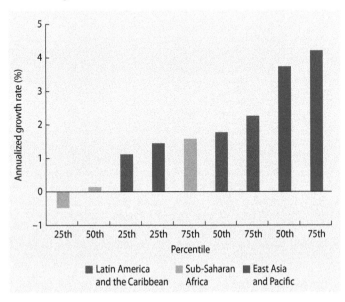

*Source:* World Bank calculations based on data from the Penn World Tables 8.1.
*Note:* Real GDP per capita growth is the annualized growth rate for each country from 1970 to 2010. Real GDP per capita is measured in 2005 US$ in purchasing power parity (PPP) terms. The sample in each region comprises countries with available data for all years from 1970 to 2010. See annex 1A for a description of all countries in each region.

the performance of the average country in each region. Figure 1.2 shows the 25th, 50th, and 75th percentiles of the regional distributions of annualized growth rates from 1970 to 2010 for all countries with available data in the three regions mentioned. The results of the exercise are stark. The 50th percentile of the growth distribution in EAP is above the 75th percentile of LAC, which means that half of EAP economies grew at faster rates than at least 75 percent of the countries in LAC. In contrast, the 50th percentile of LAC's growth distribution is above the 75th percentile of the growth distribution in SSA, which means that at least 75 percent of the countries in SSA grew at a slower pace than half the countries in LAC.

Hence, contrary to the naïve view in which all developing countries reap equal benefits of a more interconnected world, figures 1.1 and 1.2 highlight significant disparities in the growth performance of different geographic regions. Moreover, fast-growing countries appear to be located close to other fast-growing countries.

Beyond long-term growth, a strong pattern of geographic clustering is also evident for growth volatility.[6] Figure 1.3 highlights this pattern for the three regions mentioned earlier—LAC, EAP, and SSA. The figure compares the coefficient of variation, a measure of volatility calculated as the ratio of the standard deviation of annual growth divided by its average, for a similar set of countries as in figures 1.1 and 1.2. As with long-run growth, figure 1.3 shows marked differences in the distribution of volatility across regions. The 25th percentile of the distribution in SSA is higher than the 75th percentile of the distribution in LAC, suggesting that more than 75 percent of countries in SSA have higher volatility than 75 percent of the countries in LAC. On the other extreme, EAP displays values that are systematically lower than in both LAC and EAP.

The rest of this chapter explores the geographic clustering of economic performance highlighted above. Growth and volatility are only two of the many variables affecting a country's economic performance and aggregate welfare that could be affected by cross-border economic integration. However, growth has been found to be positively correlated with a large number of variables associated with a country's well-being, such as poverty reduction and health outcomes (Dollar, Kleineberg, and Kraay 2016; Easterly 1999). This suggests that studying the impact of economic integration on growth and volatility is a good first approximation to understanding the impact of economic integration on welfare more broadly.[7] With this in mind, and for the sake of brevity, the attention of this report is limited to the potential impact of economic integration on growth and volatility.

The chapter begins by looking in greater detail at the relation between geographic distance and long-term growth through a cross-country growth regression analysis. The evidence suggests that the annualized forty-year growth rate of a given country is strongly correlated with those of its nearby neighbors. In addition, a country's growth is positively correlated with the size and income per capita of nearby countries, suggesting that the characteristics of a country's neighbors may affect its long-run growth prospects.

The chapter in turn explores the relationship between geographic distance and the likelihood that economies will simultaneously experience extended periods of high growth or extended periods of low growth. The move from a simple analysis between long-run growth and geography to an analysis of the link between simultaneous episodes of growth takeoffs or downturns and geographic distance is motivated by the point made by Pritchett (2000), who argued that long-run growth rates, which by construction are stable averages, can mask important nonlinearities in the growth processes of countries.[8] The result of this finer analysis of growth once again highlights the tight commonality in growth processes observed between nearby countries—the likelihood of two countries experiencing simultaneously a growth takeoff or a growth downturn falls with distance.

FIGURE 1.3 **Regional distributions of the coefficient of variation in selected regions, 1970–2010**

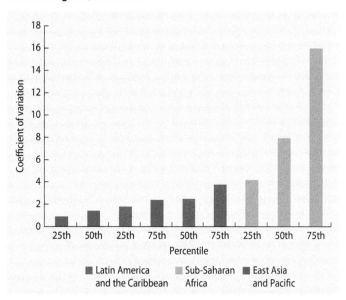

*Source:* World Bank calculations based on data from the Penn World Tables 8.1.
*Note:* The coefficient of variation is defined as the ratio of the standard deviation of real GDP per capita yearly growth over the 1970–2010 period and the average real GDP per capita yearly growth over the same period. Real GDP per capita is measured in 2005 US$ in purchasing power parity (PPP) terms. The sample in each region comprises countries with available data for all years from 1970 to 2010. See annex 1A for a description of all countries in each region.

The analysis of long-term growth is followed by analyses of business cycles. The chapter presents an analysis of short-run economic cycles similar to the one conducted by Calderón and Fuentes (2014). The results show that the likelihood of two countries facing the same phase of the business cycle (namely, a contraction, a recovery, or an expansion) decreases with the geographic distance.

Then the chapter displays results from Hevia and Servén (2016), a research paper commissioned for this report, which performs a variance decomposition exercise to understand the role played by domestic, regional, and global factors in explaining a country's GDP per capita growth volatility. The results reaffirm the conclusions from previous analyses presented in the chapter—regional factors typically carry a larger weight in explaining a country's GDP per capita growth volatility compared to global factors. Moreover, and despite the wave of globalization since the mid-1980s, the weight carried by regional factors has increased over time compared with global factors.

The chapter concludes by laying the ground for chapter 2—it discusses the impact that the geographic clustering of economic performance has on different economic integration strategies. More specifically, it argues that, regardless of the underlying factors shaping the observed geographic clustering of economic performance, the patterns observed in the chapter have important implications for a country's ability to attain high growth and stability through regional economic integration.

## The geographic clustering of long-term growth spells

Economic growth is one of the central topics in policy and academic debates, with good reason. For example, take two countries, one whose per capita income level grows at a 1 percent annual rate and another growing at a 3 percent annual rate. This difference in annual growth rates translates into significant differences in living standards over time. The first country doubles its income every 70 years, which roughly speaking means that a person living in that country is twice as rich as his grandfather. In contrast, the second country doubles its income every 23 years, which roughly speaking means that a person living in that country is twice as rich as her father.[9]

Inhabitants and policy makers of LAC are no strangers to the undeniable importance of economic growth in determining the well-being of nations. Despite brief spells of fast growth, such as the one experienced during the early 2000s, over the past fifty years the region has grown on average at a rate that more or less resembles that of the United States, preventing a strong process of convergence over time. Hence, understanding the factors behind long-term growth is of first-order importance for LAC and other developing regions.

One potential determinant of growth that has received scant attention in the literature is the type of neighborhood in which a country

is located. Two notable exceptions are Vamvakidis (1998) and Arora and Vamvakidis (2005), who find that countries whose neighbors are large, open developed economies—or that grow fast—tend to grow faster. In fact Vamvakidis (1998) shows that when adding region dummies for East Asia and SSA to their regressions, these do not have a statistically significant impact on the results, indicating that variations in growth among the regions can be explained by characteristics of neighbors rather than by simply being in a region.[10]

There are several reasons why a country's neighborhood can be important for growth. First, there is evidence that the rate of technology diffusion across countries decays with distance, suggesting that countries closer to those with large stocks of knowledge are expected to grow faster compared to those farther away.[11] Another channel through which neighbors can affect a country's growth rate is trade. The trade literature has highlighted that trade volumes fall with distance and increase with the destination's economic size, which implies that a country's trade volumes increase with the economic size of its nearby partners (see the recent survey by Head and Mayer 2014 and the vast literature on the gravity equation of trade therein). If we were to take the evidence from Frankel and Romer (1999) seriously, we would have to conclude that countries with larger partners are expected to grow faster (Vamvakidis 1998).

A preliminary exploration of this additional factor affecting growth is provided in figure 1.4. The figure uses data from the Penn World Tables 8.1 and maps GDP per capita growth rates from 1970 to 2010 (nonannualized) to a color coding where darker shades are associated with faster total growth over the period. Countries with no data in the period between 1970 and 2010 are in gray.

The exercise in figure 1.4 provides initial support for the potential role played by neighbors in explaining a country's growth—faster-growing countries are typically located next to other faster-growing countries, which

**FIGURE 1.4**   **Regional clustering of growth rates around the world, 1970–2010**

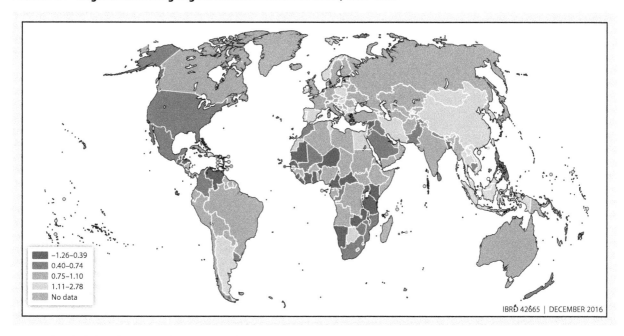

| | |
|---|---|
| ■ | −1.26–0.39 |
| ■ | 0.40–0.74 |
| ▨ | 0.75–1.10 |
| ▨ | 1.11–2.78 |
| ▨ | No data |

IBRD 42665 | DECEMBER 2016

*Source:* World Bank calculations based on data from the Penn World Tables 8.1.
*Note:* Growth rates are calculated using real GDP per capita data, which is measured in 2005 US$ in purchasing power parity (PPP) terms. The sample in each region comprises countries with available data for all years from 1970 to 2010. Dark red denotes low growth rates. Gray denotes no available data in the entire time frame analyzed. See annex 1A for a description of all countries in each region.

translates to remarkable similarities in growth rates within regions of the world. High-growth countries are largely clumped together in EAP (dark blue), countries with moderate growth rates are typically in the Americas (light blue), and countries with negative growth rates are mostly in Africa (white). The pattern of geographic clustering of growth rates is even apparent when looking within regions. Take, for example, the LAC region—over the 1970–2010 period growth rates in South America were higher than in Central and North America.

To be sure, the geographic clustering of growth rates observed in the data could be due to reasons beyond geography. It may well be the case that fundamental determinants of growth are themselves clustered geographically. For example, Acemoglu, Johnson, and Robinson (2001) find a link between the quality of current institutions, which they find affects growth, and the quality of colonial institutions, which they argue were linked to the ability of settlers to adapt to the colonies. To the extent that variables that are

geographically clustered, such as weather, climate, and diseases, determined the ability of settlers to adapt, one would expect the quality of today's institutions to display geographic clustering.

This raises the question of whether the geographic clustering of growth is driven mainly by the link between geography and some of the fundamental drivers of growth typically studied in the literature. Table 1.1 provides an imperfect attempt to tackle this question through a cross-country growth regression similar to the one presented in Vamvakidis (1998). Table 1.1 shows the results of a regression of GDP per capita growth from 1970 to 2010 on a series of controls and also includes a weighted average of growth, initial GDP per capita, and GDP of all other countries in the world. The weights used in the calculations are inversely proportional to the distance between countries. In addition to these right-hand-side variables, the controls include other typical explanatory variables in cross-country growth analyses— initial GDP per capita of the country,

**TABLE 1.1  Growth regressions with neighborhood effects**

| | Dependent variable: 1970–2010 growth | | | | | | | | |
|---|---|---|---|---|---|---|---|---|---|
| | (1) | (2) | (3) | (4) | (5) | (6) | (7) | (8) | (9) |
| Growth of nearby countries, weighted by distance | 1.489*** | 1.162*** | 1.175*** | | | | | | |
| | (0.142) | (0.141) | (0.126) | | | | | | |
| Intial GDP per capita of other countries, weighted by distance | | | | 0.154** | 0.180*** | 0.253*** | | | |
| | | | | (0.0650) | (0.0543) | (0.0520) | | | |
| Intial GDP of other countries, weighted by distance | | | | | | | 0.154** | 0.180*** | 0.253*** |
| | | | | | | | (0.0650) | (0.0543) | (0.0520) |
| Intial GDP per capita | | −0.205*** | −0.203*** | | −0.327*** | −0.375*** | | −0.327*** | −0.375*** |
| | | (0.0502) | (0.0481) | | (0.0642) | (0.0633) | | (0.0642) | (0.0633) |
| Population growth | | −0.156 | −0.382*** | | −0.227* | −0.523*** | | −0.227* | −0.523*** |
| | | (0.113) | (0.110) | | (0.137) | (0.135) | | (0.137) | (0.135) |
| Share of pop. with secondary educ. or more | | 0.0116*** | 0.00916*** | | 0.0149*** | 0.0125*** | | 0.0149*** | 0.0125*** |
| | | (0.00299) | (0.00274) | | (0.00366) | (0.00333) | | (0.00366) | (0.00333) |
| Investment/GDP | | 1.294* | 2.121*** | | 3.262*** | 4.173*** | | 3.262*** | 4.173*** |
| | | (0.681) | (0.629) | | (0.760) | (0.708) | | (0.760) | (0.708) |
| Trade/GDP | | | 0.749*** | | | 1.141*** | | | 1.141*** |
| | | | (0.253) | | | (0.328) | | | (0.328) |
| Government exp./GDP | | | 0.511 | | | 0.416 | | | 0.416 |
| | | | (0.541) | | | (0.660) | | | (0.660) |
| Terms-of-trade growth | | | 0.238*** | | | 0.256*** | | | 0.256*** |
| | | | (0.0572) | | | (0.0696) | | | (0.0696) |
| Constant | 0.0311 | 1.278*** | 1.283*** | −0.00805 | 1.466*** | 1.573*** | −0.00805 | 1.466*** | 1.573*** |
| | (0.0840) | (0.365) | (0.390) | (0.336) | (0.446) | (0.472) | (0.336) | (0.446) | (0.472) |
| Observations | 116 | 116 | 116 | 116 | 116 | 116 | 116 | 116 | 116 |
| R-squared | 0.491 | 0.635 | 0.716 | 0.047 | 0.462 | 0.580 | 0.047 | 0.462 | 0.580 |

*Source:* Authors' calculations using data from Penn World Tables 8.1.
*Note:* Country weights are inversely proportional to the distance between countries (1/distance). Standard errors in parentheses. *** p<0.01, ** p<0.05, * p<0.1.

population growth, investment rates, trade openness, government as share of GDP, education, and terms-of-trade growth. The inclusion of these variables should partly capture the effect of geography on other fundamental determinants of growth.

Columns (1), (4), and (7) confirm the simple correlations observed in the data. The growth rate of a country is positively correlated with the growth rate, the initial income, and the economic size of countries nearby. Moreover, columns (2), (3), (5), (6),

(8), and (9) show that this correlation persists even after controlling for other variables that may be affected by geographic characteristics.

While these results provide suggestive evidence of the tight link between a country's growth performance and the performance and characteristics of nearby countries, they are far from establishing any causal relationship between the two. First of all, as is typical in cross-country growth regressions, the empirical strategy is unable to successfully control for all the fundamental determinants that affect a country's growth performance, which leads to biases and potential misinterpretations of the results.[12] This is particularly problematic in the set-up of table 1.1 because of the fact that omitted variables, such as the quality of institutions, are likely to be correlated between countries, especially those that are nearby. Moreover, by design we are claiming that the growth rate of a country affects that of its neighbors and vice versa, which would then mean that the right-hand-side variable of interest is not independent of the error term. For all these reasons, the results from table 1.1 should admittedly be seen as simple correlations. Yet they are an additional indication of the geographic clustering of growth performances and, as will be discussed later, this has important implications for thinking about the potential benefits for different economic integration strategies.

Beyond the econometric problems in table 1.1, cross-country growth regressions have an additional difficulty in characterizing differences in growth processes between countries. In particular, cross-country growth regressions assume that income per capita follows a stable (log) linear path. However, Pritchett (2000) highlights that this is far from what is observed in the data.

Take, for instance, the growth experiences of Colombia and the United States, two countries whose real GDP per capita grew in the 1970–2010 period at a similar annualized rate of close to 1.3 percent. However, figure 1.5 highlights the marked difference in the growth processes of these two countries.

With the exception of short spells of economic downturns, U.S. growth can be accurately described as following a stable growth path. In contrast, over the forty years explored in figure 1.5, Colombia's growth presents three clear patterns—a decade of high growth in the 1970s, two decades of stagnant and volatile growth in the 1980s and 1990s, and close to a decade of high growth in the 2000s.[13]

The fact that the time series of a typical developing country displays both extended episodes of high growth, low growth, and sometimes negative growth has led a strand of the literature to try to identify the factors determining the transitions between episodes. One notable example of this body of work is found in Hausmann, Pritchett, and Rodrik (2005), who study the economic variables that are associated with episodes of growth. The authors find that episodes of growth accelerations are positively correlated with increases in trade and investment and with real exchange rate depreciations.

Two limitations of the analysis in Hausmann, Pritchett, and Rodrik (2005) are the arbitrary way in which they define growth acceleration episodes and the fact

**FIGURE 1.5    GDP per capita in Colombia and the United States, 1970–2010**

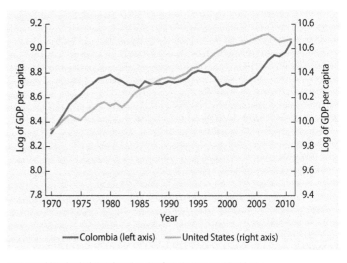

*Source:* World Bank calculations based on data from the Penn World Tables 8.1.
*Note:* Real GDP per capita is measured in 2005 US$ in purchasing power parity (PPP) terms.

that, by focusing only on growth accelerations, they neglect other types of growth episodes that are relevant for developing economies.[14] These limitations are addressed by Jones and Olken (2008), who studied episodes of both high growth and low growth by using a statistical methodology proposed by Bai and Perron (2003) to identify structural breaks in an economy's growth over time. The results in Jones and Olken (2008) highlight that growth accelerations and growth collapses are asymmetric in the sense that their correlates differ. On the one hand, similar to Hausmann, Pritchett, and Rodrik (2005), the authors argued that growth accelerations are associated with increases in trade openness, but they find no effect with regard to increasing investment. On the other hand, episodes of downturns are associated with significant reductions in investment and price volatility.

However, as highlighted earlier in this chapter, a country's growth spells (both upswings and downturns) may be correlated with those of other countries because of a multitude of factors. For example, technological transfers and economic links may lead to the transmission of growth spells from one country to another. But is the coincidence of growth episodes between pairs of countries more likely for those that are located nearby?

This question is tackled in the rest of this subsection through an analysis of growth episodes using a Bai-Perron (2003) test of structural breaks and analyzing the impact of geographic distance on the likelihood that two countries share a growth episode. In the analysis, a growth episode is defined as the years in between structural breaks identified by the Bai-Perron test. Technical details of the test are presented in annex 1B.

Before turning to the formal econometric analysis of the effect of distance on growth episodes, figure 1.6 illustrates in a nutshell the messages that will follow. The figure plots the evolution of (log) GDP per capita for four pairs of selected contiguous countries together with the dates of the structural breaks identified by the Bai-Perron test. These four examples illustrate an important point: the likelihood of two countries experiencing simultaneously a positive or negative growth spell is higher the closer the two countries are. Perhaps the starkest example is from LAC. Argentina and Brazil experienced three and four structural breaks, respectively. All of Argentina's structural breaks occur within a year of Brazil's; and the three shared breaks go in the same direction, in the sense that when one country accelerates the other does too and, conversely, when one country experiences a slowdown so does the other. Similarly, Colombia and Ecuador share a similar pattern of structural breaks—they experience three structural breaks each, one in the late 1960s / early 1970s, one in the late 1970s / early 1980s, and one in the early 2000s. Moreover, all contemporaneous breaks are in the same direction and a break identified in one country occurs within four years of the break identified for the other country, meaning that from a statistical point of view, one cannot reject the hypothesis that these breaks occur at the same time.[15] In contrast to the experience of contiguous countries, countries that are in different regions tend to experience breaks at different times; and, if breaks are relatively close together, the growth experiences that follow the breaks tend to go in opposite directions.

To test the findings of figure 1.6 in a statistically more rigorous way, table 1.2 studies the likelihood of two countries experiencing a structural break in the same direction (that is, a break followed by a high-growth episode or a break followed by a potentially negative low-growth phase) in a window of four years (panel a) and the likelihood of two countries being in the same growth phase (high-growth or low-growth episode) in a given year (panel b).[16] The four-year window is chosen to take into account that the exact timing of the structural break is uncertain. High-growth breaks are defined as breaks that mark the beginning of an episode when growth is higher than the growth in the previous phase, and low-growth breaks are defined conversely.[17]

The right-hand-side variable of interest in the econometric exercise is the (log) geographic

**FIGURE 1.6    GDP per capita and structural break dates for selected pairs of contiguous countries, 1960–2010**

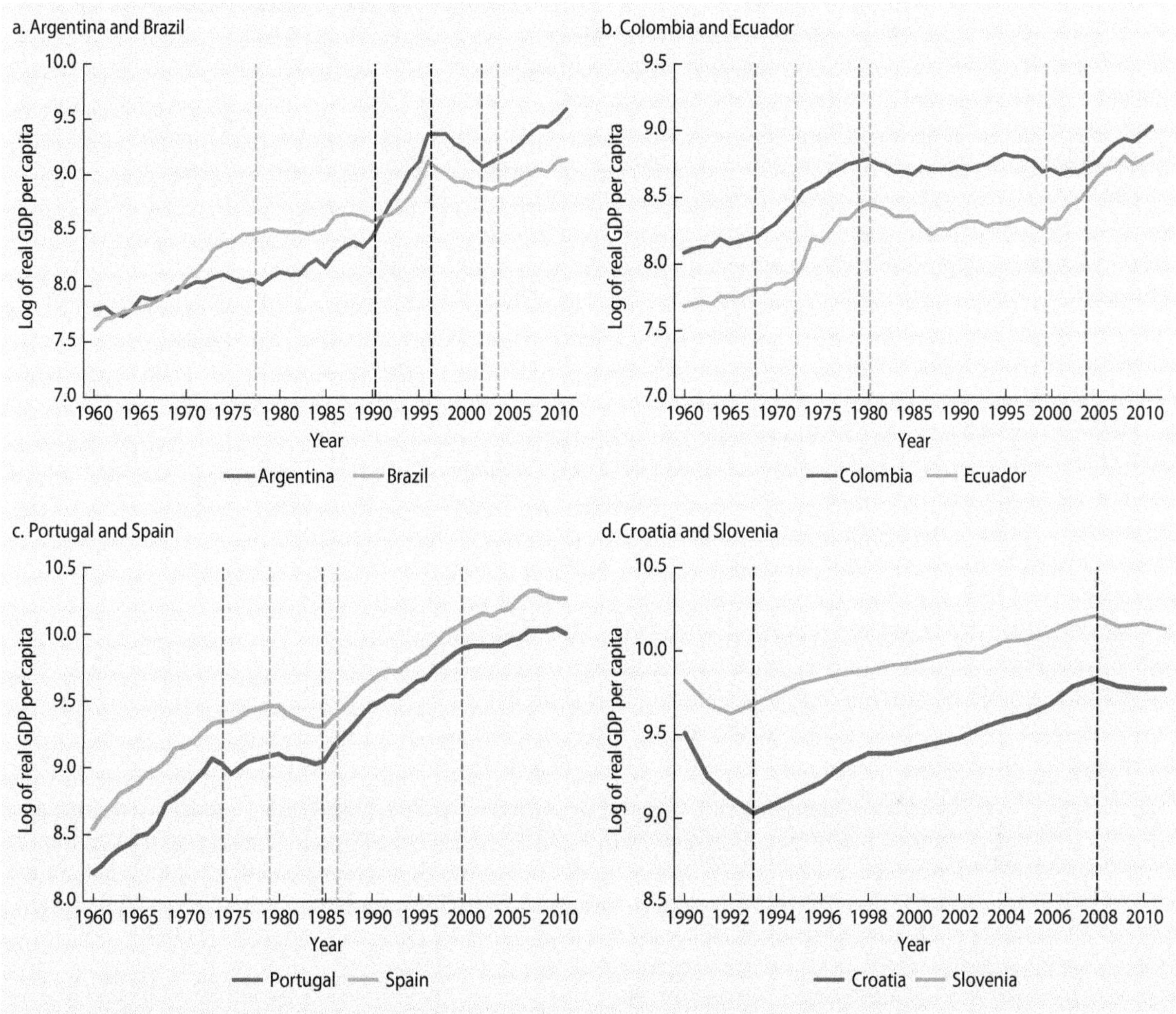

a. Argentina and Brazil

b. Colombia and Ecuador

c. Portugal and Spain

d. Croatia and Slovenia

*Source:* World Bank calculations using data from the Penn World Tables 8.1.
*Note:* Real GDP per capita is measured in 2005 US$ in purchasing power parity (PPP) terms. Vertical lines mark structural break dates for each country; black lines correspond to common years of structural breaks. Structural breaks are calculated using the Bai and Perron (2003) algorithm with data from 1950 to 2010.

distance between the pair of countries. Additional controls include the economic distance between the two countries (measured as the absolute value of the log difference of GDP per capita), which is intended to capture the fact that countries at a similar level of development may experience more similar growth processes; pairwise demographic and historical variables (such as dummies taking value 1 if the two countries share an official language,

or if the two countries have a colonial tie), intended to capture similarities in institutions between the two countries; and country-time fixed effects that capture country-specific time-varying characteristics (such as terms-of-trade fluctuations) that may affect the likelihood of a country sharing a growth spell with another country.

Table 1.2 confirms the relationship between distance and the likelihood of two

**TABLE 1.2  Structural breaks, extended growth episodes, and geographic distance**

| | Panel A. Likelihood of simultaneous breaks | | | Panel B. Likelihood of simultaneously experiencing same phase type | | |
|---|---|---|---|---|---|---|
| | All breaks Bai-Perron | High-growth breaks Bai-Perron | Low-growth breaks Bai-Perron | All phases Bai-Perron | High-growth phases Bai-Perron | Low-growth phases Bai-Perron |
| | (1) | (2) | (3) | (1) | (2) | (3) |
| Log of geographic distance | −0.00131*** | −0.000993*** | −0.000321* | −0.0233*** | −0.0112*** | −0.00830*** |
| | (0.000288) | (0.000212) | (0.000190) | (0.00397) | (0.00231) | (0.00238) |
| GDP per capita distance | −0.00114*** | −0.000424*** | −0.000722*** | −0.0101*** | −0.00250* | 0.000193 |
| | (0.000203) | (0.000156) | (0.000126) | (0.00272) | (0.00140) | (0.00164) |
| Country 1-year FE | YES | YES | YES | YES | YES | YES |
| Country 2-year FE | YES | YES | YES | YES | YES | YES |
| Other gravity dummies | YES | YES | YES | YES | YES | YES |
| Observations | 538,326 | 536,859 | 535,976 | 410,469 | 357,167 | 338,949 |
| R-squared | 0.180 | 0.195 | 0.168 | 0.355 | 0.782 | 0.700 |

*Source:* Authors' calculations using data from Penn World Tables 8.1.
*Note:* Cycles are calculated using the Bai and Perron (2003) algorithm. See appendix 1.2 for details on the methodology. OLS estimation. Standard errors in parentheses and clustered at the country pair level. Other gravity dummies include contiguity, colonial ties, formerly same country, and same official language dummies. *** $p<0.01$, ** $p<0.05$, * $p<0.1$.

countries experiencing the same type of structural break in the same direction, highlighted in figure 1.6. Column (1) in panel a shows that distance has a negative and significant coefficient on the likelihood that two countries will experience a structural break in the same direction. Everything else equal, a 1 percent increase in geographic distance translates into a 0.1 percentage point decrease in the probability of two countries sharing a structural break in the same direction.[18]

Columns (2) and (3) explore the effect of geographic distance on the coincidence of specific types of breaks. Column (2) looks exclusively at the coincidence of breaks that are followed by a high-growth episode, and column (3) looks exclusively at the coincidence of breaks that are followed by a low-growth phase. Notice that in both cases the exercise excludes episodes of coincidence of breaks of the other kind. Hence, the resulting coefficient is interpreted as an increase in the probability of the two countries sharing a

type of break relative to no coincidence of any kind of break. The results in columns (2) and (3) confirm the effect of distance on the likelihood of two countries sharing a high-growth break and a low-growth break—in both cases the effect of distance is negative and significant at least at the 10 percent confidence level. However, distance appears to have a larger effect on breaks that are followed by high-growth episodes, and these types of breaks are more precisely estimated.

The relatively low (albeit significant) marginal effect of geographic distance on the likelihood of a simultaneous break in the same direction reflects the fact that these coincidences are rare events. In fact, this is confirmed by the low R-squared of the regression, despite the fact that we include a wide array of country-time fixed effects. The logic for this is simple—as annex 1B discusses, countries experience relatively few breaks (on average, a country experiences 1.5 breaks in the 60 years of data analyzed in the exercise), and these are typically spaced over the time frame analyzed.

Given the sparse nature of episodes of coincidences in the timing of breaks, panel b of table 1.2 turns to the analysis of coincidences in the timing of growth episodes, a more common event. In fact, coincidences in growth episodes occur in 23 percent of the country pair-years in the data, whereas coincidences of break types occur only in 0.7 percent of the observations. The question that remains is whether these coincidences in growth episodes are geographically clustered.

Table 1.2, panel b, shows that, in addition to affecting the likelihood of sharing a similar break, geographic distance affects the probability that two countries have experienced a similar growth episode in a given year. Column (1) of panel b shows that geographic distance has a negative and statistically significant effect on this probability. Everything else equal, the estimated coefficient suggests that a 1 percent increase in geographic distance reduces the probability of two countries experiencing the same growth phase by 2 percentage points. A granular look at the two types of episodes (high-growth and low-growth) shows that distance plays a bigger role in shaping the coincidence of high-growth episodes—a 1 percent increase in distance lowers the probability of two countries experiencing simultaneously a high-growth phase by 1.1 percentage points (column (2), panel b). In contrast, a 1 percent increase in distance lowers the probability of two countries experiencing simultaneously a low-growth phase by 0.8 percentage points (column (3), panel b).

The two preceding exercises, presented in tables 1.1 and 1.2, underscored the geographic clustering in the growth performance of countries. Nearby countries share similar long-run average growth rates and similar extended growth phases over time. However, long-run and medium-term growth are only one dimension of economic development in developing countries. In fact, as argued earlier, short-term fluctuations are entrenched in the growth process of developing countries.

With this in mind, the rest of this chapter explores the extent to which short-term fluctuations display the same geographic clustering as medium-term and long-term growth.

## The geography of volatility

Broadly speaking, developing countries have topped the charts over the last four decades in terms of volatility. Moreover, Loayza et al. (2007) show that among the most volatile countries, most of which are developing countries, some are small economies (Dominican Republic and Togo) but there are also large ones (China and Argentina); many are predominantly commodity exporters (Ecuador and Nigeria), but some are rapidly industrializing economies (Indonesia and Peru). Hence, volatility has been an endemic characteristic of the development process in developing countries.

Moreover, developing countries appear to incur disproportionately large costs stemming from short-term swings in economic activity compared to developed economies. The larger costs inflicted by short-term fluctuations on developing countries is documented by Calderón and Fuentes (2014). The authors used quarterly data on GDP to identify high-frequency changes in economic activity. The authors implemented the algorithm proposed by Harding and Pagan (2002) to identify periods of recessions, recoveries, and expansions. They then showed that recessions in emerging economies are deeper, steeper, and more costly relative to recessions in industrialized countries.

However, as figure 1.3 exemplifies, volatility varies greatly across developing countries. Broadly speaking, African nations top the distribution of volatility, whereas East Asian economies stand on the low end of the distribution. Similar to what was documented for growth, this constitutes evidence of a geographic clustering of volatility that has not been studied in the literature.

One way to explore the geographic clustering of short-term economic fluctuations is to follow a similar approach as in table 1.2 and document the effect of geographic distance on the likelihood of two countries simultaneously going through the same economic cycle, as defined by Calderón and Fuentes (2014). More specifically, the exercise estimates the determinants of the probability in a given quarter of two countries going through the same cycle. The explanatory variables include the (log) geographic distance between each pair of countries, the economic distance between the two countries (measured as the absolute value of the log difference of GDP per capita), pairwise demographic and historical variables (such as dummies taking value 1 if the two countries share an official language or if the two countries have colonial ties), and country-quarter fixed effects that capture country-specific time-varying characteristics (such as terms-of-trade fluctuations).[19] Methodological details can be found in annex 1C.

The results of this exercise, presented in table 1.3, show a negative and significant effect of geographic distance on the likelihood of two countries simultaneously going through the same economic cycle. All other things equal, a 1 percent decrease in

geographic distance reduces the probability of two countries simultaneously going through the same economic cycle by 1.8 percentage points (column (1)). Moreover, distance plays a similar role in explaining different types of economic cycles. Columns (2)–(4) of table 1.3 show that the marginal effect of distance on the likelihood of two countries simultaneously going through a recession, an expansion, or a recovery is statistically significant and similar in magnitude; an increase in distance reduces the probability of interest by roughly 0.4 percentage points.

Additional evidence on the geographic clustering of short-term economic performance and volatility is found in the literature on international business cycles. Motivated by the increasing interconnectedness of the global economy, this body of work initially aimed at quantifying the relative importance of domestic, regional, and global factors in explaining a country's GDP volatility. An early example of studies in this strand of the literature is Kose, Otrok, and Whiteman (2003), who used data up to 1990 and found that a single global factor explains the bulk of the volatility in high-income economies,

**TABLE 1.3   Short-term cycles and geographic distance**

| | Dependent variable: Same cycle dummy | | | |
|---|---|---|---|---|
| | All | Contraction | Recoveries | Expansions |
| | (1) | (2) | (3) | (4) |
| Log of geographic distance | −0.0188*** | −0.00440*** | −0.00391*** | −0.00485*** |
| | (0.00313) | (0.00120) | (0.00137) | (0.00165) |
| GDP per capita distance | −0.0336*** | −0.0106*** | −0.00178 | −0.00407** |
| | (0.00331) | (0.00133) | (0.00136) | (0.00192) |
| Country 1-quarter FE | YES | YES | YES | YES |
| Country 2-quarter FE | YES | YES | YES | YES |
| Other gravity dummies | YES | YES | YES | YES |
| Observations | 210,223 | 183,536 | 92,697 | 111,040 |
| R-squared | 0.509 | 0.909 | 0.602 | 0.831 |

*Source:* Data from Calderón and Fuentes (2014).
*Note:* Cycles are calculated using the Harding and Pagan (2002) algorithm. See annex 1C for details on the methodology and data. OLS estimation. Standard errors in parentheses and clustered at the country pair level. Other gravity dummies include contiguity, colonial ties, formerly same country, and same official language dummies. *** $p<0.01$, ** $p<0.05$, * $p<0.1$.

whereas country factors play by far the dominant role in developing countries. In contrast, regional factors play a very small role in explaining GDP volatility.

More recently, the international business cycle literature finds that the weight carried by regional factors in explaining GDP growth volatility has increased substantially since the mid-1980s. For example, Hirata, Kose, and Otrok (2013) reassess the questions of Kose, Otrok, and Whiteman (2003) by means of a dynamic factor model and find that regional factors explain a larger share of output volatility relative to global factors in the 1960–2010 period, and that the weight carried by regional factors has increased over time.

In this vein, Hevia and Servén (2016), in a background paper prepared for this report, attempt to dig deeper into the regional nature of economic business cycles. The authors used GDP growth data from 1960 to 2011 and decompose growth volatility into global, regional, and country-specific shocks using a factor model similar to those used in previous studies. In particular, the authors estimated the evolution of three variables affecting a country's GDP growth: a global factor, a region-specific factor, and a country-specific factor. The authors assumed that the global and the regional factors do not affect all countries equally; they are amplified or dampened by a variable called "factor loading." The methodology used by Hevia and Servén (2016) differs from previous work, most notably Hirata, Kose, and Otrok (2013), in that it allows regional factors to be correlated between themselves. The interested reader can find more details on the methodology used in this exercise in annex 1D. The baseline results of the exercise from Hevia and Servén (2016) are presented in figure 1.7.

Figure 1.7 shows that the lion's share of growth volatility in the average country in the world over the period 1960–2011 is explained by country-specific factors. More precisely, idiosyncratic shocks explain about 65 percent of the total variance of the average country in the world. Interestingly,

**FIGURE 1.7    Variance decomposition by region, 1960–2011**

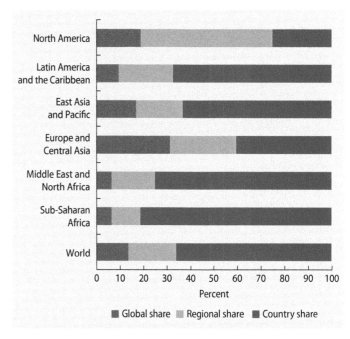

*Source:* Hevia and Servén (2016).
*Note:* Numbers for each region correspond to the contribution of each of the three factors to growth variance in the average country in the region. Global share is the share of a country's real GDP growth variance that is explained by a global factor—that is, a factor that is common to all countries in the world. Regional share is the share of a country's real GDP growth variance that is explained by a regional factor—that is, a factor that is common to all countries in the region. Finally, country share is the share of a country's real GDP growth variance that is explained by an idiosyncratic factor. See annex 1D for more details on the methodology and annex 1A for countries included in the analysis.

when looking exclusively at external factors, the results suggest that regional factors explain a larger share of the variance than do global factors; the former explains close to 20 percent, whereas the latter explains about 15 percent.

Going beyond world averages, figure 1.7 shows that there are substantial differences in terms of the contribution of each of these three factors across regions. On one extreme, North America, and to a lesser extent Europe, display a pattern where country-specific factors explain a relatively small share of GDP volatility.[20] In contrast, developing regions display a pattern that resembles more closely that of the average country—country-specific factors play the largest role in explaining volatility. One feature that is shared by most regions is that

## FIGURE 1.8 Variance decomposition by region and subperiod

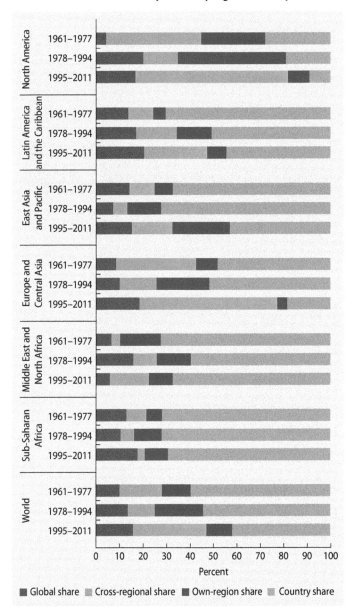

■ Global share  ■ Cross-regional share  ■ Own-region share  ■ Country share

*Source:* Hevia and Servén (2016).
*Note:* Numbers for each region correspond to the contribution of each of the three factors to the growth variance in the average country in the region. Global share is the share of a country's real GDP growth variance that is explained by a global factor—that is, a factor that is common to all countries in the world. Regional share is the share of a country's real GDP growth variance that is explained by a regional factor—that is, a factor that is common to all countries in the region. The regional factor for each region is split into two components, one that is orthogonal to other regions (own region) and one that is correlated with those of other regions. Finally, country share is the share of a country's real GDP growth variance that is explained by an idiosyncratic factor. See annex 1D for more details on the methodology and annex 1A for countries included in the analysis.

the balance between external factors, namely global and regional, tilts in favor of regional factors. Moreover, in most cases the differences between these two factors is quite large—in North America, Latin America, and the Middle East and North Africa, the regional factors explain twice as much of GDP variance as do the global factors.

One caveat should be added to the results in figure 1.7, which indicate that idiosyncratic factors explain the largest share of GDP volatility (followed by regional factors). The results assume that the way in which each of these factors affects GDP growth (the factor loadings) has remained constant over the past 50 years. As discussed at the beginning of this chapter, there are good reasons to believe this assumption may be flawed. One would expect the technological and policy changes that led to the current wave of globalization to dramatically affect the exposure of countries to global and regional shocks. To address this caveat, Hevia and Servén (2016) reestimated their model for three separate time periods: 1960–1977, 1978–1994, and 1995–2011. The results of this additional exercise are presented in figure 1.8.

The evidence from the three periods mentioned above leads to interesting conclusions. First, the weight carried by idiosyncratic factors appears to fall over time, with only the exception of the Middle East and North Africa region.[21] This is arguably the result of improvements over time in macrofundamentals, especially in developing countries, and of more exposure to external factors. Second, the lion's share of the increase in the weight carried by external factors in explaining GDP growth volatility is attributable to an increase in regional factors rather than global factors. Moreover, figure 1.7 shows that the increased weight of the regional factors comes mainly from the part that is correlated across regions. This suggests that, during the most recent wave of globalization, economic shocks tended to affect various regions at the same time, although not all.

## The geographic clustering of economic performance and its relevance for economic integration strategies

The analysis presented above provides evidence that over the last thirty years, as the world has become increasingly interconnected, the link between economic performance and geography has been alive and well. Whether we look at the short or long run, at growth or volatility, economic performance appears to be markedly clustered at a geographic level, suggesting that distance is far from dead.

To be sure, the link between economic performance and geography can be intermediated by a number of factors. Take, for instance, LAC. More than half the countries in the region share a common colonizer, a common official language, a similar legal system, and, arguably, similar institutional arrangements and quality of institutions. Most South American countries are net exporters of minerals and hydrocarbons, whereas many Central American and Caribbean economies are not. Hence, the geographic clustering of these attributes, which the literature has identified as potential factors affecting economic performance, may be another explanation for the results documented above.

However, it is hard to explain the link between economic performance and geography exclusively through these country characteristics. After all, the factors that are listed above are time invariant or highly persistent. In contrast, the results in Hevia and Servén (2016) show that the geographic clustering of economic performance has been changing over time, suggesting that other time-varying factors are also weighing in to explain these patterns. Furthermore, some of the evidence showcased in this chapter in favor of the geographic clustering of economic performance is conditional on both a common institutional heritage and an economic structure.

Regardless of the fundamental reasons shaping it, the robust correlation between a country's economic performance and that of its neighbors poses important questions for policy makers around the world when thinking about economic integration strategies. A first question concerns the desirability of integration with nearby countries: Are the benefits of integrating with nearby countries in terms of growth and stability greater than those of integrating with the rest of the world? If the answer is yes, and given that geography already plays a role in favor of regional economic integration, a second question arises: Should policy act in favor of reinforcing regional integration or be neutral and let geography alone play its part? Answering these questions is of particular importance for Latin America and the Caribbean, a region that throughout its development path has been afflicted by low growth and volatility and that once more faces the important challenge of finding engines of growth to help it break from its past. The rest of this report digs deeper into these questions in hopes of enhancing our understanding of both the causes and consequences of regional economic integration.

## Annex 1A. Classification of regions

Many parts of the report emphasize differences in outcomes across regions. For that purpose, this annex presents the list of countries included in each region. With some exceptions that will be properly highlighted, the list of countries below will be respected throughout the report.

East Asia and Pacific (EAP) includes Australia; Brunei Darussalam; Cambodia; China; Fiji; Hong Kong SAR, China; Indonesia; Japan; Kiribati; the Democratic People's Republic of Korea; the Republic of Korea; the Lao People's Democratic Republic; Malaysia; Mongolia; Myanmar; New Zealand; Palau; Papua New Guinea; the Philippines; Samoa; Singapore; the Solomon Islands; Thailand; Tonga; Tuvalu; Vanuatu; and Vietnam.

Europe and Central Asia (ECA) includes Albania; Armenia; Azerbaijan; Belarus;

**TABLE A.1.1  Summary statistics for structural breaks**

| | All Countries | LAC | EAP | ECA | EU15 + | MENA | North America | South Asia | Sub-Saharan Africa |
|---|---|---|---|---|---|---|---|---|---|
| **Panel A. Total breaks** | | | | | | | | | |
| All breaks | 236 | 46 | 27 | 44 | 26 | 29 | 2 | 10 | 52 |
| High growth breaks | 132 | 24 | 18 | 32 | 6 | 16 | 0 | 6 | 30 |
| Low growth breaks | 114 | 22 | 9 | 12 | 20 | 13 | 2 | 4 | 32 |
| **Panel B. Average by country** | | | | | | | | | |
| All breaks | 1.51 | 1.59 | 1.59 | 1.52 | 1.73 | 1.71 | 1.00 | 1.67 | 1.33 |
| High growth breaks | 0.78 | 0.83 | 1.06 | 1.10 | 0.40 | 0.94 | 0.00 | 1.00 | 0.77 |
| Low growth breaks | 0.73 | 0.76 | 0.53 | 0.41 | 1.33 | 0.76 | 1.00 | 0.67 | 0.56 |

*Source:* Authors' calculations.
*Notes:* Breaks are identified using the Bai and Perron (2003) methodology. High growth breaks are breaks that mark the beginning of a phase where average growth exceeds the average growth of the previous phase. Conversely, low growth breaks are identfied as breaks that mark the beginning of a phase with average growth smaller than the average growth of the previous phase.

Bosnia and Herzegovina; Bulgaria; Croatia; Cyprus; the Czech Republic; Estonia; Faeroe Islands; Georgia; Greenland; Hungary; Kazakhstan; the Kyrgyz Republic; Latvia; Lithuania; the former Yugoslav Republic of Macedonia; Moldova; Montenegro; Poland; Romania; the Russian Federation; Serbia; the Slovak Republic; Slovenia; Tajikistan; Turkey; Turkmenistan; Ukraine; and Uzbekistan.

European Union 15 extended (EU15+) includes Austria; Belgium; Denmark; Finland; France; Germany; Greece; Iceland; Ireland; Italy; Luxembourg; Netherlands; Norway; Portugal; Spain; Sweden; Switzerland; and the United Kingdom.

Latin America and the Caribbean (LAC) includes Argentina; The Bahamas; Barbados; Belize; Bolivia; Brazil; Chile; Colombia; Costa Rica; Dominica; the Dominican Republic; Ecuador; El Salvador; Grenada; Guatemala; Guyana; Haiti; Honduras; Jamaica; Mexico; Nicaragua; Panama; Paraguay; Peru; St. Kitts and Nevis; St. Lucia; St. Vincent and the Grenadines; Suriname; Trinidad and Tobago; Uruguay; and República Bolivariana de Venezuela.

Middle East and North Africa (MENA) includes Algeria; Bahrain; Djibouti; the Arab Republic of Egypt; the Islamic Republic of Iran; Iraq; Israel; Jordan; Kuwait; Lebanon; Libya; Malta; Morocco; Oman; Qatar; Saudi Arabia;

the Syrian Arab Republic; Tunisia; the United Arab Emirates; and the Republic of Yemen.

North America includes Canada and the United States.

South Asia (SAR) includes Afghanistan; Bangladesh; Bhutan; India; Maldives; Nepal; Pakistan; and Sri Lanka.

Sub-Saharan Africa (SSA) includes Angola; Benin; Burkina Faso; Burundi; Cabo Verde; Cameroon; the Central African Republic; Chad; Comoros; the Democratic Republic of Congo; the Republic of Congo; Côte d'Ivoire; Equatorial Guinea; Ethiopia; Gabon; The Gambia; Ghana; Guinea; Guinea-Bissau; Kenya; Liberia; Madagascar; Malawi; Mali; Mauritania; Mauritius; Mozambique; Niger; Nigeria; Rwanda; São Tomé and Príncipe; Senegal; Seychelles; Sierra Leone; Somalia; South Africa; Sudan; Tanzania; Togo; Uganda; Zambia; and Zimbabwe.

## Annex 1B. Identification of structural breaks

The Bai and Perron (2003) method finds and tests for multiple structural breaks within a time series. In the case of our exercise, we look at a growth series within a country,

$$g_t = \alpha_R + e_t, \qquad (1B.1)$$

where $g_t$ is the annual growth rate in purchasing power parity (PPP) per capita income, $\alpha_R$ is the mean growth rate during phase R, and $e_t$ is an error term. Data are taken from the Penn World Tables 8.1.

The intuition for the Bai and Perron method is as follows. First, an algorithm searches all possible sets of breaks (up to a maximum number of breaks) and determines for each number of breaks the set that produces the maximum goodness-of-fit (R-squared). The statistical tests then determine whether the improved fit produced by allowing an additional break is sufficiently large, given what would be expected by chance (due to the error process), according to asymptotic distributions the authors derive. Starting with a null of no breaks, sequential tests of $k$ vs. $k+1$ breaks allow one to determine the appropriate number of breaks in a data series. Bai and Perron determine critical values for tests of various size and employ a "trimming" parameter, expressed as a percentage of the number of observations, which constrains the minimum distance between consecutive breaks. For our main results, we focus on a specification with a 10 percent trimming parameter, which means that each phase has to have about 6 years.

We find a total of 236 breaks around the world, 136 high-growth breaks (up breaks) and 84 low-growth breaks (down breaks) (table 1B.1, panel a). This amounts to an average of 1.5 breaks per country (panel b). The three regions with the most total breaks are Sub-Saharan Africa (SSA), Latin America and the Caribbean (LAC), and East Asia and Pacific (EAP). However, in EAP most breaks are up breaks, whereas in SSA and LAC breaks are evenly distributed between up and down breaks.

## Annex 1C. Identification of economic cycles

A point of contention in business cycle analysis is how to identify turning points in economic activity—that is, points at which the economy switches from expansion to contraction or vice versa. We date the turning points of the business cycle using an algorithm developed by Harding and Pagan (2002) and used by Calderón and Fuentes (2014). The algorithm is as follows:

A cyclical peak in the level of real output of country $i$ occurs at time $t$ if

$$(1 - L^2)y_{it} > 0, (1 - L)y_{it} > 0, \text{ and}$$
$$(1 - L)y_{i,t+1} < 0, (1 - L^2)y_{i,t+2} < 0, \quad (1C.1)$$

and a cyclical trough in the level of real output in country $i$ occurs at time $t$ if

$$(1 - L^2)y_{it} < 0, (1 - L)y_{it} < 0, \text{ and}$$
$$(1 - L)y_{i,t+1} > 0, (1 - L^2)y_{i,t+2} > 0, \quad (1C.2)$$

where $L$ is the lag operator, such that $L^k y_t = y_{t-k}$, and $y_{it}$ is the GDP growth of country $i$ at time $t$. These conditions ensure that the turning points are a maximum or minimum relative to two quarters on either side of any identified time $t$. In addition, the algorithm requires that

- Complete cycles run from peak to trough and have two phases: contractions (peak to trough) and expansions (trough to peak). Additionally, peaks and troughs must alternate.
- The minimum duration of a cycle is 5 quarters. Each phase of the cycle must last at last 2 quarters.

In our analysis we also define recovery as the period in which growth is above the previous peak but has not yet reached a new peak.

## Annex 1D. Variance decomposition using a multilevel factor model

Factor models are a common methodology used to analyze cross-sectional dependence in time series data. The basic idea is that the modeler chooses "factors" that are thought to exert a common influence.

In their paper Hevia and Servén (2016) consider the following two-level factor model of real GDP growth:

$$y_{m,it} = \beta_{m,i} G_t + (\lambda_{m,i})' F_{m,t} + \mu_{m,it} \quad (1D.1)$$

with $i = 2,..N_m$; $m = 1,...,M$; and $t = 1,...,T$. Here $y_{m,it}$ denotes the growth rate of GDP in country $i$ of region $m$ over period $t$, $G_t$ is a set of $r_G$ common world (global) factors, and $F_{mt}$ is a set of $r_m$ region-specific factors. $\beta_{m,i}$ and $\lambda_{m,i}$ are the factor loading terms, and $\mu_{m,it}$ is an error component that may be heteroskedastic and serially and/or cross-sectionally (weakly) correlated. Stacking observations for region $m$ at time $t$, the model can be written

$$Y_{mt} = \tau_m G_t + \Lambda_m F_{mt} + \mu_{mt} \qquad (1D.2)$$

and further combining all regions into a $T \times N$ matric ($N = \Sigma r_m$), the model can be written in matrix form:

$$Y = G\tau' + F + U, \qquad (1D.3)$$

where $G$ and $F$ are $(T \times r_G)$ and $(T \times \Sigma r_m)$ matrixes of factors $\tau$ and $\Lambda$ are $(N \times r_G)$ and $(N \times \Sigma r_m)$ matrixes of global and regional factor loadings. $\Lambda$ is block diagonal, with the $m$th block containing the loadings of the $N_m$ countries in the $m$th region on their $r_m$ regional factors.

The model requires the following restrictions to identify the loading factors:

1. $\dfrac{G'G}{T} = I_{rG}$ and $\dfrac{F'_m F_m}{T} I_{rm}$ for all $m$
2. $\tau'\tau$, and $\Lambda'_m \Lambda_m$, $m = 1,...,M$ are diagonal matrices
3. $F'_m G = 0$ for all $m$

These assumptions normalize the factors and impose the condition that the regional and global factors are independent and allow for the identification of the factor-loading terms.

## Notes

1. World Bank (2002) identified two previous waves of globalization. A first wave started in 1870 and lasted for about 40 years. Sharp reductions in transportation costs during this period eased the movements of goods and people, leading to an increase in trade and migration flows, especially between industrialized countries. A second wave of globalization took place from the end of World War II until the early 1980s. Following the protectionism of the interwar period, industrialized countries embraced internationalization by removing the trade barriers that were put in place in the early years of the twentieth century, yielding visible increases in global trade flows over that period—from 5 percent of global GDP in 1950 to about 15 percent of GDP in 1980.

2. A World Trade Organization (WTO) brochure shows that from 1996 to 2013 the bound most-favored-nation tariff for the average WTO member, which is the maximum tariff a country can impose on other countries, has fallen from about 11 percent to close to 8 percent. The reduction was even sharper for applied tariffs (see https://www.wto.org/english/thewto_e/20y_e/wto_20_brochure_e.pdf).

   Reductions in transportation costs are documented in Hummels (2007).

3. Trade in tasks, which is an essential aspect of global value chains (GVCs), is tightly linked to the communication costs between producers of different tasks. For instance, Grossman and Rossi-Hansberg (2012) show in a theoretical model that reductions in communication costs increase the likelihood of trade in tasks. This is consistent with the observation that GVCs and outsourcing have gained prominence in tandem with tariff reductions and the rise of ICTs.

   Data from the United Nations Conference on Trade and Development show the rapid growth of foreign direct investment (FDI) flows, which are a proxy for Multinational Activity, since the 1980s. In the 30 years from 1980 to 2010, the dollar amount of FDI flows grew at a yearly rate of 10.8 percent, higher than the 7.8 percent yearly growth rate of the dollar amount of trade over the same period.

   Freund and Weinhold (2002) find evidence that Internet connectivity is associated with growth in export of services. The authors use data on exports of services to the United States and find that countries with deeper Internet penetration experience higher growth of exports to the United States.

4. The terms the "death of distance" and "the world is flat" were introduced in two books, *The Death of Distance: How the*

*Communications Revolution Is Changing Our Lives* by Frances Cairncross (1997) and the international best-seller *The World Is Flat: A Brief History of the Twenty-First Century* by Thomas L. Friedman (2007), respectively.

5. Throughout this report, countries are grouped in regions according to several definitions of regions. One regional grouping used extensively is a slight modification of the World Bank regional classification. See annex 1A for a detailed explanation of this regional classification.

   Annual data on GDP per capita and GDP per capita growth come from the Penn World Tables version 8.1. In particular, the analysis uses real GDP per capita in purchasing power parity (PPP) terms, which is constructed as the ratio between demand-side real GDP per capita in PPP terms and population. GDP per capita in PPP terms helps take into account differences in the purchasing power across countries in the assessment of income per capita differences.

6. See Loayza et al. (2007) for a discussion of the impact of volatility on welfare.

7. Dollar, Kleineberg, and Kraay (2014) show that growth is positively and significantly correlated with various functional forms of the social welfare function. Easterly (1999) has previously shown that GDP per capita is strongly correlated with a plethora of alternative proxies of the quality of life across countries.

8. Pritchett (2000) identified six growth patterns in the nearly 30 years of data he analyzed (his analysis starts in 1960 and finishes in an end year that varies between 1985 and 1992). First, there are some countries with processes he labeled as "accelerations." These are countries that experienced a break in their growth process, moving from an initially moderate growth rate to a high growth rate. An example of this type of process is Chile. This a rare process—only 6 percent of the countries in his sample experience such a process. A second process he identified is "steep hills." These are countries that experienced a high and relatively stable growth rate throughout the 30 years analyzed in the paper. This process comprises about 10 percent of the countries in the sample and includes all the Asian Tigers. A third process is what Pritchett calls "hills." These are countries that experienced a moderate and

relatively stable growth rate throughout the 30 years analyzed in the paper. This process comprises about 30 percent of the countries in the sample and includes most high-income countries. A fourth process is what the author labeled "plateaus," in which countries experience a break in their growth process, moving from an initially high growth rate to a moderate growth rate. This process includes countries like Brazil and about 14 percent of the countries in the sample. The fifth process identified by the author is what he labeled "plains," encapsulating countries with a virtually zero growth rate throughout the 30 years he analyzes. Finally, the most common pattern he identified, comprising close to 30 percent of the countries in the sample, is what he labeled "mountains." This pattern includes countries that experienced a period of positive growth followed by a period of negative growth.

9. Nobel Laureate Robert Lucas Jr. made similar calculations in his 1988 *Journal of Monetary Economics* paper titled "On the Mechanics of Economic Development." In this widely cited paper, he famously stated that "once one starts thinking about them (differences in growth and its consequences), it is hard to think about anything else."

10. Control variables used by Vamvakidis (1998) include investment, secondary school enrollment, growth in terms of trade, infant mortality, population growth, openness to trade, years having an open policy toward trade, and average annual trade share.

11. See Keller (2002) and Bravo-Ortega, Cusolito, and Lederman (2016) for evidence on the link between technology diffusion and distance.

12. One way to partly overcome the problem of omitted variables is to include country fixed effects in the regression, an approach that was common in a series of empirical growth papers in the 1990s. However, as highlighted in Pritchett (2000), this approach has problems of its own.

13. The differences in growth processes between high-income and developing countries transcend the arbitrary example presented above. Pritchett (2000) shows that most industrialized countries follow a growth process that he labels as "hills," characterized by an upward and stable path. In contrast, developing countries have a much wider range of growth processes that range from accelerations to

"mountains," that is, long spells of positive growth followed by long spells of negative growth. Similar insights are uncovered in Aguiar and Gopinath (2007), who argue that, whereas growth processes in industrialized countries are well approximated by small deviations around a stable trend, in developing countries the process is one of substantial volatility in the trend.

14. Hausmann, Pritchett, and Rodrik (2005) define a growth acceleration as an eight-year period where the growth rate is at least 3.5 percent per year and 2 percent higher than it was before the acceleration began.

15. The econometric test in Bai and Perron (2003) calculates a confidence interval for the date of the structural break of each country. In the case of the growth series analyzed in the exercise, the 90 percent confidence interval of the average structural break is approximately +/–3.5 years around the identified break year.

16. The exercise is performed through an ordinary least squares (OLS) estimation (linear probability model) of a dummy variable taking value 1 if two countries experience a break in the same direction, in the case of the regression presented in panel a, and a dummy taking value 1 if two countries are in the same phase in a given year, in the case of panel b.

17. In a robustness exercise we define up and down breaks in a slightly different way. In particular, up breaks and up phases are identified as breaks that start phases where (i) growth is higher than in the previous phase and (ii) growth exceeds 3 percent annually throughout the phase. In contrast, down breaks and down phases are identified as breaks that start phases where (i) growth is lower than in the previous phase and (ii) growth is lower than 0.5 percent annually throughout the phase. Using these alternatives does not change the qualitative results presented in what follows.

18. Notice that economic distance also has a negative, statistically significant effect on the likelihood of the two countries experiencing a break in the same direction. Moreover, the effect is of similar magnitude as that of geographic distance.

19. Economic distance is intended to capture the fact that countries of similar level of development may experience similar growth processes; demographic dummies are intended to capture similarities in institutions between the two countries, and country-quarter fixed effects capture time varying country characteristics that may affect the likelihood of a country sharing a growth spell with another country.

20. The regions in Hevia and Servén (2016) are defined as follows: Mexico is included in North America, as opposed to Latin America as in the rest of this report; and Bangladesh, India, and Pakistan are included in East Asia, as opposed to Central Asia.

21. In another paper commissioned for this report, Bennett et al. (2016) find a similar decline in the country-specific component of trade volatility.

## References

Acemoglu, Daron, David Laibson, and John List. 2014. "Equalizing Superstars: the Internet and the Democratization of Education." *American Economic Review Papers and Proceedings* 104 (5): 523–27.

Acemoglu, Daron, Simon Johnson, and James A. Robinson, 2001. "The Colonial Origins of Comparative Development: An Empirical Investigation." *American Economic Review* 91 (5): 1369–1401.

Aguiar, Mark, and Gita Gopinath. 2007. "Emerging Market Business Cycles: The Cycle Is the Trend." *Journal of Political Economy* 115: 69–102.

Arora, Vivek, and Athanasios Vamvakidis. 2005. "How Much Do Trading Partners Matter for Economic Growth?" *IMF Staff Papers* 52 (1): 24–40.

Bai, Jushan, and Pierre Perron, 2003. "Computation and Analysis of Multiple Structural Change Models." *Journal of Applied Econometrics* 18 (1): 1–22.

Bennett, Federico, Daniel Lederman, Samuel Pienknagura, and Diego Rojas. 2016. "The Volatility of International Trade Flows in the 21st Century: Whose Fault is it Anyway?" Policy Research Working Paper 7781, World Bank, Washington, DC.

Berthelon, Matias, and Caroline Freund, 2008. "On the Conservation of Distance in International Trade." *Journal of International Economics* 75 (2): 310–20.

Bravo-Ortega, Claudio, Ana P. Cusolito, and Daniel Lederman, 2016. "Faraway or Nearby?

Domestic and International Spillovers in Patenting and Product Innovation." Policy Research Working Paper 7828, World Bank, Washington, DC.

Cairncross, Frances. 1997. *The Death of Distance: How the Communications Revolution Is Changing Our Lives.* Boston: Harvard Business School Press.

Calderón, César, and Rodrigo Fuentes. 2014. "Have Business Cycles Changed over the Last Two Decades? An Empirical Investigation." *Journal of Development Economics* 109 (July): 98–123.

de la Torre, Augusto, Tatiana Didier, Alain Ize, Daniel Lederman, and Sergio Schmukler. 2015. *Latin America and the Rising South: Changing World, Changing Priorities.* Washington, DC: World Bank.

Dollar, David, Tatjana Kleineberg, and Aart Kraay. 2014. "Growth, Inequality, and Social Welfare: Cross-Country Evidence." Policy Research Working Paper 6842, World Bank, Washington, DC.

Dollar, David, Tatjana Kleineberg, and Aart Kraay, 2016. "Growth Still Is Good for the Poor." *European Economic Review* 81 (January): 68–85.

Easterly, William. 1999. "Life during Growth." *Journal of Economic Growth* 4 (3): 239–76

Frankel, Jeffrey A., and David H. Romer. 1999. "Does Trade Cause Growth?" *American Economic Review* 89 (3): 379–99.

Freund, Caroline, and Diana Weinhold. 2002. "The Internet and International Trade in Services." *American Economic Review* 92 (2): 236–40.

———. 2004. "The Effect of the Internet on International Trade." *Journal of International Economics* 62:171–89.

Friedman, Thomas L. 2007. *The World Is Flat: A Brief History of the Twenty-First Century.* New York: Picador/Farrar, Strauss and Giroux.

Grossman, Gene, and Esteban Rossi-Hansberg, 2012. "Task Trade Between Similar Countries." *Econometrica* 80 (2): 593–629.

Harding, D. and A. Pagan. 2002. "Dissecting the Cycle: A Methodological Investigation." *Journal of Monetary Economics* 49 (2): 365–81.

Hausmann, Ricardo, Lant Pritchett, and Dani Rodrik, 2005. "Growth Accelerations." *Journal of Economic Growth* 10 (4): 303–29.

Head, K., and T. Mayer. 2014. "Gravity Equations: Workhorse, Toolkit and Cookbook." In Vol. 4 of *Handbook of International Economics*, edited by Gita Gopinath, Elhanan Helpman, and Kenneth Rogoff. Amsterdam: Elsevier.

Hevia, Constantino, and Luis Servén, 2016. "International Business Cycles: Global or Regional?" Background paper prepared for this report.

Hirata, Hideaki, Ayhan Kose, and Christopher Otrok. 2013. "Regionalization vs. Globalization." IMF Working Papers 13/19, International Monetary Fund, Washington, DC.

Hummels, David. 2007. "Transportation Costs and International Trade in the Second Era of Globalization." *Journal of Economic Perspectives* 21 (3): 131–54.

Jones, Benjamin F., and Benjamin A. Olken. 2008. "The Anatomy of Start-Stop Growth." *The Review of Economics and Statistics* 90 (3): 582–87.

Keller, Wolfgang. 2002. "Geographic Localization of International Technology Diffusion." *American Economic Review* 92 (1): 120–42.

Kose, Ayhan, Christopher Otrok, and Charles Whiteman, 2003. "International Business Cycles: World, Region, and Country Specific Factors." *American Economic Review* 93 (4): 1216–39.

Lendle, A., M. Olarreaga, S. Schropp, and P. Vezina. 2012. "There Goes Gravity: How eBay Reduces Trade Costs." Policy Research Working Paper 6253, World Bank, Washington, DC.

Loayza, Norman, Romain Ranciere, Luis Servén, and Jaume Ventura. 2007. "Macroeconomic Volatility and Welfare in Developing Countries: An Introduction." *World Bank Economic Review* 21 (3): 343–57.

Lucas, Robert Jr. 1988. "On the Mechanics of Economic Development." *Journal of Monetary Economics* 22 (1): 3–42.

Pritchett, Lant. 2000. "Understanding Patterns of Economic Growth: Searching for Hills among Plateaus, Mountains, and Plains." *World Bank Economic Review* 14 (2): 221–50.

Vamvakidis, Athanasios. 1998. "Regional Integration and Economic Growth." *World Bank Economic Review* 12 (2): 251–70.

World Bank. 2002. *Globalization, Growth and Poverty: Building an Inclusive World Economy.* Washington, DC: World Bank.

# Regional Trade in the Americas: A Stepping-Stone toward Stable Growth?

## Introduction

Regional trade integration is seen as a potential source of efficiency and growth. In fact, intraregional trade agreements explicitly or implicitly claim that one of their key objectives is to accelerate economic growth. For example, an objective of the Pacific Alliance—the 2012 integration agreement between Chile, Colombia, Mexico, and Peru—is "driving further growth, development, and competiveness of the economies of its members." Similarly, the Dominican Republic–Central America Free Trade Agreement (CAFTA-DR) lists the creation of "new opportunities for economic and social development" and "new employment opportunities and improved working conditions and living standards in their respective territories" as some of its resolutions. Mercosur—the customs union comprising Argentina, Brazil, Paraguay, Uruguay, and República Bolivariana de Venezuela—began to see itself explicitly as a vehicle for stimulating growth in South America even earlier (see, for example, Fanelli 2007).

However, although the link between regional integration and economic outcomes appears to be taken for granted in the minds of many policy makers, the economics literature is far less decisive regarding this link. There is abundant literature studying the potential role of trade integration, broadly speaking, in boosting income levels. Hence, to the extent that regional integration is a natural process of global integration, the arguments linking trade integration and growth should apply to regional integration. Nonetheless, it is hard to find compelling arguments in the academic literature suggesting that regional integration per se can become a stepping-stone for higher and more stable long-term growth.[1] Even less evidence can be found in the literature with regard to the link between regional trade integration and other economic outcomes, such as volatility. As such, it is unclear in what way, if any, regional integration is indeed preferable to global integration, and how regional integration efforts relate to global integration efforts.

In a modest attempt to fill this gap in the literature, we posit three related questions that are crucial to an open regionalism (OR) strategy in Latin America and the Caribbean (LAC):[2] (i) Can LAC achieve higher levels of intraregional trade through policy efforts, assuming this is a desirable outcome?

(ii) Can these efforts help LAC achieve a higher, more stable growth path? (iii) Are there complementarities between regional and global integration?

The rest of this chapter begins by reassessing the extent of LAC's intraregional trade. Understanding the factors affecting intra-LAC trade is important because, despite a growing number of regional trade agreements, the incidence of intra-LAC trade in total trade has remained flat. The assessment presented follows the so-called gravity model of trade, which posits that bilateral trade flows are determined by the economic size of trading partners and by the frictions that hamper bilateral trade flows. Trade frictions, in turn, are assumed to be a function of geographic distance. Controlling for size and distance is important in a region like LAC, where more than half its countries have populations of less than 5 million people and where country pairs are relatively distant. The findings of this exercise suggest that LAC's intraregional trade levels are consistent with what the size of LAC's economies and the distances between regional trading partners predict. There is, however, some scope for formal agreements, especially between South America and the rest of the region, to increase intra-LAC trade.

Importantly, the empirical exercise presented in this chapter highlights that LAC faces higher costs associated with distance compared to other regions. This is partly the reason why LAC's trade with both regional and nonregional partners appears to be relatively low. Thus, region-wide efforts to pursue policies that lower LAC's trade costs, such as investments in infrastructure, could have a big impact on the region's trade competitiveness and should be part of LAC's OR agenda.

The chapter then critically assesses the merits of arguments favoring regional trade integration as a way to achieve efficiency and a stable, high-growth development path. To do this, the chapter does not directly quantify the potential benefits of different integration strategies. Rather, it relies on the economics literature to identify accepted channels through which different forms of international economic integration can stimulate growth and stability, which in turn can be quantified as an indirect way of assessing the priorities for the renewal of OR in the Americas. The report draws upon two prominent strands of economic theory. The first is the idea that the gains from trade depend on differences between countries. In these "neo-classical" models, these differences are usually modeled as arising either from factor supplies (for example, being "labor abundant" or "capital abundant") or from technology. The second is the idea that trade facilitates learning, either through the experience of exporting or from the exposure to new products and ideas that are embodied in imports. Although these are not the only theories that explain trade and the gains from trade, these are two that have perhaps the longest and most established history in international economics.[3]

The analysis shows that, on average, LAC countries have very similar patterns of revealed comparative advantage (RCA), which implies that the efficiency gains from trade integration between LAC countries are expected to be small compared to integration with the rest of the world. However, the conclusions emerging from studying the average pair of countries hides the potential efficiency gains of trade integration between countries with specific traits, such as different economic sizes. Indeed, the analysis shows that there may be unexploited efficiency gains from trade integration between regional partners with large differences in economic size, as they typically display a negative correlation in their trade structure. This contrasts with the high degree of similarity between countries of comparable economic size and suggests that small economies in LAC would probably benefit, from an efficiency point of view, from deeper integration with larger countries in the region.

Regarding the objective of reducing macroeconomic volatility, trade integration between regional partners might even be detrimental in the absence of economic reforms by key regional players. The detrimental effects of regional integration on stability stem from the high variance of import demand seen in countries in the region and the high covariance of import demands across countries in LAC. This high correlation is arguably linked to the similar economic structures shared by LAC countries. The chapter quantifies the impact of deeper regional integration on volatility through two counterfactual exercises, both of which show that increasing trade integration among countries in LAC would increase export volatility for all the countries in the region that are included in the exercise.

Turning to long-term growth, trade between LAC countries is unlikely to deliver knowledge spillovers and learning from imports, one of the channels through which trade integration can boost long-term growth. This is due to the relatively low stock of knowledge in the region, a result of historically low research and development (R&D) efforts. A conclusion of the analysis is that, if LAC wants to reap the pro-growth benefits of trade integration with regional partners, countries like Brazil and Mexico, which exert substantial gravitational pull in the region from the point of view of trade, need to increase their R&D efforts.[4]

Finally, the chapter explores the potential complementarities between regional and global integration efforts. First, it assesses the role of regionally traded goods in LAC's integration. These are goods and services where the costs associated with distance are so high that they are typically only exchanged by neighboring countries and the policy-related barriers to trade are not import tariffs per se, but rather differences in regulatory schemes. For these goods and services, regional integration efforts are equivalent to global integration. Notable examples of these goods and services are electricity and land transportation. Hence, regional efforts to assure the quality and the efficient provision of these types of goods and services will be crucial for the growth and stability prospects of LAC and for the ability of the region to gain international competitiveness in sectors that use these "regionally traded goods" intensively.

Then it studies the role that trade openness has in facilitating learning from interactions with nearby countries. The central idea relates to learning from international trade—in this case, about what can be learned from trading with our neighborhood about exporting to farther away markets. The results suggest that, in general, regional integration facilitates exports to extraregional markets, but this stepping-stone effect in early stages is not independent of the characteristics of regional partners—having richer, globally integrated regional partners increases a country's likelihood of entry and survival in new, extraregional export markets. This finding is thus strictly consistent with our claim that a new "open regionalism" should have a renewed outward-looking orientation.

## Regional trade integration in LAC: International comparison and determinants

Regional trade flows are an integral part of international trade flows. Indeed, over the past 25 years intraregional export flows closely followed total trade flows; they grew rapidly until 2008, dropped during the global financial crisis of 2009, recovered between 2010 and 2011, and have been stagnant since then (figure 2.1, panel a).[5] Moreover, intraregional exports represent a significant share of total trade. Between 1990 and 2014, intraregional exports accounted for approximately 45 percent of total trade.[6]

The aggregate picture presented in figure 2.1, panel a, however, masks important differences in the incidence of intraregional trade flows in total flows across regions. At one extreme stand EU15+ (European Union 15 extended) and East Asia and the Pacific (EAP), regions where intraregional exports accounted for 60 and 50 percent of total trade in 2014, respectively (figure 2.1, panel b). At the other extreme stand regions such as South Asia (SAR), Sub-Saharan Africa (SSA), and the Middle East and North Africa (MENA), where intraregional exports accounted for a meager 10 to 15 percent of total trade in 2014.

FIGURE 2.1   **Intraregional trade around the world**

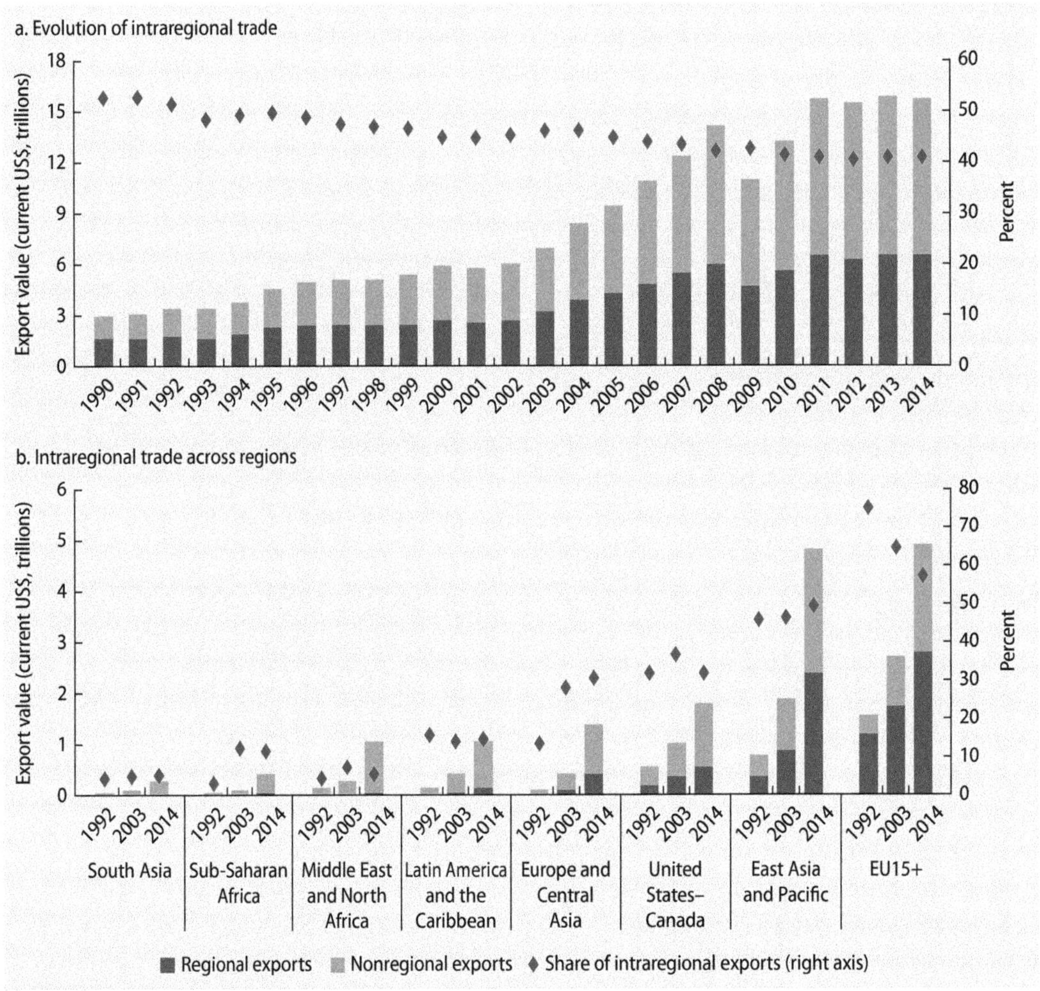

a. Evolution of intraregional trade

b. Intraregional trade across regions

■ Regional exports   ■ Nonregional exports   ◆ Share of intraregional exports (right axis)

*Source:* World Bank calculations based on data from UN COMTRADE.
*Note:* The share of intraregional exports is calculated as the ratio between intraregional exports and total exports. See annex 1A for a list of countries in each region.

The remarkable performance of EAP in terms of regional trade integration has caught the attention of other developing regions for at least two reasons. First, the incidence of intraregional exports in total trade in EAP has been on a steady upward path since the early 1980s, increasing from about 35 percent of total exports in 1985 to over 50 percent in 2014. More importantly, the rise in regional trade integration in EAP has occurred in tandem with rapid growth of total trade flows and a marked process of convergence to the living standards of developed countries. LAC is no exception in this global admiration of the EAP experience, something that should not come as a surprise. After all, LAC intraregional trade flows have been flat, at about 20 percent of total trade flows, while economic convergence has remained elusive.

However, replicating EAP's experience has proven a difficult challenge for LAC. The region has pursued regional integration efforts through formal trade integration agreements since the 1960s, efforts that have only intensified since the mid-1990s. Indeed, prior to the year 2000 the average country in LAC held a preferential trade agreement with about 4 regional partners; by 2013 this number had risen to nearly 10. Despite these efforts, intraregional exports in LAC have remained stagnant.

This discussion raises a question: What are the constraints that policy makers in LAC face in their goal of boosting regional trade integration? To answer this question the rest of this section explores in detail a potential explanation behind LAC's relatively low share of intraregional trade, namely, the role that economic size and geography play in shaping trade flows. In particular, the analysis follows the insights of the international trade literature that point to economic size and trade frictions induced by geographic distance as gravitational forces shaping trade flows.[7]

## Economic size and geographic distance as fundamental determinants of trade flows

Understanding the determinants of international trade patterns is a research goal that dates back to the early 1800s. Neoclassical models of international trade focused on the role of technology (Ricardian models) and differences in factor endowments (Heckscher-Ohlin model) in explaining observed trade patterns. As appealing as the insights of these models are, however, studies from the 1970s, 1980s, and 1990s found little empirical support for these theories as explanations for observed trade patterns because most global trade was between wealthy and nearby countries.[8]

One empirical model that appears to fit the trade data particularly well is the so-called gravity model of trade (Tinbergen 1962). Its central tenet is that trade flows should be proportional to the gross domestic product (GDP) of trading partners and inversely proportional to their geographic distance. The positive relationship between bilateral trade flows and the GDP of trading partners captures the idea that large, wealthy countries demand and supply more goods from and to the rest of the world relative to smaller countries, yielding high levels of trade between them.[9] The inverse relationship between trade and distance captures the idea that trade implies moving goods, and that the cost of moving goods is expected to increase with distance.[10] Hence, the price charged by more distant producers is expected to be higher compared to those of producers nearby, resulting in lower demand for exports (varieties) from more distant countries. The effects of distance, therefore, may prevent countries from realizing the benefits of trade predicted by neoclassical models.

The relationship predicted by the gravity model has important implications for understanding the regional integration patterns discussed above. First of all, the negative relationship between trade flows and distance predicted by the gravity model and observed in the data implies that, all other things equal, trade flows between nearby partners are expected to be higher than between faraway partners. In other words, even if trade policy around the world were nondiscriminatory, the gravity model predicts that trade should be largely regional because of trade costs that vary systematically with geographic distance.

Another important implication of the gravity model is that differences in the size and distance between countries within regions can play an important role in explaining differences in the incidence of regional trade across regions. In particular, regions comprising countries with large GDP values and with short distances between them are expected to exhibit higher regional trade flows as a share of total trade than others, all else equal.

Table 2.1 provides a preliminary look at some of the gravity characteristics that may be behind the cross-regional differences in regional integration patterns depicted in figure 2.1, panel b. For example, Europe and the United States and Canada, two regions that stand among the most integrated in terms of trade flows, are also the two regions with the highest average GDP and the

**TABLE 2.1   Gravity variables, by region**

| | Within-region country pairwise distance | | 2014 GDP (as % of U.S. GDP) | | 2014 GDP pc (as % of U.S. GDP pc) | |
|---|---|---|---|---|---|---|
| | Mean | Median | Mean | Median | Mean | Median |
| Sub-Saharan Africa | 3,360 | 3,120 | 0.24% | 0.07% | 4.91% | 1.91% |
| East Asia and Pacific | 4,840 | 4,464 | 5.23% | 1.07% | 29.45% | 7.92% |
| Europe and Central Asia | 2,190 | 1,864 | 1.00% | 0.30% | 19.22% | 16.78% |
| EU15+ | 1,260 | 1,242 | 6.55% | 3.08% | 90.98% | 87.87% |
| Latin America and the Caribbean | 2,816 | 2,531 | 1.08% | 0.17% | 16.06% | 13.63% |
| Middle East and North Africa | 2,193 | 1,952 | 1.04% | 0.63% | 35.69% | 12.27% |
| South Asia | 1,735 | 1,710 | 2.14% | 0.43% | 4.59% | 2.44% |
| Central America and Mexico | 795 | 571 | 1.23% | 0.25% | 11.62% | 7.29% |
| Caribbean | 1,366 | 1,236 | 0.07% | 0.02% | 18.41% | 15.20% |
| South America | 2,504 | 2,376 | 2.40% | 1.18% | 16.63% | 13.52% |

*Source:* World Bank calculations from World Development Indicators and Centre d'Études Prospectives et d'Informations Internationales (CEPII).

shortest average distance between regional pairs of countries. EAP, another highly integrated region, ranks poorly in terms of distance, but has the third-largest GDP among all regions. In contrast, SSA, the region with the second-lowest level of regional integration, has the lowest average GDP and the second-highest average pairwise distance. Thus the logic of the gravity model seems consistent with the data.

The points made in table 2.1 can be further illustrated by an alternate definition of regions. Figure 2.2, panel a, shows the levels of regional integration in the Americas, comprising LAC plus the United States and Canada, and EAP without Japan. Hence, the exercise adds two large countries to LAC (pushing in favor of regional integration compared to LAC alone) and subtracts one big country from EAP (pushing against regional integration compared to the original EAP definition). The results confirm the importance of the size of countries in a region for its level of integration—the incidence of regional exports in the Americas (LAC plus the United States and Canada) stands at about 50 to 60 percent of total trade, higher than the 20 percent for LAC and the

35 percent of the United States and Canada in the original regional classification. Likewise, EAP's regional integration falls from 50 percent in the case where Japan is included to 40 percent when it is excluded.

In addition, the exercise with alternative regional definitions demonstrates the importance of distance in shaping regional integration. Under standard regional definitions, figure 2.2, panel b, shows that South America displays the highest levels of regional integration with LAC as a whole (20–25 percent of total trade flows) and that Central America has the lowest levels (below 10 percent). When the United States and Canada are included to make up the Americas, the rankings are reversed (figure 2.2, panel c). Hence, while the inclusion of two big countries increases regional integration levels across the board, it disproportionately favors countries that are close to them.

The insights of the gravity equation suggest that, in order to carefully assess LAC's standing in terms of regional integration, one should take into account the impact of geography and size on trade flows. One initial attempt to do such assessment is presented in the work of Frankel, Stein, and Wei (1995).

**FIGURE 2.2   An illustration of the gravity forces of international trade**

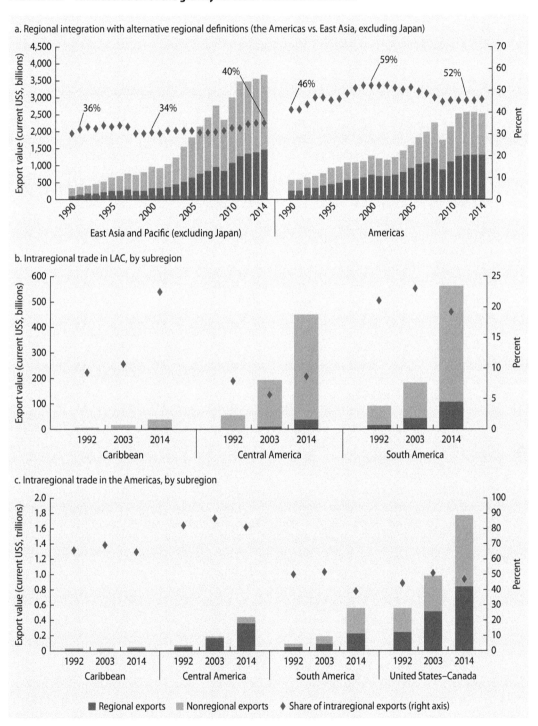

a. Regional integration with alternative regional definitions (the Americas vs. East Asia, excluding Japan)

b. Intraregional trade in LAC, by subregion

c. Intraregional trade in the Americas, by subregion

■ Regional exports    ■ Nonregional exports    ◆ Share of intraregional exports (right axis)

*Source:* World Bank calculations based on data from UN COMTRADE.
*Note:* The share of intraregional exports is calculated as the ratio between intraregional exports and total exports. Americas = LAC plus the United States and Canada; LAC = Latin America and the Caribbean. See annex 1A for a list of countries in each region.

The authors follow the gravity approach by estimating a regression of bilateral trade flows (in logs) on log GDP of each of the countries, a set of bilateral variables that includes distance and a dummy variable taking value 1 if the two countries are members of a preferential trading arrangement. The authors include Mercosur, the Andean Pact (the free trade agreement [FTA] between Bolivia, Colombia, Ecuador, Peru, and República Bolivariana de Venezuela), and the North American Free Trade Agreement (NAFTA).[11] The results presented in Frankel, Stein, and Wei (1995) show that, once GDP, distance, and other bilateral variables are taken into account, intra-Mercosur and intra–Andean Pact trade in the 1990s were statistically higher than the average pair of countries that are not in the trade blocs studied in the paper.[12] In contrast, NAFTA's trade falls within the predictions of gravity variables.

The work of Frankel, Stein, and Wei (1995) was revisited and expanded in a background paper prepared for this study by Artuc, Hillberry, and Pienknagura (2016). On the estimation side, the authors use an alternative econometric approach aimed at correcting for two limitations of the early gravity literature. First, they estimate a modified gravity equation where, instead of controlling for GDP, the authors include a full set of exporter and importer fixed effects. The inclusion of these fixed effects (as opposed to GDP) captures the so-called multilateral resistance term, a term that arises from the formal theoretical derivation of the gravity equation. It captures the fact that the trade relationship between a country that supplies a good and a country that demands that good is affected by the (frictions corrected) price of similar varieties of that good offered by other exporters. In other words, trade between two countries in a particular product depends on the global market conditions for that product as well as the trade relations between each of the two countries and the rest of the world. The omission of this term introduces biases in the elasticities of trade with respect to distance and size.

Second, instead of estimating the gravity equation with a log-linear ordinary least squares (OLS) approach, as in Frankel, Stein, and Wei (1995), the authors use the Poisson–Pseudo Maximum Likelihood (PPML) estimator proposed by Santos-Silva and Tenreyro (2006), which corrects for biases common in the log-linear OLS model. (See annex 2A for details on the specification and the advantages of PPML.)

In addition to the technical differences highlighted above, Artuc, Hillberry, and Pienknagura (2016) address—in a more comprehensive way than previous work—the question of whether LAC's intraregional trade is higher or lower compared to what is predicted by gravity variables. Rather than focusing on specific trade blocs within LAC, the authors provide an assessment of intraregional trade integration for various definitions of regions: LAC as a whole, subregions in LAC, and contiguous countries. The results presented below broaden the analysis of Artuc, Hillberry, and Pienknagura (2016) by studying additional definitions of regions: the Americas (LAC plus the United States and Canada) and the FTA partners of Latin American countries (see annex 2A for details on the different specifications presented). As in figure 2.1, panel b, in most cases LAC's results are compared to those of other regions.

The results of the gravity estimations show that the average pair of countries in regions such as SSA, SAR, and LAC, which originally ranked poorly in terms of the incidence of regional trade (see figure 2.1, panel b), have intraregional trade flows that are in line with or exceed what is predicted by gravity variables (figure 2.3, panel a).[13] In particular, SSA displays intraregional trade flows that are significantly higher, from a statistical point of view, than those predicted by gravity variables. SAR and LAC show levels of intraregional trade that are higher than the gravity predictions, albeit not significantly so. In contrast, EAP, a region that ranked second in the original comparison of intraregional trade flows, presents levels of intraregional trade that are statistically lower than those predicted by gravity variables. Three regions where the inclusion of gravity variables does not seem to affect performance in terms of intraregional trade are MENA, EU15+, and Eastern Europe and Central Asia (ECA). In the former, the incidence of intraregional trade in total trade was among the lowest compared to other regions, a conclusion that holds when we control for gravity variables. In the latter two cases, the opposite is true.

Although the results in figure 2.3, panel a, suggest that, on average, countries in LAC trade according to what is predicted by the gravity model, the results may mask potential differences across countries in the region. To address this possibility, figure 2.3, panels b and c, presents the results of a gravity specification where the intra-LAC dummy is allowed to vary by subregions within LAC. In particular, the exercise benchmarks imports (panel b) and exports (panel c) of the average country in South America, Central America, and the Caribbean, respectively, to and from other countries in LAC. On average, South American and Caribbean countries display intra-LAC import levels that are

**FIGURE 2.3    Benchmarking regional integration through a gravity model of trade**

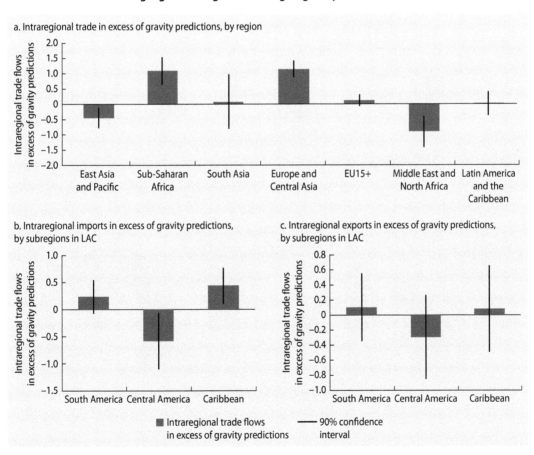

*Source:* World Bank calculations based on Artuc, Hillberry, and Pienknagura (2016).
*Note:* In all panels the coefficients capture the excess intraregional trade of a region relative to its trade with nonregional partners conditional on gravity characteristics. Vertical lines capture 90 percent confidence intervals. Standard errors are clustered at the importer level. In panels b and c, the dummy variable for LAC–LAC trade is allowed to vary by subregion within LAC. The treatment for other regions is the same as in panel a. CA = Central America including Mexico; LAC = Latin America and the Caribbean. See annex 1A for a list of countries in each region.

in line with or exceed those predicted by size and geography, whereas Central America shows intra-LAC imports that are lower than those predicted by gravity. On the export side, intra-LAC flows appear to be consistent with gravity across all LAC subregions—in all subregions the estimated dummies are not statistically different from zero.

Naturally, differences in regional integration within LAC are sensitive to the definition of region, because the inclusion or exclusion of countries changes the averages of certain gravity variables, and as a result, trade patterns in a given region. For instance, an assessment of

integration in the Americas provides substantially different conclusions relative to the assessment in figure 2.3. The analysis of megaregions shows that intra-Americas trade is statistically larger compared to what gravity variables would predict, suggesting that the inclusion of the United States and Canada boosts trade in LAC beyond what would be predicted by their economic size and distance to LAC countries (figure 2.4, panel a). Also, the inclusion of the two North American countries changes the performance of LAC's subregions in terms of regional integration. On the import side, all subregions in the

**FIGURE 2.4   Benchmarking regional integration through a gravity model of trade, alternative regional definitions**

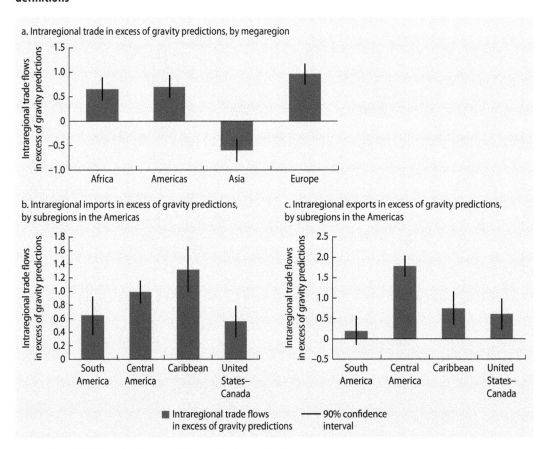

*Source:* World Bank calculations based on Artuc, Hillberry, and Pienknagura (2016).
*Note:* In all panels the coefficients capture the excess intraregional trade of a megaregion relative to its trade with nonregional partners conditional on gravity characteristics. Vertical lines capture 90 percent confidence intervals. Standard errors are clustered at the importer level. In panels b and c, the dummy variable for Americas–Americas trade is allowed to vary by subregion within the Americas. The treatment for all other regions is the same as in panel a. Africa = Sub-Saharan Africa plus Middle East and North Africa; Americas = Latin America and the Caribbean plus United States and Canada; Asia = East Asia and the Pacific plus South Asia; CA = Central America including Mexico: Europe = EU15+ plus Europe and Central Asia. See annex 1A for a list of countries in each region.

Americas display intra-Americas trade that is higher than the gravity variables would predict (figure 2.4, panel b). On the export side, the results for Central America in figure 2.3, panel b, are reversed—it exhibits export levels to the Americas that exceed gravity predictions (South America and the Caribbean perform according to gravity characteristics; figure 2.4, panel c).

One important limitation of most analyses of regional trade, including the one presented above, is that they use only merchandise trade data. That is, the analysis does not take into account trade in services. This may be particularly important in regions with a high prevalence of small economies, where, as will be discussed later in this chapter, services constitute a significant share of total trade. Services are typically neglected from the analysis of regional integration because until recently there was no database with bilateral service flows.[14] More recently, data sets like Francois and Pindyuk (2013) have partially overcome certain data constraints. Nevertheless, given the sources used in the construction of the data set, a large share of bilateral pairs within LAC and other emerging regions are not considered in the data (see box 2.1), implying that even these new data sources are not well suited for an analysis of regional integration. With the caveat of the exclusion of trade in services in mind, the rest of this section explores potential explanations of the patterns in figures 2.3 and 2.4.

---

## BOX 2.1    Trade-in-services data for LAC countries

Exports of services in LAC made up roughly 20 percent of total exports in 2009 (figure B2.1.1, panel a). Although this number represents a slight decline from earlier in the decade, it is in line with that in most other developing regions. Given both the weight of services exports in total exports and the importance of trade in services for regional trade networks, it is natural to extend the gravity model analysis described above to trade in services. Specifically, given adequate bilateral trade-in-services data (TSD), the gravity specification detailed in chapter 1 can be used to compare predicted and actual services trade flows in addition to merchandise trade flows.

Nonetheless, it is important to take note of several restrictions concerning TSD, which are more challenging to collect than merchandise trade data, for several reasons. First, there is often overlap between goods and services trade statistics, meaning that it is difficult to disaggregate the two types of exports. Second, because of the challenging nature of tracking services flows, TSD are often missing. Furthermore, a lack of correspondence between the commonly used extended balance of payments classification—a detailed balance of payments classification covering services—and standard industry classifications (such as the International Standard Classification of all Industrial Economic Activities) makes it challenging to report TSD in a unified way across countries. Finally, even when these challenges are overcome at the total economy level, mapping services flows between bilateral pairs proves particularly difficult.

Panel b of figure B2.1.1 shows the percentage of bilateral services exports by region and by LAC country for which there are unattributed partners. LAC ranks second highest, with close to 34 percent of bilateral services exports being attributed to an "unknown" partner. In other words, we are sure of the recipient country of services exports only two-thirds of the time, even at the total economy level. Breaking this down by individual LAC country, we see that the quality of bilateral TSD is most thorough for those countries belonging to the Organisation for Economic Co-operation and Development (OECD)—namely, Mexico and Chile—as well as other relatively small countries that do not have sizable services export shares in total exports. In terms of the gravity model analysis in this chapter, therefore, extensions to bilateral trade in services would be limited in country scope.

*(continued)*

## BOX 2.1   Trade in services data for LAC countries *(continued)*

### FIGURE B2.1.1   Trade in services

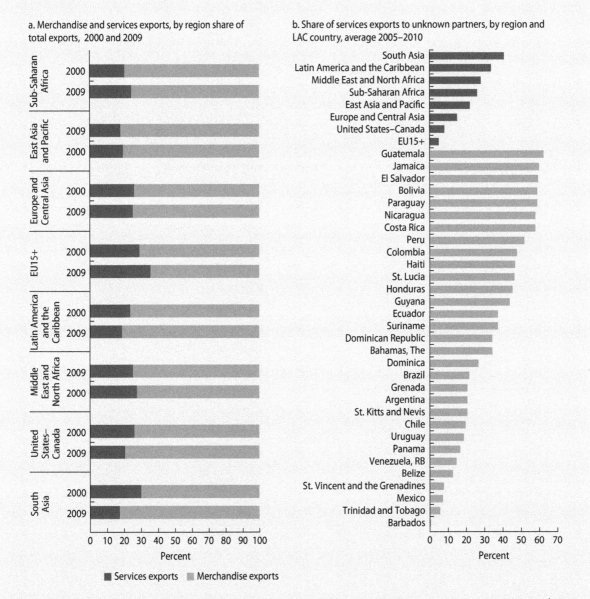

a. Merchandise and services exports, by region share of total exports, 2000 and 2009

b. Share of services exports to unknown partners, by region and LAC country, average 2005–2010

■ Services exports   ■ Merchandise exports

*Source:* World Bank calculations based on data from International Monetary Fund Direction of Trade Statistics (DOTS), Francois and Pindyuk 2013, and Centre d'Études Prospectives et d'Informations Internationales (CEPII).

## Explaining patterns of trade integration

The previous section showed that there is no evidence indicating that LAC underperforms in terms of intraregional trade once standard gravity variables such as distance, contiguity, and FTAs are taken into account. If anything, there is weak evidence of overtrading in the region. LAC's same-region coefficient, which captures the extent to which there is excess trading between regional partners, is positive, albeit not statistically significant. This result seems to contradict the somewhat popular belief that LAC is "behind" in intraregional trade compared to EAP, a region that also appears to perform according to what is predicted by standard gravity controls.

However, the conclusions emerging from the analysis presented above are subject to one important caveat. The benchmark exercise, the results of which are shown in figure 2.3 and repeated in figure 2.5, panel a, assumes that gravity variables affect all

**FIGURE 2.5  Benchmarking regional integration through a gravity model of trade, with homogeneous and heterogeneous gravity coefficients**

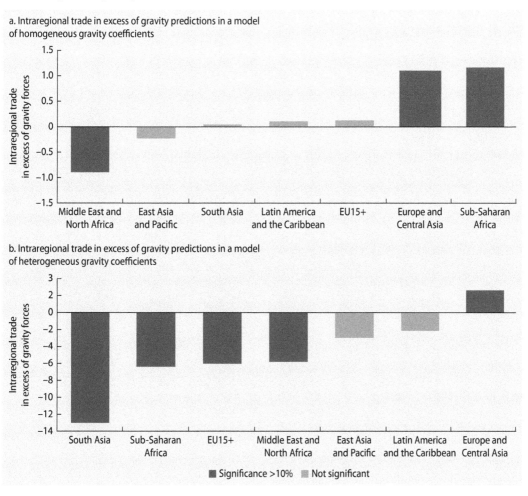

a. Intraregional trade in excess of gravity predictions in a model of homogeneous gravity coefficients

b. Intraregional trade in excess of gravity predictions in a model of heterogeneous gravity coefficients

■ Significance >10%   ■ Not significant

*Source:* Calculations based on Artuc, Hillberry, and Pienknagura 2016.
*Note:* Bars capture excess regional trade relative to trade with the rest of the world conditional on gravity characteristics. Standard errors are clustered at the importer level. See annex 1A for a list of countries in each region.

countries equally. That is to say, regardless of income level, institutional quality, natural geographic barriers, and infrastructure developments, the elasticity of trade flows with respect to distance, contiguity, and trade agreements is the same across countries. Although this assumption is commonly made in the gravity literature, there is evidence suggesting that allowing for heterogeneity in elasticities may be more appropriate. In the specific case of LAC, Mesquita Moreira, Volpe, and Blyde (2008) showed that the region's transport costs appear to be higher than those observed in high-income countries and even some emerging economies. Moreover, to the extent that countries in a region share fundamental factors affecting trade costs, trade elasticities may vary not only by region but also by partner. For example, the costs faced by U.S. exporters when crossing the United States–Canada border may be significantly different from those faced when crossing the United States–Mexico border. Importantly, assuming a single elasticity when in reality elasticities vary by country can bias the same-region dummies presented in figure 2.5, panel a.

To address these concerns and to study their implications for trade policy, the rest of this section expands on the previous analysis by relaxing the constant elasticity assumption in the benchmark model. The benchmark gravity equation is expanded to allow the elasticities of trade flows with respect to distance, contiguity, and trade agreements to vary across regions and by type of partner (partners within a county's region and partners outside a country's region).

Most of the coefficients of the same-region dummies turn negative after allowing for heterogeneous elasticities to distance, contiguity, and FTAs (figure 2.5, panel b). The predominantly negative sign across all regions (except ECA) points toward a global tendency to undertrade with regional partners. In the specific case of LAC, the same-region coefficient turns negative, but one cannot statistically reject the hypothesis that the coefficient is zero.[15] Moreover, there are no significant differences in intraregional patterns between

LAC and EAP because both regions display coefficients for their same-region dummies that are not statistically significant.

Turning to the analysis of the elasticities, figure 2.6, panel a, shows that the elasticities with respect to FTAs of trade flows between LAC countries and their regional and nonregional partners are relatively small in magnitude and, in the case of trade flows with regional partners, not statistically significant. Moreover, they are similar to those observed in other regions. The elasticities of trade flows between LAC countries and their regional and nonregional partners with respect to FTAs are not statistically different from those observed in regions such as EAP, MENA, or EU15+.

A clearer difference between LAC and other regions is observed in terms of the elasticities of trade flows with respect to distance and, to a lesser extent, contiguity (figure 2.6, panels b and c). Not only does LAC display the highest elasticity of trade flows with regional partners with respect to distance (in absolute value), but the region also has one of the highest distance elasticities of trade flows with nonregional partners (third, behind MENA and SSA). Moreover, LAC's distance elasticities on both accounts are statistically larger in magnitude when compared to those of EAP.[16] Similarly, LAC stands out as the region with the highest elasticity of trade flows with nonregional partners with respect to contiguity. A point to be made when interpreting the latter elasticity is that the only nonregional contiguous pair of countries is the United States and Mexico. This particular trade link is very strong, driving up the aforementioned coefficient, and is not very representative of the rest of LAC. In fact, when looking at the effect of contiguity on LAC's trade flows with regional partners, it appears on the shallow end and in line with that of other regions.

The high distance elasticity observed in LAC suggests that behind its relatively low levels of trade integration (with regional and nonregional partners) are factors hampering trade, especially trade with more distant partners. Studies such as Mesquita Moreira et al. (2013) or Mesquita Moreira, Volpe, and Blyde (2008) point to inadequate infrastructure,

**FIGURE 2.6    Coefficients for contiguity, FTAs, and distance in a heterogeneous coefficients gravity model of trade**

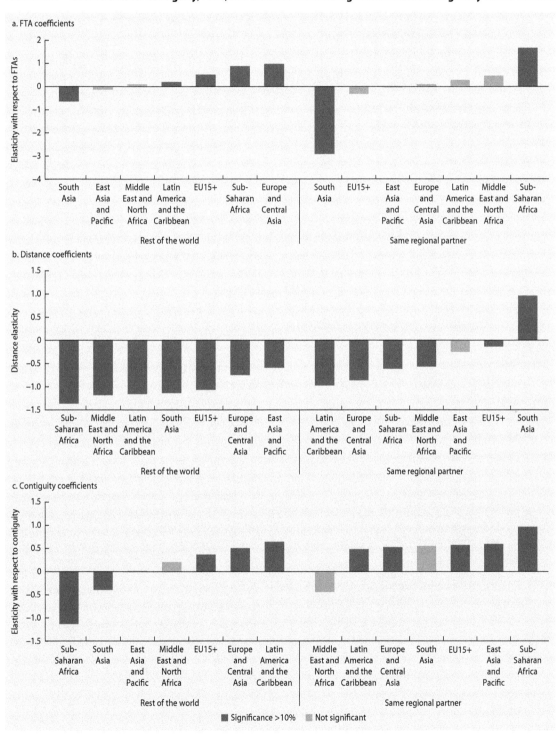

*Source:* Calculations based on Artuc, Hillberry, and Pienknagura 2016.
*Note:* Bars capture excess regional trade relative to trade with the rest of the world conditional on gravity characteristics. Standard errors are clustered at the importer level. See annex 1A for a list of countries in each region.

**FIGURE 2.7    Average cost of trading in 2013**

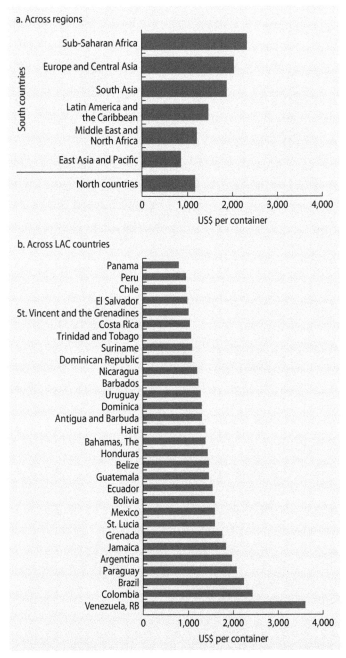

*Source:* World Bank calculations based on the Doing Business Indicators.
*Note:* This figure shows the average cost associated with exporting and importing a standardized cargo of goods by sea transport in 2013 across regions (panel a) and across LAC countries (panel b). The cost of trading is measured by the fees (in U.S. dollars) levied on a 20-foot container (excluding tariffs). All the fees associated with completing the procedures to export or import the goods are taken into account. For exporting goods, procedures range from packing the goods into the container at the warehouse to their departure from the port of exit. For importing goods, procedures range from the vessel's arrival at the port of entry to the cargo's delivery at the warehouse. For landlocked economies, these include procedures at the inland border post, since the port is located in the transit economy. Cross-country averages are reported in panel a. North countries comprise the G-7 and Western European economies. All other countries are classified as South. The regional classification of South countries follows the World Bank classification.

inefficient customs, challenging topography, and low competition among shipping companies as potential factors driving transport costs up for LAC. Others, such as Estevadeordal and Talvi (2016), point to the "spaghetti bowl" problem created by the large number of rules of origin (RoOs) introduced by FTAs as another factor hampering trade. The next section delves deeper into LAC's transport costs and the factors that might be driving a higher distance elasticity in the region. A discussion of the role of RoOs is deferred to the next chapter.

## In search of the costs of distance

The ability of economies to integrate efficiently into the global economy depends to a great extent on the quality of hard and soft infrastructure services, ranging from transportation, telecommunications, and financial services to border processes and customs practices to business and regulatory environments.[17] In fact, internal (domestic) trade and transaction costs can have a large impact on a country's external (international) competitiveness. The extent of red tape and access to efficient transport networks feature prominently among the cost factors that determine whether firms can meet external demand in a competitive and timely fashion.

The World Bank's Doing Business database captures the internal costs associated with shipping goods from the factory gate to ports (for exports) and from ports to retail outlets (for imports) through its "cost of trading" index.[18] This indicator measures the fees (excluding tariffs and trade taxes) associated with exporting and importing a standardized cargo of goods by sea transport, accounting for the time and cost necessary to comply with every official procedure (the time and cost for sea transport itself are not included) (Djankov, Freund, and Pham 2010).

The results show that, on average, it is more expensive to export and import in developing countries than in the high-income economies (East Asian economies are a marked exception) (figure 2.7, panel a).

On average, LAC countries are well positioned with respect to other emerging economies, with internal costs associated with cross-border trading lower than in all regions except MENA and EAP. There is, however, great heterogeneity within LAC (figure 2.7, panel b). Panama is the least expensive country (ranked 38th worldwide), followed by Peru (52nd) and Chile (53rd). At the other extreme, among the most expensive countries in the world for trade are República Bolivariana de Venezuela (175th), Colombia (162nd), and Brazil (156th). Access to efficient and competitive international transport networks is also crucial for integration into global markets. The availability of effective transport connections, including ancillary services, affects the location decisions of production. Trade in intermediate goods is especially sensitive to transport costs (World Bank 2009). Transportation infrastructure may also play a role in facilitating knowledge diffusion and spillovers (Agrawal, Galasso, and Oettl 2014). The relatively poor quality of transport networks in LAC countries seems to act as a trade barrier, constraining the ability of economies in the region to integrate efficiently into the global economy. On average, LAC countries seem to underperform compared with both high-income countries and some developing countries on a range of indicators capturing accessibility to and the quality of transport networks. There is some evidence that the region is not spending sufficiently or effectively on infrastructure, even though infrastructure development offers significant potential to speed the pace of growth in the region (Calderón and Servén 2010; Fay and Morrison 2007). There is wide heterogeneity within the region, however.

*Land transport* Detailed data on the value of trade by different modes of transportation are sparse, but data on the United States and LAC indicate that trade with land neighbors occurs mostly by surface modes (such as truck, rail, and pipeline); only 10 percent of trade takes place by air or ocean (Hummels 2007). About 10–20 percent of total trade by

LAC countries is with land neighbors. The development of the land transport network is therefore an important factor behind intraregional integration.

Data on road and railway density reveal a gap between high-income and developing countries. Adjusted by population density, these measures indicate that LAC lags behind high-income countries, though the evidence is more nuanced with respect to other developing regions (figure 2.8, panel a).[19] On average, LAC outperforms MENA and SAR in both road and rail density and performs about the same as SSA. LAC has denser railway networks but sparser road coverage than EAP. A caveat of this analysis is that measures of road and railway density are imperfect indicators of the quantity of transport services, especially services relevant for the development of cross-border links, because they do not indicate whether production centers are effectively connected to markets or trade outlets.

Data on the quality of land transport infrastructure suggest some scope for improvement in LAC. The quality of the road network, proxied by the share of unpaved roads, is relatively poor when contrasted with other developing regions; almost 70 percent of the roads in LAC are unpaved—a far larger share than in EAP and MENA (less than 30 percent) and South Asia (less than 50 percent) (see figure 2.8, panel b). LAC also seems to lag behind in the quality of its railway network. Panama is the highest-ranked LAC country in terms of the quality of its railroad infrastructure (ranked 30th in the Global Competitive Forum Index); no other LAC country features in the top 50. Moreover, 10 of the world's 20 worst performers, including Brazil, Colombia, and Peru, are in LAC.

*Maritime transport* For trade with non-neighboring countries, which corresponds to about 80 percent of world trade by value, nearly all goods trade moves by ocean and air (Hummels 2007). Most manufactured and semimanufactured goods are transported in liner vessels, as are bulk commodities like oil

FIGURE 2.8    **Land transportation, by region, 2011**

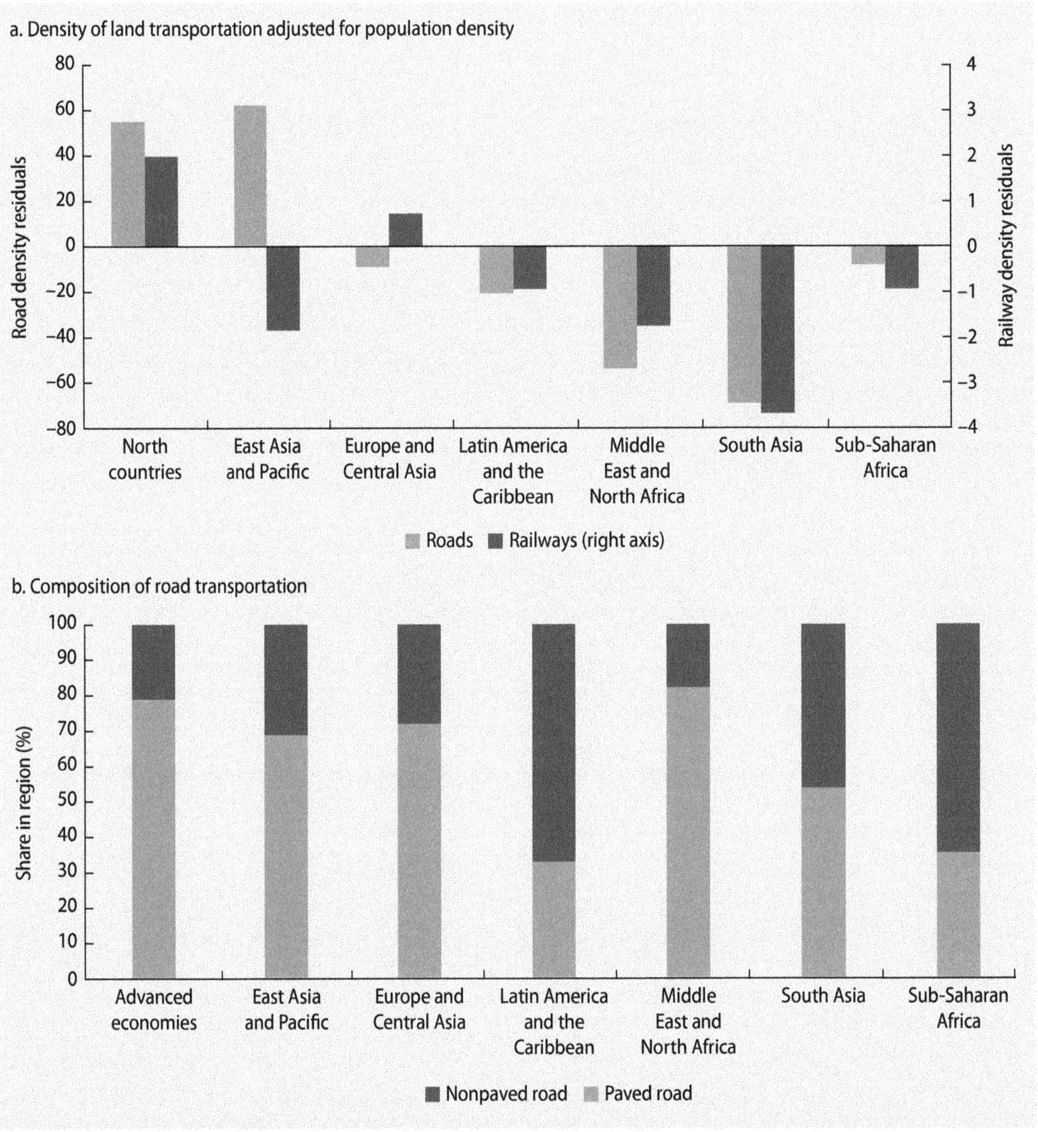

a. Density of land transportation adjusted for population density

Roads    Railways (right axis)

b. Composition of road transportation

Nonpaved road    Paved road

*Source:* World Bank calculations based on World Development Indicators.
*Note:* Panel a reports residuals of regressions of measures of density of land transportation (road density and railway density) against population density at the country level. Cross-country averages are reporterd. Density of land transportation is measured by the number of kilometers of roads or rails per 100 square kilometers of land area. Rail lines are the length of railway route available for train service, irrespective of the number of parallel tracks. Paved roads are roads surfaced with crushed stone (macadam) and hydrocarbon binder or bituminized agents, with concrete or cobblestones. All other roads are considered unpaved. The North countries includes the G-7 members and other Western Europe countries. Singapore and Hong Kong SAR, China, are excluded from the EAP average because of the physical characteristics of these economies. See annex 1A for a list of countries in each region.

and petroleum products, iron ore, coal, and grains. The international shipping industry carries about 90 percent of world trade in terms of volume, according to the Maritime International Secretariat Services (2013). The quality of maritime shipping services is thus an important determinant of competitiveness. It directly affects countries' engagement in global trade and indirectly increases per capita income.

The use of maritime transportation is not homogeneous across countries. Some freight routes are much more developed than others because most shipping companies adopt a hub-and-spokes operating structure. This operating structure consists of hub ports, lateral ports, main lines (long-haul lines that connect hub ports and involve a set of sequential port calls, typically across the oceans), and branch lines (short-haul lines connecting several lateral ports in one region to serve the main lines), which together form a complex transportation network system (Rodrigue and Comtois 2006; Ducret and Notteboom 2012). This hub-and-spokes arrangement has led to an unbalanced geographical distribution of hub ports around the world, with most of them located in Asia and Europe (Hu and Zhu 2009). Ports in Hong Kong SAR, China; Singapore; and Rotterdam are central hubs in the global network. Panama and Kingston (Jamaica) are hubs in LAC.

A map of marine traffic for cargo ships during the second half of 2013 shows this heterogeneity (de la Torre et al. 2015). The highest intensity of marine traffic is in Europe, the United States, and the Pacific coast of Asia. Traffic along Latin American coasts is significantly less dense.

Data from the World Shipping Council (n.d.) confirm that LAC countries are not at the center of the world's main shipping routes. In 2012 only 3 million 20-foot equivalent units (TEUs, a standard measure of container ship capacity) were shipped between Asia and South America, the most active route for LAC countries. This volume is an order of magnitude smaller than the 22 million TEUs shipped along the main trading route between Asia and North America.

LAC countries have accessibility to this global network, through its branch lines. A proxy for the ease of access to high-capacity and high-frequency global maritime freight transport systems is the Liner Shipping Connectivity Index (figure 2.9).[20] In 2013 the export-oriented economies of East Asia took the top five spots: China and Hong Kong SAR, China, were the highest-ranking economies, followed by the transshipment hub of

Singapore. High-income countries, including Belgium, Germany, Japan, the Netherlands, the United Kingdom, and the United States, took most of the other top 15 spots.

Within LAC only Panama features in the top 30 (at 25th). Mexico is the second-highest-ranking country in the region (32nd), followed by Colombia (38th) and Brazil (39th). In general, Central America and Caribbean countries typically reveal more restricted use of the liner shipping network than do South American countries. Adjusting the index for country size (proxied by population and land area) does not improve the rankings of LAC countries—the top countries in the region actually move significantly down; Mexico falls to 80th place, Brazil to 76th, and Colombia to 86th. The top three East Asian economies remain at the top of the ranking.

The spatial design of the maritime transport network reflects an equilibrium outcome in which both demand and supply effects are at play. Demand factors include demand for containerized transport and demand for specific transport service characteristics. Central to supply-side considerations are the strategies of container shipping liners, which aim to maximize profits and take advantage of increasing economies of scale through the strategic choice of market coverage (the hub-and-spokes operating structure is particularly important in this regard). Other important factors are port infrastructure, port system development, and internal transport and logistics infrastructure in the hinterland for port access (see, for example, Notteboom 2009).

These factors may be a constraint in many LAC countries, where port performance is typically poor, although there is wide heterogeneity within the region.[21] Panama is one of the top 10 countries in the world in port efficiency, but Bolivia (ranked 142nd), Brazil (131st), and Costa Rica (128th) are among the least efficient, according to the *Global Competitiveness Report 2013–14* (Schwab and Sala-i-Martin 2013). The determinants of port efficiency include excessive regulation, the prevalence of organized crime,

**FIGURE 2.9 Liner Shipping Connectivity Index in selected economies, 2013**

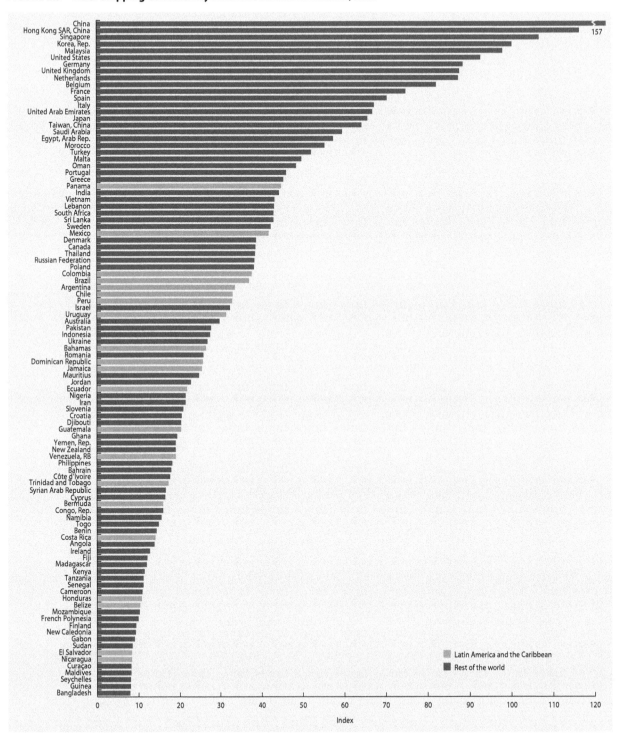

*Source:* Calculations based on UNCTAD data. Underlying data come from Containerization International Online.
*Note:* Index based on five components of the maritime transport sector: (i) the number of ships, (ii) their container carrying capacity, (iii) the maximum vessel size, (iv) the number of services, and (v) the number of companies that deploy container ships in an economy's ports. The highest value (100) represents the value for the economy with the highest average index in 2004. All reported values are relative to this economy-year observation. Only the top 100 economies are reported.

congestion, and the general condition of the country's infrastructure.

*Air transport*    Although the global air cargo industry is still relatively small compared with the maritime shipping industry, it has become a viable alternative for high-value and low-volume as well as time-sensitive products. A growing emphasis on speed in cross-border shipments—which has accompanied the expansion of just-in-time business models—highlights the increased importance of air freight transport.[22]

Global air cargo grew significantly between 1990 and 2013, more than doubling in volume, from 56 billion ton km to almost 175 billion ton km. According to the International Air Transport Association (IATA), 35 percent of world merchandise trade in value was transported by air in 2013.[23] Air traffic is concentrated in high-income economies, which accounted for almost 50 percent of all air freight transport in 2013 (figure 2.10). Within developing regions, EAP (20 percent of world air freight) and MENA (13 percent) captured the largest shares of world air freight. LAC accounted for just 3 percent; Brazil (21st), Chile (24th), and Colombia (31st) were the highest-ranked countries in the region (although once country size, proxied by population and land area, is controlled for, these countries drop significantly in the rankings).

Like the maritime transport network, the air transport network is characterized by a hub-and-spokes structure. This structure may explain at least in part the geographical heterogeneity in the concentration of air traffic.

## Similarity in comparative advantages and trade integration

The discussion in the previous subsection focused exclusively on the role played by gravity variables in explaining patterns of intraregional trade across regions. Yet, as highlighted earlier in this chapter, economic theory has traditionally emphasized comparative advantage (explained by differences in technologies or factor endowments) as a crucial determinant of trade flows and of the gains from trade. More precisely, trade theory predicts that countries with similar patterns of comparative advantage will trade less than those with patterns that differ, and the gains from trade are realized precisely because countries produce goods with different (relative) production costs.

Understanding the role played by comparative advantage in explaining intraregional trade patterns is especially important for LAC, a region where exports of natural resources represent a significant share of total exports in many countries. In fact, as will be illustrated later in this chapter, countries in LAC have very similar export baskets, something that does not necessarily hold in other regions. This could serve as a further impediment beyond gravity factors to regional trade flows in LAC and, if the neoclassical theories of trade are correct, to the attainment of efficiency gains due to intraregional trade. Hence, this section provides an assessment of the extent to which trade integration in LAC may be capturing patterns of comparative advantage within the region.

Artuc, Hillberry, and Pienknagura (2016) estimated 10 separate gravity equations, one per industry defined at the Standard International Trade Classification (SITC) Rev. 3, 1-digit code. These results are then combined with measures of revealed comparative advantage (RCA) to illustrate the relation between the two.[24]

Figure 2.11 confirms the patterns predicted by economic theory. Once gravity forces are controlled for, intraregional trade in LAC is higher in sectors where a lower number of countries in the region have a revealed comparative advantage, and vice versa. Hence, sectors like Foods and live animals (SITC code 0), Crude materials, inedible, except fuels (SITC code 2), and Mineral fuels, lubricants, and related materials (SITC code 3), all in which more than 45 percent of countries have an RCA, have intra-LAC trade levels that stand below what gravity variables predict. In contrast, sectors like Chemicals and related products (SITC code 5), Manufactured goods (SITC Rev 3, code 6),

**FIGURE 2.10    Air freight transport in selected economies, 2013**

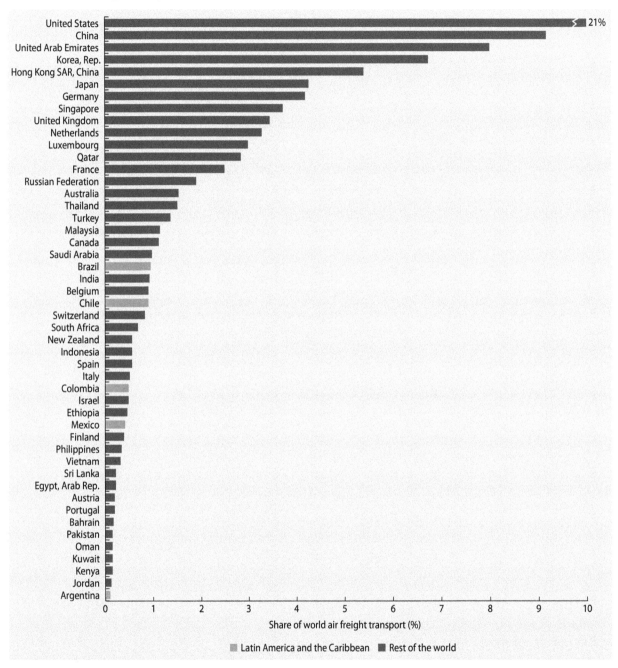

*Source:* World Bank Doing Business indicators.
*Note:* Air freight is measured by the volume of freight, express, and diplomatic bags carried at each flight stage (operation of an aircraft from takeoff to next landing), measured in metric tons times kilometer traveled. Only economies with at least 0.01 percent of world transport are reported.

and Machinery and transport equipment (SITC Rev 3, code 7), in all of which, less than 25 percent of countries in LAC have a positive RCA, have intra-LAC trade that exceeds what is predicted by gravity variables. Hence, RCA similarity within LAC presents an additional constraint to deeper regional integration in the region, and to the potential efficiency gains that can be reaped from intraregional trade.

## Intraregional connectivity and export basket diversification

Beyond trade values, a region's performance in terms of regional trade integration can be further evaluated through other margins of trade. In particular, despite having low trade levels, countries in a region can have a large number of active trade links, even more so relative to the rest of the world. Similarly, the size of the typical export basket between two countries in a region may be different than what is observed with countries outside the region. The behavior of these two dimensions of trade—the extensive margin of trade and the size of export baskets—within regions can provide additional information regarding the extent to which countries in a region are integrated.

Moreover, there are at least two reasons why studying these two margins may be important as part of an assessment of a region's standing in terms of regional integration. First, if the interest of policy makers pursuing integration is fostering stable growth, the extensive margin of trade and the size of a country's export basket may be equally as important as the intensive margin (values). For example, the literature has highlighted a positive correlation between export concentration (both in products and destinations) and volatility (Lederman and Maloney 2012; Lederman, Pienknagura, and Rojas 2015; Lederman and Lesniak, forthcoming). Hence, to the extent that regional integration can favor diversification in products and destinations relative to global integration, it can provide economic benefits to regionally

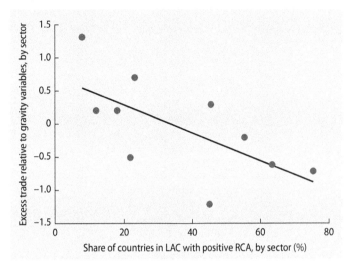

**FIGURE 2.11**  **Sector-level intraregional trade: The role of comparative advantage**

*Source:* World Bank calculations based on Artuc, Hillberry, and Pienknagura (2016).
*Note:* Revealed comparative advantage (RCA) is calculated following Vollrath 1991. More details can be found in main text. LAC = Latin America and the Caribbean. See annex 1A for a list of countries in this region.

integrated economies in terms of volatility reduction, a point that will be discussed further later in this chapter.

Second, the extensive margin of trade is also shaped by economic size and geography. For instance, Helpman, Melitz, and Rubinstein (2008) show that the probability that two countries have an active trade connection (that is, non-zero trade) decreases with distance. This suggests that gravity forces also affect patterns of export diversification across countries.

A cursory look at the number of intraregional trade connections shows that there are three distinct sets of regions. At one extreme stand ECA, EU15+, and North America, where on average close to 90 percent of all possible trade connections were active during 2010–14 (figure 2.12, panel a). Moreover, all of the countries in each region in this group have a high degree of connectivity, highlighted by the low range between the 95th and 5th percentile in each region. A second group, comprising South Asia, MENA, LAC, and EAP, has average (and median) connectivity that stands between

**FIGURE 2.12** **Extensive margin of trade with regional partners and with the rest of the world, number of partners, by region**

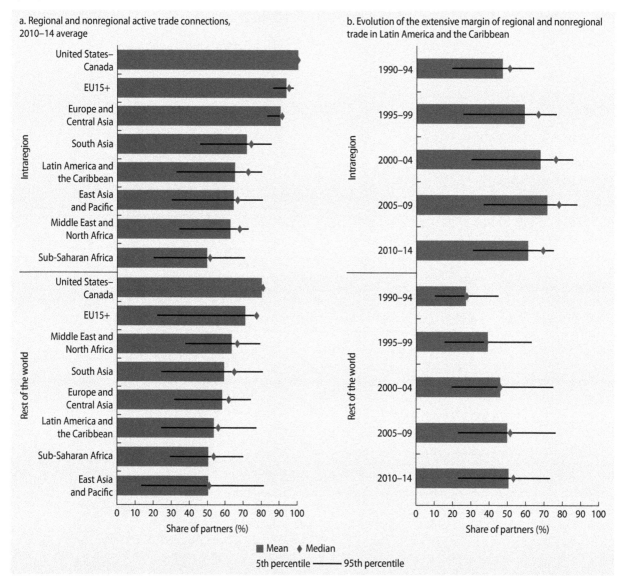

a. Regional and nonregional active trade connections, 2010–14 average

b. Evolution of the extensive margin of regional and nonregional trade in Latin America and the Caribbean

■ Mean ◆ Median
5th percentile ——— 95th percentile

*Source:* World Bank calculations using data from UN's COMTRADE.
*Note:* Connectivity is measured as the share of trading partners relative to the number of potential partners. EAP = East Asia and the Pacific; See annex 1A for a list of countries in each region.

60 and 70 percent of all possible intraregional connections. However, these are also regions where there is a high degree of heterogeneity in terms of the intraregional connectivity of individual countries. In LAC, for example, the country at the 95th percentile of connectivity trades with close to

80 percent of all regional partners whereas the country at the 5th percentile trades with only 40 percent of regional partners. Finally, SSA stands at the bottom of the pack, with only 50 percent of all possible connections active, albeit with a large degree of dispersion across countries in the region.

Regional differences in terms of connectivity with the rest of the world follow closely those of within-region connectivity. Regions like North America, EU15+, and ECA lead the pack, whereas LAC, EAP, and SSA stand at the bottom end. To be sure, in all regions there is a wider dispersion across countries in terms of their connectivity with nonregional partners compared to connectivity within regions. This is perhaps most noticeable in EAP, where the country at the 95th percentile of the distribution trades with close to 80 percent of all possible destinations, whereas the country at the 5th percentile trades with only 20 percent. This reflects the fact that EAP comprises large economies such as China, Japan, and the Republic of Korea, all of which are highly integrated with the rest of the world, but also includes small islands in the Pacific that tend to be highly specialized in terms of export products and markets (see Lederman and Lesniak, forthcoming).

Although the cross-regional comparison puts LAC behind other regions, both in terms of intra-LAC connectivity and connectivity with the rest of the world, the number of active trade connections has been increasing over time in both categories. Intra-LAC connectivity increased from an average of 50 percent in the early 1990s to close to 75 percent in the 2004–08 period (figure 2.12, panel b). Similarly, the average extra-LAC connectivity increased from close to 30 percent in the early 1990s to 50 percent in the mid-2000s. These trends stalled during the global financial crisis of 2009 and its aftermath, especially in the case of intraregional connections. Nevertheless, the levels in the latest period exceed those from the earlier periods.

In short, the raw numbers show that LAC does have a significant number of established connections within the region relative to the potential, and LAC's regional connectivity exceeds its connectivity with the rest of the world. Still, although the most connected countries in LAC do appear to match the levels of connectivity of other regions, the average country in the region is typically less connected relative to those in regions like EU15+ and ECA. The patterns evidenced in LAC are similar to those in EAP, patterns that are partly explained by the fact that a large number of countries in these regions are small island economies.

Figure 2.13 examines export product diversification with regional and nonregional partners. It presents the share of the total number of SITC Rev. 3 products at the 4-digit level that countries in each region export to regional and nonregional partners. All countries in all regions appear to have larger export baskets with regional partners than with nonregional partners. Moreover, with the exception of the North America region, which comprises just two countries, the dispersion within regions between the country at the 95th percentile of the distribution of export basket size and the country at the 5th percentile is much larger than the extensive margin numbers, regardless of the type of partner. But there are notable differences across regions. The share of total export products that the United States and Canada and the average country in EU15+ export to regional partners and to nonregional partners is substantially larger compared to other regions. The United States and Canada export close to 95 percent of all export products to each other and close to 40 percent to other countries; the average EU15+ country exports close to 50 percent of all export products to other EU15+ countries and about 20 percent to other markets. The distant third in the ranking is ECA, where the average country exports close to 20 percent of the total number of export products to regional partners and less than 10 percent to nonregional partners. The two regions that stand at the bottom of the pack are LAC and SSA. Both regions are highly specialized. The average countries in LAC and SSA export less than 10 percent of the total number of export products to regional partners and an even smaller number to countries elsewhere.

LAC's poor performance compared to other regions notwithstanding, countries in the region do appear to be more diversified today than they were in the early 1990s.

**FIGURE 2.13   Share of total products exported to regional partners and to the rest of the world**

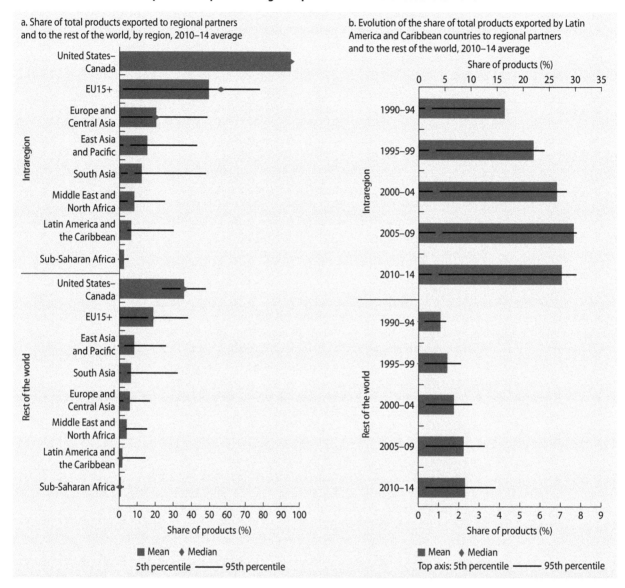

a. Share of total products exported to regional partners and to the rest of the world, by region, 2010–14 average

b. Evolution of the share of total products exported by Latin America and Caribbean countries to regional partners and to the rest of the world, 2010–14 average

*Source:* World Bank calculations using data from UN COMTRADE.
*Note:* Calculations are made using SITC Rev. 3, at the 4-digit level. Values are calculated as shares of the total number of SITC Rev. 3, 4-digit products. See annex 1A for a list of countries in each region.

The average country in LAC exported close to 4 percent of the total number of products to regional partners and close to 1 percent to partners in other corners of the world in the early 1990s. These numbers rose to 7 percent and 2 percent, respectively, by the early 2010s. However, these trends appear to be dominated by a few countries that have seen a noticeable process of export diversification over the past 20 years. In fact, the median country in the region has seen more modest increases over time. This lack of diversification may be related to growth volatility, which is discussed later in the chapter.

The regional patterns displayed in figures 2.12 and 2.13 may be driven by similar factors to those driving export values. As was anticipated earlier, the literature has provided evidence that gravity variables can also affect fixed costs of exporting (costs that determine the extensive margin of trade) and can constrain the diversification of export portfolios (see Lederman and Lesniak, forthcoming; and Lederman, Pienknagura, and Rojas 2015). With this in mind, table 2.2 assesses regional integration performance across regions in terms of export basket size and the extensive margin of trade. In particular, table 2.2 shows the results of two regressions: one of a dummy

**TABLE 2.2    The gravity forces behind the extensive margin of trade and the size of export baskets**

|  | Extensive margin (1) | Number of products (2) |
|---|---|---|
| Log distance | −0.0576*** | −0.376*** |
|  | (0.00183) | (0.00433) |
| Common language | 0.142*** | 0.306*** |
|  | (0.00310) | (0.00637) |
| Colonial ties | −0.0250*** | 0.302*** |
|  | (0.00588) | (0.0104) |
| Free trade agreement | 0.0795*** | 0.389*** |
|  | (0.00280) | (0.00556) |
| East Asia and Pacific | 0.170*** | −0.0142 |
|  | (0.00732) | (0.0123) |
| Latin America and the Caribbean | 0.376*** | 0.721*** |
|  | (0.00629) | (0.0134) |
| Sub-Saharan Africa | 0.248*** | 1.086*** |
|  | (0.00676) | (0.0170) |
| South Asia | 0.169*** | 0.123** |
|  | (0.0199) | (0.0555) |
| Europe and Central Asia | 0.340*** | 1.022*** |
|  | (0.00734) | (0.0112) |
| EU15+ | −0.404*** | −0.690*** |
|  | (0.00464) | (0.00858) |
| Middle East and North Africa | 0.0413*** | 0.252*** |
|  | (0.00814) | (0.0180) |
| Constant | −1.997*** | 2.012*** |
|  | (0.0379) | (0.0935) |
| Observations | 1,010,160 | 1,010,160 |
| R-Squared | 0.376 | 0.707 |
| Exporter FE | YES | YES |
| Importer FE | YES | YES |

*Source:* World Bank calculations based on data from UN COMTRADE, World Development Indicators, and Centre d'Études Prospectives et d'Informations Internationales (CEPII).
*Note:* FE = fixed effects. See annex 1A for a list of countries in each region. Standard errors are clustered at the importer level and are reported in parentheses.
*** p<0.01, ** p<0.05, * p<0.1.

variable taking value 1 if one country exports to another on a set of controls that includes exporter and importer fixed effects (to capture the role of size and other country specific variables), gravity variables (distance, colonial ties, common language, FTAs), and region-specific dummies; and one of the number of products exported from one country to another on the same set of controls.

The results of table 2.2, column (1), show that on the extensive margin, all regions with the exception of EU15+ have a probability of trade between regional partners that exceeds what is predicted by gravity factors. Interestingly, the coefficient for LAC stands as the second largest among all regions. A similar pattern emerges for the size of export baskets—most developing regions, including LAC, have export baskets with regional partners that are larger than what is predicted by gravity factors.

The above results indicate that the same factors that restrain export values in LAC also prevent the region from achieving higher regional connectivity and more diversified export baskets within the region. Hence, growth and the reduction of costs associated with distance will yield not only higher intraregional trade volumes but also more connectivity and diversification in intraregional trade.

In sum, the results highlighted in this section show that, if one of their objectives is to increase intra-LAC or intra-Americas trade flows, Latin American policy makers have two options. Countries in the region could grow at a rate that is higher than that of the average country in the world, or they could reduce trade frictions associated with policies and distance. But clearly growth is a policy goal in its own right, and arguably a more important one than regional integration per se. Thus, instead of focusing on policy actions that have the sole objective of boosting regional integration, the rest of this chapter explores integration strategies that can help LAC achieve high and stable growth.

## Revisiting the arguments in favor of regional integration

Thus far, the analysis has focused on explanations of differences in intraregional trade across regions. An implicit assumption was that fostering deeper regional trade links is indeed a desirable goal from the viewpoint of the region's growth agenda. As will be discussed below, there are at least two reasons for thinking that regional trade integration can affect efficiency, growth, and stability. First, the gains from trade predicted by different models depend on the characteristics of a country's trading partners. Similar points can be made about the ability of a country to use trade links as a tool to mitigate volatility. Thus, an assessment of the characteristics of LAC countries can provide a preliminary answer as to whether policies that seek to deepen trade ties with regional partners at the expense of partners outside the region are expected to deliver efficiency, growth, or stability dividends. Second, the next section presents evidence that there are important unexploited complementarities between regional and global integration efforts, which can be exploited through an OR strategy.

To be clear, the analysis presented below does not test the hypothesis of whether intraregional integration is good for growth. Rather, it takes mechanisms that have been identified in the literature as potential channels through which trade can affect growth, assumes that they are in fact operational, and then establishes the extent to which integration in each region can affect income levels and growth through these channels. In addition, the analysis assumes that all countries have the same ability to benefit from a given partner. The validity of these assumptions will be discussed below.

### Trade with nearby countries: In search of efficiency gains

One of the rationales for trade liberalization is to raise national income by increasing efficiency. Traditional international trade models predict that trade openness increases economy-wide income by reallocating factors of production (workers, labor, and land) toward sectors in which they are the most productive.[25] More recently, the literature has emphasized additional channels through which international trade can foster productivity increases. One argument is provided by Melitz (2003), who presents a model where international trade allows for reallocations within sectors by shifting resources from low-productivity firms to high-productivity ones. In this case, the productivity gains would come from within industry improvements purely because of the exit of low-productivity firms and the survival of high-productivity firms.

Regardless of the mechanism, an important insight is that the magnitude of the gains that a country can attain from trade depends on the characteristics of its trading partners and the structure of trade. For example, the gains arising from trade links between countries with a very similar productivity structure across sectors will be lower than trade links between countries with very different cross-sectoral productivity structures.

One implication of these theoretical perspectives is that, leaving commercial policy aside, the productivity gains from trade a country can attain will be shaped by the characteristics of nearby countries. This is due to the fact that, as is highlighted repeatedly in this report, the costs associated with distance bias trade toward closer countries. As a result, in a world of nondiscriminatory commercial policies, the gains from trade will typically be heterogeneous across countries and across regions because of the characteristics of a country's neighbors.

With this in mind, the exercise that follows compares the potential efficiency benefits from trade with regional partners and those from trade with the rest of the world, under the assumption that the aforementioned effects of trade can be realized. The analysis can also be interpreted as an indication of the desirability, from the standpoint of improving efficiency, of pursuing commercial policies that favor regional partners.

To this end, we study the most basic theoretical channel through which trade can affect welfare and income, namely, trade between partners that have different patterns of comparative advantage, as highlighted by neoclassical models of trade. This channel fosters productivity enhancements through the reallocation of resources across sectors in the economy. The exercise calculates for every pair of potential trading partners the Spearman rank correlations of the countries' trade baskets. A high correlation is interpreted as an indicator of similarity in comparative advantage. Country-specific average correlations are aggregated at the regional level.

In most regions, the average bilateral similarity of comparative advantage is greatest between countries with common borders and lowest between nonregional, noncontiguous partners. The similarity between regional partners (that do not share borders) is in the middle (figure 2.14). From the neoclassical theory point of view, these findings suggest that economies in most regions could benefit more from integration with the rest of the world than with regional partners.

However, there are differences across regions concerning the bilateral similarity of comparative advantage between country pairs that share borders and country pairs from the same region. Perhaps surprisingly, the countries from North America and EU15+ have the *lowest* RCA similarity between contiguous and regional partners in the whole sample. There is also significant variation among developing economies. EAP and ECA, on average, have the least similar patterns of comparative advantage. In contrast, LAC's average similarity is the second highest among all regions, behind only SSA.

To be sure, the results for LAC mask heterogeneity within the region. Central America and South America have relatively high similarity indexes compared to the Caribbean countries[26] (figure 2.15, panel a). This suggests, in theory, that countries in the Caribbean could attain a higher benefit from trade with other Caribbean economies

**FIGURE 2.14** **Trade similarity with regional partners and with the rest of the world, by region**

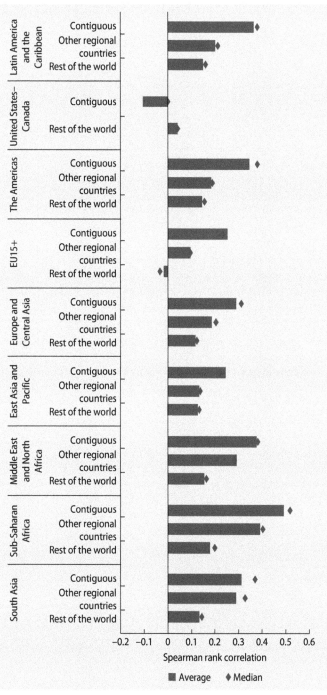

Spearman rank correlation

■ Average ◆ Median

*Source:* World Bank calculations using data from UN COMTRADE.
*Note:* Calculations are made using data for 2014. Export similarity between any pair of countries is calculated as the Spearman rank correlation of the vector of revealed comparative advantages of the two countries. The ranking ranges from −1 (most dissimilar) to 1 (most similar). For the bilateral correlations all products with zero trade in both countries are excluded. Regional numbers correspond to the average correlation between countries in the region and partners in the relevant partner group. See annex 1A for a list of countries in each region.

compared to intra-South America and intra-Central America trade.

However, the highest potential benefits of regional trade integration for all subregions in LAC come from trade across subregions within LAC. In particular, in all subregions the average country has a similarity index with LAC partners outside of its own subregion that is close to that with partners from the rest of the world. This suggests that, if anything, from the point of view of patterns of specialization, countries in LAC should be seeking integration with partners outside their own subregion or outside LAC.

With this in mind, one can ask whether trade blocs within LAC are structured in such a way as to bring together trading partners with differences in terms of their patterns of comparative advantages. The answer to this question varies by trade bloc. In the case of Mercosur and the Pacific Alliance, both of which comprise mostly South American countries, the answer seems to be no (figure 2.15, panel b). In both cases, the patterns of comparative advantage vary more between members and nonmembers than between members of the bloc. In the case of NAFTA and CAFTA-DR, the answer appears to be yes. In both, average differences in RCA patterns within the bloc are more favorable for pro-efficiency reallocations than those with nonmember countries. Chapter 3 expands this analysis by studying preferences within trade blocs in LAC and their treatment of outside parties.

The first look at patterns of similarity in trade structures for the average pair of countries in LAC indicates that, broadly speaking, the region may be too similar to achieve efficiency gains from integration. This conclusion emerges from an analysis of the most recent trade data available.

RCAs may change over time, however. In fact, Proudman and Redding (2000) and Levchenko and Zhang (2016) provide evidence that this is the case. Patterns of RCA can evolve because of changes in the endowment of factors of production (physical capital, human capital, labor, and land) or

**FIGURE 2.15    Trade similarity with regional partners and with the rest of the world, by subregions and trade blocks in LAC**

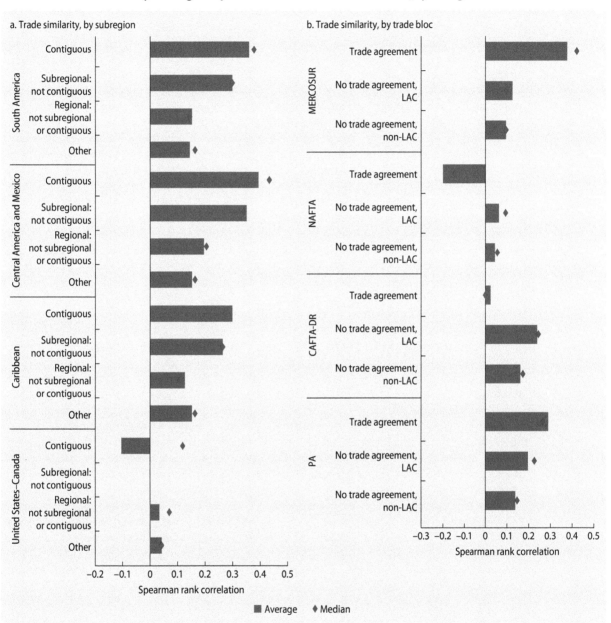

Source: World Bank calculations using data from UN COMTRADE.
Note: Calculations are made using data for 2014. Export similarity between any pair of countries is calculated as the Spearman rank correlation of the vector of revealed comparative advantages of the two countries. The ranking ranges from –1 (most dissimilar) and 1 (most similar). For the bilateral correlations all products with zero trade in both countries are excluded. Subregional and trade bloc numbers correspond to the average correlation between countries in each of these and partners in the relevant partner group. NAFTA = North American Free Trade Agreement; MERCOSUR: Argentina, Brazil, Paraguay, Ururguay, and Venezuela. NAFTA: Canada, Mexico, and the United States. CAFTA-DR: Costa Rica, the Dominican Republic, El Salvador, Guatemala, Honduras, Nicaragua, and the United States.

because of changes in the factors driving observed productivity differences between sectors (for example, technology, taxes, and institutions). This implies that, to the extent that countries in LAC can enact policies that create changes in either factor accumulation or productivity at the sectoral level, the potential for efficiency gains stemming from regional integration may improve in the future.

But it is unlikely that these changes will occur overnight. After all, accumulating factors of production and accruing the benefits of policies aimed at unleashing the productivity of a given sector can take time. Moreover, for these changes to yield dissimilar trade structures within the region, they must occur in such a way that countries end up specializing in different sectors. This would be the case, for example, if countries accumulate specific factors of production at different speeds, such that the relative stocks of these factors change over time. Only time will tell whether this type of process will materialize in the region. What is clear is that it requires a level of regional policy coordination that may be hard to achieve.

Turning back to the current trade structures, even if the broad patterns of RCA provide a sobering message regarding the potential for efficiency gains from regional integration in LAC, there are some bright spots worth highlighting. These bright spots are discussed below.

*Efficiency gains from trade with nearby countries: The role of economic size and distance* The analysis of the potential gains from trade integration between countries of different subregions suggests that the economic size of a country and its trading partners, as well as the distance between them, may shape the potential efficiency gains from integration. After all, the analysis shows that small countries in the Caribbean and Central America appear to be more differentiated in terms of RCAs when compared to South American countries. This suggests that when studying the potential gains from regional integration, one should

not ignore that they may vary depending on the countries one is looking at within a region.

Existing evidence already argues in favor of the idea that economic size and distance can affect the efficiency gains from trade integration. Lederman and Lesniak (forthcoming) show that the size of a country's trade basket increases with economic size, where size is proxied with the country's labor force. This result holds even after controlling for a country's trade openness. This implies that the trade structures of small economies, which are typically highly specialized in a few goods, and large economies, which hold relatively large trade baskets, are expected to differ significantly. The similarity of trade structures in small economies will depend on whether the two countries specialize in similar goods or not. This, in turn, is expected to be affected by their distance. For example, nearby countries may share similar endowments of arable land or crops, leading to similar patterns of comparative advantage.

To explore in more detail the role of size and distance in explaining patterns of trade similarity, table 2.3 shows the results of a regression of the Spearman rank correlation of a pair of countries is against the (log) geographic distance between the two countries and the bilateral distance in economic size between the two countries. Bilateral distance in economic size is proxied with the absolute value of the difference of the log of the labor force of the two countries. This regression is run for two samples (all pairs and LAC pairs) and two specifications (with and without country fixed effects).

The results in table 2.3 confirm the idea that the trade structures of countries of different size differ more compared to those of countries of similar size. The coefficient of the distance on economic size (column (1)) is negative and statistically significant, suggesting that the larger the difference in size between the pair of countries, the lower the Spearman rank correlation of their trade baskets. The same is true for geographic distance. The results are robust to the inclusion of country fixed effects (columns (2)

TABLE 2.3 **Export similarity: The role of size and distance**

| | Bilateral Spearman rank correlation | | | |
|---|---|---|---|---|
| Dependent variable | All (1) | LAC–LAC (2) | All (3) | LAC–LAC (4) |
| Geographic distance (log) | −0.00815*** | −0.0506*** | −0.0413*** | −0.0321*** |
| | (0.00196) | (0.00578) | (0.00120) | (0.00457) |
| Economic distance (log difference) | −0.0156*** | −0.0420*** | −0.0199*** | −0.0389*** |
| | (0.000875) | (0.00234) | (0.000636) | (0.00171) |
| Constant | 0.324*** | 0.794*** | 0.740*** | 0.548*** |
| | (0.0170) | (0.0436) | (0.0968) | (0.0719) |
| Observations | 15,835 | 589 | 15,835 | 589 |
| R-squared | 0.023 | 0.472 | 0.747 | 0.837 |
| Exporter FE | YES | YES | YES | YES |
| Importer FE | YES | YES | YES | YES |

*Source:* World Bank calculations based on data from UN COMTRADE, World Development Indicators, and Centre d'Études Prospectives et d'Informations Internationales (CEPII).
*Note:* Economic distance refers to the log difference of the GDP per capita of the reporting country and its partner. FE = fixed effects. LAC = Latin America and the Caribbean. See annex 1A for a list of countries included in LAC. Standard errors are reported in parentheses. *** $p<0.01$, ** $p<0.05$, * $p<0.1$.

and (4)) and to different samples (columns (3) and (4)).

This does not necessarily imply that small economies will have incentives to grant preferences to large economies, however. This will ultimately depend on two forces. On the one hand, in very small and specialized economies import tariffs are used as consumption taxes, which means that granting preferential treatment can lead to the problem of trade diversion, while at the same time lowering fiscal revenue. This follows from the observation that these countries can optimally choose higher tariffs in a large number of goods compared to large economies because they do not suffer from distortions in domestic production, one of the costs associated with tax collection (see Corden 1997). On the other hand, granting preferences to a large economy may be desirable if it facilitates preferential access into that market for local exporters.

From the point of view of the large economy, efficiency gains are expected to be small, suggesting that, at first glance, there are few incentives to reduce tariffs and favor imports from small economies. This point notwithstanding, there are two reasons that

may lead large economies to grant preferences to small countries. One is associated with geopolitical interests (see Lederman and Özden 2007) and the other has to do with the fact that, because integration with small economies leads to small reallocations, the potential losses to workers in affected sectors are small.

## Trade with nearby countries: In search of knowledge

Trade can also affect growth rates in countries that are not knowledge production hubs by facilitating transfers from those that are. This occurs through interactions between economic agents or through the knowledge embodied in the goods that are traded. Under this premise, the stock of knowledge of a country, which is an input in its total factor productivity (TFP) growth, is a function of both its own stock of knowledge and those of the countries with which it has trade links. Thus, even if a country invests little in knowledge creation, it can "import" knowledge from other countries. This insight was initially proposed by Grossman and Helpman (1991) and tested empirically by Coe and

Helpman (1995). In particular, the latter estimate the elasticity of a country's TFP growth with respect to stocks of domestic R&D and those of its trading partners. The study found large and positive elasticities for both domestic and foreign stocks, suggesting that both types of investments are inputs in the production of knowledge. Moreover, the authors also find that the elasticity of TFP growth with respect to the R&D stock of a country's trading partners is a function of the country's openness.

This point is further explored in the work of Lumenga-Neso, Olarreaga, and Schiff (2005), who argue that once a country "imports" knowledge, this additional stock of knowledge is added to the domestic stock and the sum of the two is what will be contained in the country's exports to the rest of the world. Hence, the authors argue that there are three stocks of knowledge affecting a country's growth: domestic R&D efforts, the R&D investments of a country's trading partners embodied in the partners' exports (first-round effects), and the knowledge from a country's trading partners' partners that is embodied in their exports (second-round effects). The authors find that the second-round effects are at least as important as the first-round effects.

What does the literature on international diffusion of knowledge through trade imply for regional integration? The answer to this question will depend on the rate at which knowledge depreciates with each transfer. Take, for instance, an extreme where depreciation is close to one (very high frictions to the diffusion of knowledge). In this case all that will matter for a country's growth is its own stock of knowledge. In contrast, if depreciation is very low (low frictions), the second-order effects are so large that all countries have access to a world stock of knowledge. In between these two extremes, own knowledge and first-order effects will dominate, and the identity of a country's trading partners will be important for its stock of knowledge.

To further illustrate the role of depreciation on the overall stock of knowledge, figure 2.16 depicts for each region the stock of R&D under two scenarios—one where depreciation is 90 percent (high friction), and one with 10 percent (low friction). In both cases we calculate the diffusion of R&D as in Lumenga-Neso, Olarreaga, and Schiff (2005).[27] In the low-friction case the second-order effect dominates all other effects and the total stock of knowledge of all regions is very similar. In the high-friction case, in contrast, a country's own R&D stock and that of its trading partners have a higher weight. In this case LAC stands well below high-income regions as well as other developing countries such as EAP and ECA.

Hence, in a scenario where frictions are low, a bias toward regional integration is very much irrelevant for a country's growth prospects—the important thing is being open to trade. In contrast, when frictions are high and first-order effects are important, high R&D efforts of a its trading partners mean that a country has better growth prospects from integrating with them. This suggests that, under these assumptions, LAC would be better off pursuing integration with high-income countries, and less so with its regional partners.

The analysis of Coe and Helpman (1995) and Lumenga-Neso, Olarreaga, and Schiff (2005) assumes that the frictions to knowledge diffusion are homogeneous across countries. That is, the impact of the stock of knowledge of two countries on the growth rate of a third country is the same, conditional on the two countries having the same import intensity with the third country. However, the literature has presented evidence suggesting that this may not be the case. Keller (2002) shows that the elasticity of TFP growth of a country with respect to the stock of knowledge of another country is positive but decreases with distance. This, the author argues, is one of the reasons behind the lack of convergence observed around the world (see chapter 1 for more on this). Similarly, Bravo-Ortega, Cusolito, and Lederman (2016) estimate patent production functions, taking into account not only the effect of a country's own R&D

**FIGURE 2.16**   **Knowledge stocks across regions: The role of frictions in the diffusion of knowledge**

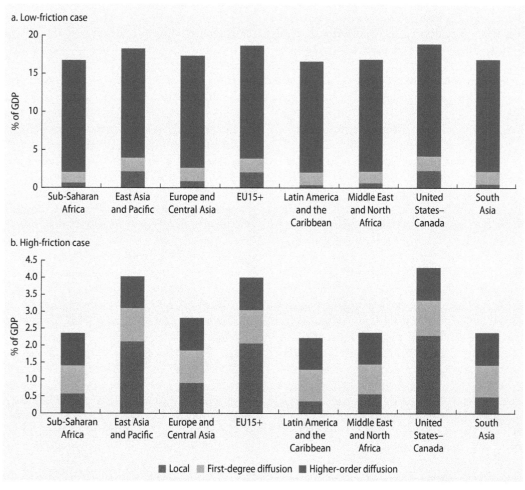

*Source:* World Bank calculations based on Lumenga-Neso, Olarreaga, and Schiff 2005.
*Note:* Panel a assumes $p = 0.1$; panel b assumes $p = 0.9$. See main text for details on the construction of R&D stocks. See annex 1A for a list of countries in each region.

investments and stock of patents but also the stock of patents in the world. Moreover, the authors allow the elasticity of patenting activity with respect to the stock of patents of external countries to vary by economic distance (that is, different levels of income per capita between the country in analysis and the external country) and by geographic distance. The results show that the diffusion of knowledge is localized (is highest for nearby countries), and is higher the more similar countries are in their level of development.

The observation that frictions to knowledge diffusion are increasing in distance, both geographic and in terms of levels of development, provides some support for the role of regional trade integration as a way to boost growth. However, there are two caveats to this idea. First, so far we have assumed that knowledge diffusion occurs through trade. But, as suggested by Keller (1998) and Bahar and Rapoport (2016), other forms of integration such as migration or foreign direct investment (FDI) flows can act as conduits for knowledge diffusion. Hence, LAC countries can potentially achieve similar outcomes (for example, boosting growth) by pursuing other forms of economic integration (for example, migration). Indeed, the fact that RCAs across LAC countries are similar suggests that, although trade may be low because of this, there is scope for migration to help share best practices and technological advances in industries in which countries in the region share relative comparative advantages.

The second caveat is related to the low R&D levels in the region, a problem that has been recognized in previous flagship reports in this series (see Lederman et al. 2014). Even if lower frictions with nearby countries may facilitate knowledge absorption from these countries, there has to be knowledge to absorb in the first place. The fact that Brazil and Mexico (two countries where R&D would be expected to be high, given their relatively high income levels by regional standards and the size of their population) have relatively low R&D levels is particularly problematic for the scope of knowledge transmission within the region (see Lederman and Maloney 2003). After all, gravity forces suggest that these are the natural focus points of trade in the region. Hence, for LAC to really benefit from proximity in terms of

knowledge diffusion, key actors in the region need to increase their R&D investments.

*Knowledge diffusion and trade with nearby countries: The role of economic size* The benefits of an increase in the investment of knowledge by big countries in LAC would be especially important for small economies in the region. After all, there are arguments that suggest that these are countries that have a disadvantage in the production of knowledge. This disadvantage stems from the fact that the production of knowledge requires large fixed investments that range from materials and equipment to the time that researchers have to invest prior to developing a new idea. These fixed investments require devoting a non-negligible fraction of GDP and of the labor force to knowledge-producing activities at the expense of other productive activities, an effort that many small countries cannot afford.

The relationship between knowledge production and economic size is clearly illustrated by figure 2.17. The figure plots the log of R&D/GDP, or R&D intensity, together with the log of a country's labor force, and the fitted line of a regression of the former against the latter. The result points to a positive correlation between R&D intensity and a country's size.

**FIGURE 2.17  R&D intensity and economic size**

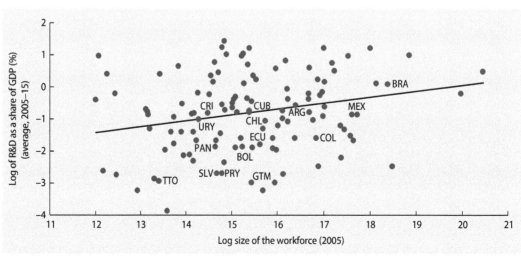

*Source:* World Bank calculations using data from World Development Indicators.
*Note:* R&D (research and development) intensity is defined as R&D/GDP.

The results in figure 2.17 imply that bigger countries that do not integrate with knowledge production hubs are not as affected by it as a small country would be. The reason behind this is that a larger country can produce its own knowledge, whereas a smaller country will have more difficulty doing so. As a result, regional integration efforts by small economies are expected to have a larger impact on growth, especially in a world with frictions to the transfer of knowledge.

In sum, the conclusions of the analysis presented above regarding comparative advantages and knowledge spillovers from trade do not give much support to the idea that higher growth can be attained by pursuing deeper regional integration in trade. Rather, the results suggest that, if anything, internationalization toward extraregional markets can be a more conducive path to growth. However, regional partners may play a role in this internationalization process by facilitating entry and survival of exporters in extraregional markets. This possibility is explored below.

## Trade with nearby countries: In search of stability

The previous sections focused exclusively on whether regional integration can boost efficiency and growth in LAC. Yet, as discussed in chapter 1, the region's growth path is not only characterized by its low mean, but it is also marked by its relative volatility compared to other regions. High volatility is a matter of policy concern in its own right because it can have a direct impact on many important economic outcomes; it can reduce growth (Ramey and Ramey 1995; Hnatkovska and Loayza 2004) and increase poverty and inequality (Gavin and Hausmann 1998; Laursen and Mahajan 2005). Hence, equally important in assessing the desirability of deeper regional integration is determining the extent to which it can dampen or exacerbate LAC's volatility relative to an integration strategy that does not discriminate against nonregional partners.

To be sure, the economics literature has pointed to international integration as a potential cause of volatility, with three empirical regularities backing this claim. First, exports and imports rank among the most volatile components of GDP, coming second only to investment. Second, there is evidence of a positive correlation between trade openness and volatility (di Giovanni and Levchenko 2009). Finally, trade volatility has closely followed the behavior of GDP volatility over the past 20 years—with a slight downward trend from the mid-1990s until 2008, followed by a sharp increase after the global financial crisis of 2008–09.[28]

However, the link between trade integration and volatility depends on a number of factors. First, in some instances trade integration can reduce volatility. This can happen, for example, in countries with unreliable and volatile local inputs producers. In these circumstances, trade integration, by giving final goods producers access to less volatile inputs producers, can mitigate GDP growth volatility (see Caselli et al. 2015). Even in circumstances where trade integration can increase volatility, there are some structural factors that can mitigate or amplify this adverse effect. The domestic economic policy framework is one such factor. A country's trade structure is a second factor affecting the link between openness and GDP growth volatility.[29] The identity of a country's trading partners is a final factor affecting the link between integration and GDP growth volatility because different countries may have more volatile profiles of external demand and supply than other (Jansen, Lennon, and Piermartini 2016; Bennett et al. 2016). From the standpoint of understanding the effect of regional integration on volatility, the latter is perhaps the most relevant factor. After all, regional trade integration is precisely about promoting deeper trade ties with countries that may have attributes affecting volatility that differ from those of other countries.

The rest of this section delves into this factor. In particular, following Bennett et al. (2016), a background paper commissioned for this report, and Jansen, Lennon, and

Piermartini (2016), this section analyzes regional integration through the lens of portfolio theory. Under this view, deeper regional integration is desirable if it lowers a country's volatility profile compared to integration with other countries. The contribution of trade partners to a country's volatility profile will depend on three elements: the inherent volatility of the partners' trade flows, the covariance of the partners' trade flows with those of the country, and the covariance between the trade flows of different partners. Hence, the analysis focuses on understanding how these three elements behave in LAC countries and what their total effect implies for volatility.

*Regional integration through the lens of portfolio theory* Observed patterns of trade integration are affected by a number of variables. One of these variables is commercial policy. Moreover, commercial policy, when applied in a preferential manner, can end up affecting the relative weight that a trading partner has in a country's total trade.

Given the impact that trade policy has on trade weights, it is reasonable to think that a country's trade policy partly responds to objectives that are affected by trade weights. Previous sections of the chapter have emphasized one such objective, namely, growth. However, there may be other economic and noneconomic objectives behind commercial policy.[30] The analysis that follows focuses on managing volatility as an additional objective of trade policy.

Interestingly, when growth and volatility are taken together, the choice of a country's set of partners and the weight attached to each partner resembles the choice described in modern portfolio theory (MPT). MPT, a commonly used tool in finance, characterizes the optimal choice of assets by an investor who wants to minimize the risk inherent to a portfolio subject to a given return. This problem reduces to choosing the weight (or allocation) that the optimal portfolio gives to each asset considered by the investor. One of the main insights of MPT is that this choice not only depends on the individual assets'

volatilities but it should also factor in the covariance that specific assets have with the rest of the portfolio. In this sense, variance minimization calls for assets with low variance and a negative correlation with the rest of the portfolio.

The logic behind MPT can be easily extended to trade policy choices. For simplicity, the parallel will be viewed focusing on exports. In this case the return a country gets from trading with a partner is growth, which can be proxied by export growth. The contribution to volatility that each trading partner adds to the portfolio will depend on the volatility of the partner's demand for imports, the covariance between the partners' demand for imports and the country's supply for exports, and the covariance between each partner's demand for imports. Hence, taking export supply and import demand patterns as given, the policy choice is to choose trade weights in order to minimize export volatility.

Can the call for deeper trade integration in LAC be rationalized from the point of view of MPT? Answering this question requires estimating the growth and volatility of a country's supply for exports and its partners' demand for imports, as well as the covariances discussed above. This is precisely the estimation that Bennett et al. (2016) pursue. In particular, the authors estimate a year-by-year, sector-level gravity equation that allows the authors to recover an exporter-specific effect and an importer-specific effect, which can be interpreted as proxies of aggregate supply and demand.[31] Moreover, in the estimation the authors control for other gravity variables as well as the sectoral fixed effect. These additional controls are important to separate the effect of supply and demand from the composition of a country's trade basket or the remoteness of a country (see box 2.2 for details on the methodology applied). With this estimation, one can approximate the growth of a country's export as the sum of six terms—a term capturing the growth of global trade, a term capturing the growth of the country's supply of exports, the weighted average of the growth of the

## BOX 2.2 Estimating the components of export growth volatility

What are the factors affecting a country's export growth volatility? This is the question that Bennett et al. (2016) try to answer. The authors explore the role played by country-specific factors, factors associated with the sectoral composition of a country's export basket, global factors, factors associated with a country's trading partners, factors associated with distance and its elasticity, and the potential interaction between each of these factors.

To achieve this objective, the authors follow the methodology proposed by Koren and Tenreyro (2007) to decompose the variance of exports. In particular, the authors begin by estimating a year-by-year sector-level gravity equation:

$$\ln(X_{ijkt}) = \alpha_t + \gamma_{it} + \lambda_{jt} + \eta_{kt} + \xi_{ijt} + \epsilon_{ijkt}, \quad (B2.2.1)$$

where $\ln(X_{ijkt})$ is the logarithm of sectoral bilateral real export flows from country $i$, $(i \in I)$ in a given year $t$, to importer $j$ (in the set of $i$'s trade partners $J_{it}$) in sector $k$ (in the set of industries traded from $i$ to $j$ denoted as $K_{ijt}$). Focusing on country $i$'s exports, the first component in (B2.2.1), $\alpha_t$, is a global effect, common to all exporters, importers, and sectors for a given year. This captures shocks to trade flows that affect all sectors and countries in the same magnitude. The second component $(\gamma_{it})$ is a country-specific component and captures shocks to country $i$'s exports that impact all destinations and sectors equally. This, for example, captures economy-wide macroeconomic policies. Analogously, $\lambda_{jt}$ is an importer-specific effect that captures shocks common to all origins and sectors. This, for instance, captures changes in the income level of the importer that affect the demand of all goods from all origins. The fourth component $(\eta_{kt})$ is the sectoral effect and captures shocks to trade in sector $k$ common to all origins and destinations. Importantly, the exporter, importer, and sectoral effects are normalized such that the sum of all these effects across origins, destinations, and sectors, respectively, sum to zero each period.[a] In this sense, the exporter, importer, and product effects capture movements along these dimensions that are not captured by the common effect (that is, that do not cut across origins, destinations, and products). The fifth component $(\xi_{ijt})$ represents the sum of bilateral resistance effects common in the gravity trade liter-

ature. This term explains the fraction of trade from exporter $i$ and importer $j$ due to distance, a shared border, common legal system, colonial ties, common language, and the presence of free trade agreements between the pair at time $t$. The remaining term $(\epsilon_{ijkt})$, referred to as the error effect, is the part of exports that is unexplained by the previous components.

Having estimated (B2.2.1), the authors approximate aggregate trade growth for country $i$ in period $t$ as:[b]

$$\ln(\widehat{X_{it}}) = \ln(X_{it}) - \ln(X_{it-1}) \cong \sum_{j \in J_{it}} \sum_{k \in K_{ijt}} a_{ijkt-1}$$
$$\times (\ln(X_{ijkt}) - \ln(X_{ijkt-1})) \quad (B2.2.2)$$

Replacing (B2.2.1) into (B2.2.2) leads to:

$$\ln(\widehat{X_{it}}) \cong \widehat{\alpha_t} + \widehat{\gamma_{it}} + \sum_{j \in J_{it}} a_{ijt-1} \times \widehat{\lambda_{jt}} + \sum_{j \in J_{it}} \sum_{k \in K_{ijt}} a_{ijst-1}$$
$$\times \widehat{\eta_{kt}} + \sum_{j \in J_{it}} a_{ijt-1} \times \widehat{\xi_{ijt}}$$
$$+ \sum_{j \in J_{it}} \sum_{k \in K_{ijt}} a_{ijkt-1} \times \widehat{\epsilon_{ijkt}} \quad (B2.2.3)$$

where $a_{ijt}$ and $a_{ikt}$ are the trade shares of partner $j$ and sector $k$ over $i$'s total exports respectively. Equation (B2.2.3) states that country $i$'s aggregate trade growth can be expressed as the sum of the growth of a global effect, the growth of country $i$'s exporter effect, and the trade-weighted sum of the growth of its partners' effects, sectorial effects, resistance effects, and idiosyncratic effects.[c]

There are two important things to mention with regard to equation (B2.2.3). First, each of the elements in (B2.2.3) can be potentially correlated with other elements. This is true statistically, but it is also economically plausible. For instance, macroeconomic policies, which affect country-specific shocks, can respond to shocks in sectors that are economically relevant in the country. Also, equation (B2.2.3) is an accounting identity because the error term captures everything that is not accounted for by the other effects and because we do not place any restrictions on the covariances across elements. As such, while being a convenient way to partition the data, the elements in (B2.2.3) cannot be matched directly to a specific theory.

*(continued)*

---

From equation (B2.2.3) it is straightforward to decompose trade growth volatility and arrive at equation (2.1) in the text.

The variances and covariances are calculated across the $T$ years in the sample. In particular, for each pair of variables $x$ and $y$, we calculate variances and covariances as

$$Var(x) = \left( \frac{1}{T} \sum_{t=t0}^{T} (x_t - \bar{x})^2 \right),$$

$$Cov(x,y) = \left( \frac{1}{T} \sum_{t=t0}^{T} (x_t - \bar{x})(y_t - \bar{y}) \right)$$

a. The restrictions imposed on each set of fixed effects are arbitrary. For example, Koren and Tenreyro (2007) perform a similar empirical exercise to the one presented but impose a zero-sum restriction on the country-specific effect. The restrictions chosen in the empirical exercise in this book are more fitted for the questions that are at the heart of it.

b. This stems from the identity $g_{ijkt} = \sum_{j=1}^{J} \sum_{k=1}^{K} a_{ijt} \times g_{ijt}$ and the approximations $g_{it} \cong \ln(X_{it}) - \ln(X_{it-1})$ and $g_{ijt} \cong \ln(X_{ijkt}) - \ln(X_{ijkt-1})$.

c. For more details on the exact calculation of each of these effects, see annex 2A.

country's partners' demand for imports, the weighted average of the growth of the sectors' trade volumes, the growth attributable to changes in gravity variables and the elasticity of trade volumes to each of them, and a term that is exporter-importer-sector specific. Finally, export growth volatility will be a sum of the volatilities of each of the six terms described above and the respective covariances between them. Mathematically, export growth volatility is equal to:

$$Var(gX_{it}) \cong \underbrace{Var(\widehat{\alpha_t})}_{global\ effect} + \underbrace{Var(\widehat{\gamma_{it}})}_{country\ effect}$$

$$+ Var \underbrace{\left( \sum_{j \in J_{it}} a_{ijt} \times \widehat{\lambda_{jt}} \right)}_{partners\ effect}$$

$$+ Var \underbrace{\left( \sum_{k \in K_{it}} a_{ikt} \times \widehat{\eta_{kt}} \right)}_{sectoral\ effect}$$

$$+ Var \underbrace{\left( \sum_{j \in J_{it}} a_{ijt} \times \widehat{\xi_{ijt}} \right)}_{average\ resistance\ effect}$$

$$+ Var \underbrace{\left( \sum_{j \in J_{it}} \sum_{k \in K_{it}} a_{ijkt} \times \widehat{\epsilon_{ijkt}} \right)}_{residual\ effect}$$

$$+ Cov$$

$$(2.1)$$

where $gX_{it}$ is the growth of exports of country $i$ in period $t$; $\widehat{\alpha_t}$ captures the growth of global trade (global effect), $(\widehat{\gamma_{it}})$ captures the growth of country $i$'s supply of exports (country effect), $\sum_{j \in J_{it}} a_{ijt} \times \widehat{\lambda_{jt}}$ is the weighted average of the growth of country $i$'s partners' demand for imports (partner effect, where $a_{ijt}$ are the weights and $\widehat{\lambda_{jt}}$ is the growth rate of $j$'s demand for imports), $\sum_{k \in K_{it}} a_{ikt} \times \widehat{\eta_{kt}}$ is the weighted average of the growth of the sector-specific growth rates (sectoral effect), $\sum_{j \in J_{it}} a_{ijt} \times \widehat{\xi_{ijt}}$ captures the weighted average of the growth of gravity-related trade (average resistance effect), $\sum_{j \in J_{it}} \sum_{k \in K_{it}} a_{ijkt} \times \widehat{\epsilon_{ijkt}}$ is the weighted average of the growth of exporter-importer-sector specific term (residual effect), $Var(.)$ is the variance operator, and $Cov$ is (twice) the sum of all the covariances. Regional integration efforts will typically affect the trade weights (the $a$'s) in the equation above.

The export growth variance equation provides a useful tool to address the question of how deeper regional integration in LAC affects the volatility of the region's exports. However, before analyzing the answer to this question in more detail, it is useful to first understand the behavior of each of the components affecting trade volatility across countries in different regions.

A word of caution regarding the data used in the analysis by Bennett et al. (2016) is warranted. The results that follow use a sample of about 40 countries and 4 sectors for which there is non-zero trade in the 22 years between 1990 and 2011 for all exporter-importer-sector triads.[32] Countries and years are chosen for data reliability reasons (see Berthelon and Freund 2008) and for the technical requirements assuring proper estimation of each of the effects in (2.1). Although the sample covers the bulk of global trade and a large share of each country's trade flows, the country coverage amounts to only about 20 percent of all countries. In the case of LAC, the sample includes six countries—Argentina, Brazil, Chile, Colombia, Mexico, and Peru. Hence, the results regarding the impact of deeper regional integration in LAC on volatility are limited to these countries. Later in this section, additional suggestive evidence will be provided to assess the impact of deeper trade integration in LAC on the volatility of other countries in the region.

This caveat notwithstanding, figure 2.18 shows some of the factors highlighted in equation (2.1), through which changes in regional integration patterns (changes in the weights) can affect volatility. In particular, it shows by region the simple average of the variance of the exporter and importer effects as well as some of the (simple) average covariances that enter the term $Cov$ in equation (2.1). In the case of covariances, it shows averages with regional and nonregional partners.

The first point to notice is that the volatility of export supply growth for the average country among the six LAC countries in the sample is among the highest for all regions (figure 2.18, panel a). This suggests that LAC's export growth is volatile in part because the supply of exports from LAC to the world is more volatile than in other regions. Hence, export growth volatility in LAC is partly self-inflicted. Moreover, LAC countries' demand for imports is more volatile than in countries in other regions. This suggests that, through the partner effect term in equation (2.1), raising the weight carried

by intra-LAC exports on total exports will have an adverse effect on export volatility.

However, as was discussed earlier, the weight put on different partners can also affect volatility through the covariance terms. Zooming into the covariance across import demand terms and the covariance between important demand and export supply terms, one can see that the average correlation between the exporter effects of LAC countries and the importer effects appears to be small with both regional and nonregional partners. In contrast, there are stark differences in the correlation of import demand terms within LAC and between LAC and other countries. The former are on average positively correlated and large; the latter are negative and smaller in magnitude.

Put together, the evidence in figure 2.18 already suggests that deepening trade integration within LAC is expected to increase export volatility in the region. However, for simplicity, figure 2.18 presents only a few of the variances and covariances that are affected by trade weights. Trade weights also affect the variance of the average resistance term, the variance of the error term, and other covariances not shown in figure 2.18.

Figure 2.19 quantifies the overall effect that deeper regional trade integration would have on export volatility in LAC countries. The analysis performs two counterfactual exercises: one where the overall weight carried by LAC partners is doubled at the expense of nonregional partners, and another where the weight carried by non-LAC partners is slashed by half in favor of regional partners. The exercise imposes a number of assumptions on the trade weights. First, the increase in the overall regional weight is distributed uniformly. This means that if Argentina sends 40 percent of its exports to LAC partners—30 percent to Brazil and 10 to the rest of LAC—the counterfactual shares in the first exercise are such that Argentina sends 40 percent of its exports to Brazil and 20 percent to the rest of LAC, and in the second exercise that Argentina sends 52.5 percent of its exports to Brazil and 17.5 percent to the rest of LAC (70 percent in total).

**FIGURE 2.18** **Variances and correlations of supply and demand effects, by region**

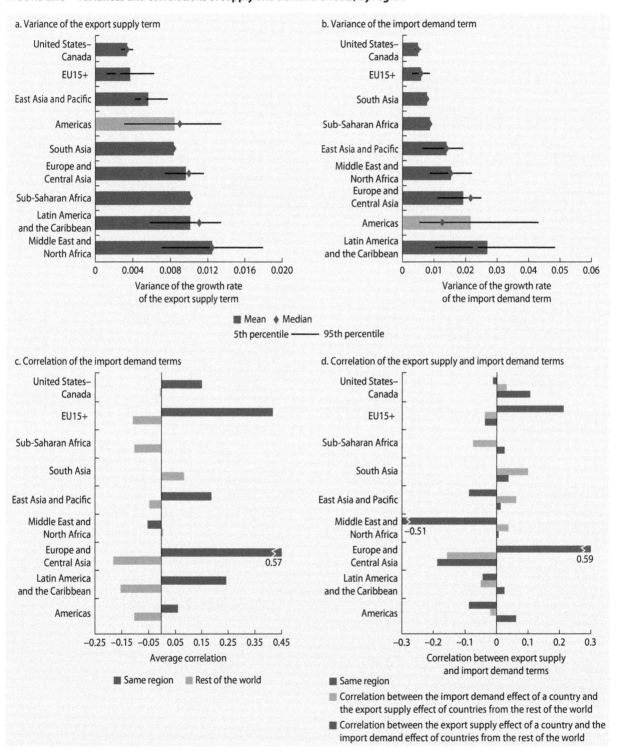

Similarly, the reduction in trade weights of nonregional partners is distributed uniformly. Second, the distribution of export shares across sectors from one country to another is the same in the counterfactual exercises as in the observed data. Finally, the exercise assumes that the variances and covariances of all the terms in (2.1) are not affected by the new shares.[33] Some of these assumptions are admittedly strong and are imposed to simplify the analysis of the exercise. Hence, the results should be taken with caution. Nevertheless, the counterfactuals provide a tentative answer to the question pursued in this section.

The results in figure 2.19 show that under the first counterfactual exercise, all countries in LAC experience an increase in volatility compared to the original level of volatility. Argentina, Brazil, and Peru display the largest percentage increases in standard deviations under the first counterfactual exercise; in contrast, Chile and Mexico experience relatively small increases. To some extent the observed heterogeneity across countries in their change in volatility stems from differences in initial intra-LAC shares. Countries like Argentina, Brazil, and Peru have high initial intra-LAC shares (between 20 and 40 percent), which means that under the counterfactual exercise, these shares are even bigger (between 40 and 80 percent). In contrast, Mexico has a very low observed share of intra-LAC exports (3 percent), resulting in a relatively small share in the first counterfactual exercise (6 percent).

The role played by initial intra-LAC weights is further illustrated by the second counterfactual exercise. In this case, Mexico experiences the largest absolute increase in the intra-LAC, moving from 3 percent to 51.5 percent of total exports, a number that stands substantially above the one obtained in the first counterfactual exercise. As a result, Mexico experiences the biggest percentage increase in export volatility—the standard deviation of Mexico's export growth is 50 percent higher relative to the observed standard deviation. In contrast, Argentina has a lower intra-LAC share in the

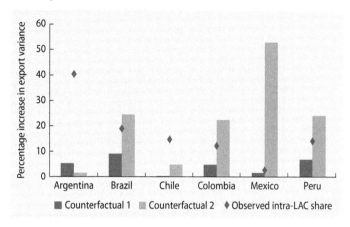

**FIGURE 2.19**  **Regional integration and its effect on export volatility in selected countries**

*Source:* World Bank calculations, based on Bennett et al. 2016.
*Note:* Changes in export variance are calculated under two counterfactual exercises. The first assumes that for each country, intra-LAC export shares double compared to the observed share. The second assumes that the rest of the world share (the non-LAC share) halves compared to the observed shares. See the main text for more details on the exercise. LAC = Latin America and the Caribbean. See annex 1A for a list of countries in this region.

second counterfactual exercise compared to the first one, resulting in a smaller percentage increase in the standard deviation of export growth.

In sum, all other things equal, deeper regional integration is expected to increase export volatility in LAC countries. However, these increases will vary on the initial levels of integration and the specific partners with which countries integrate. The analysis that follows explores in more detail the latter point. In particular, it analyzes whether specific patterns of regional integration may be better than others from a volatility management point of view.

As was discussed earlier, a limitation of the conclusions from figure 2.19 is that it focuses on a narrow set of countries in LAC. This limitation arises from data constraints and technical issues arising in the methodology used in Bennett et al. (2016). However, the authors also explore an alternative exercise that—although not fully capable of separating the contribution to export growth of supply, demand, and product specific factors—allows one to assess in a qualitative way the impact of deeper regional integration in LAC for a wider set of countries.

Instead of using bilateral sector-level flows, the authors perform a decomposition exercise as described in box 2.2 using sector-level export and import data for different countries. This alternative decomposition extracts a year-by-year, export-related country fixed effect from the export data and a year-by-year, import-related country fixed effect from the import data.[34] Because of the use of aggregate flows (as opposed to bilateral flows), both these effects may capture supply and demand factors. Despite this limitation, the exercise is useful as it allows one to correlate these country-specific export- and import-related fixed effects and allows an analysis of the contribution of deeper regional integration on export growth volatility in a larger number of countries.[35] However, given the limitations described above, this broader analysis provides a qualitative view similar to the one presented in figure 2.18 instead of the counterfactual exercise in figure 2.19.

Figure 2.20 shows the average and median variance of the export- and import-related fixed effects. The results include a larger sample of countries, including 23 LAC countries. The first thing to notice is that, in broad terms, the average regional rankings follow closely what was observed in figure 2.18. In particular, regions like the United States and Canada and EU15+ have the lowest average export and import volatilities, whereas LAC, MENA, and SSA have the largest export and import volatilities. The magnitudes and the specific rankings of some regions change, partly as a result of the inclusion of a wider set of countries. However, it does appear that the volatilities of the exporter and importer fixed effects obtained from the aggregate data are highly correlated with the volatilities of the supply and demand effects obtained from the bilateral data (figure 2.21)

So the question remains, is there evidence of benefits in terms of volatility reductions

**FIGURE 2.20    Volatility of exporter and importer effects by region, sector-level trade data**

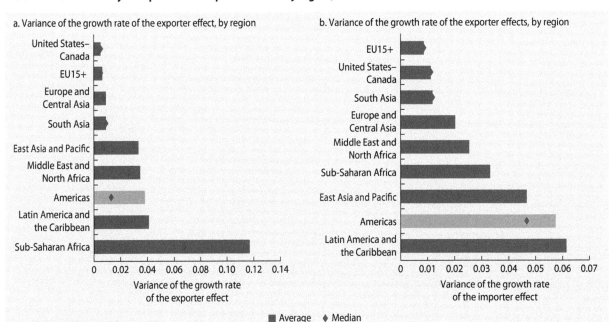

Source: World Bank calculations, based on Bennett et al. 2016.
Note: Exporter and importer effects are estimated by running a simple ordinary least squares (OLS) regression of sector-level trade data by year, controlling for sector and country fixed effect. Then, the year-by-year growth rate of the fixed effect is calculated. Finally, the variance of the growth rate is calculated for the 1990–2011 period. See annex 1A for a list of countries in each region.

**FIGURE 2.21** **A comparison of the variances estimated using bilateral sector-level data and aggregate sector-level data**

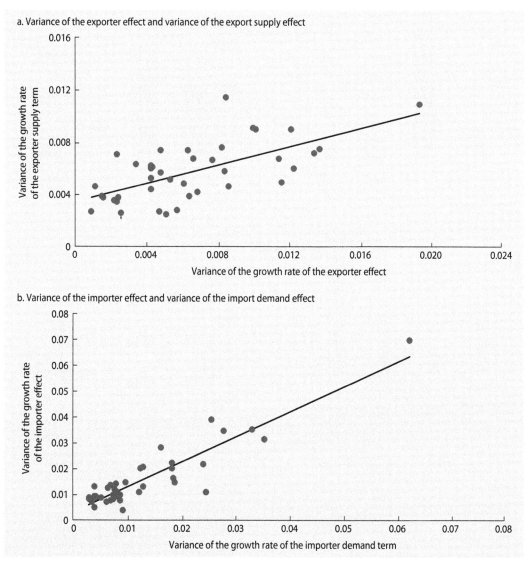

*Source:* World Bank calculations, based on Bennett et al. 2016.
*Note:* Exporter and importer effects are estimated by running a simple ordinary least squares (OLS) regression of aggregate, country-sector-level trade data by year, controlling for sector and country fixed effect. Export supply and import demand terms are estimated using bilateral, sector-level trade data. See annex 1A for details on the regions and box 2.2 for details on the estimation.

from deeper regional integration in LAC? To answer this question in more detail, figure 2.22 presents the variances and covariances for the different subregions in LAC. The evidence suggests that exports in the Caribbean are far more volatile compared to those in Central America and South America, even after controlling for sectoral composition. On the import side, the Caribbean and Central America have similar volatilities, both of which are almost twice as high as the one observed in South America. On the covariance side, import-related fixed effects are highly correlated within subregions, and

**FIGURE 2.22** Variances and correlations of the exporter and importer effects, by subregions in LAC

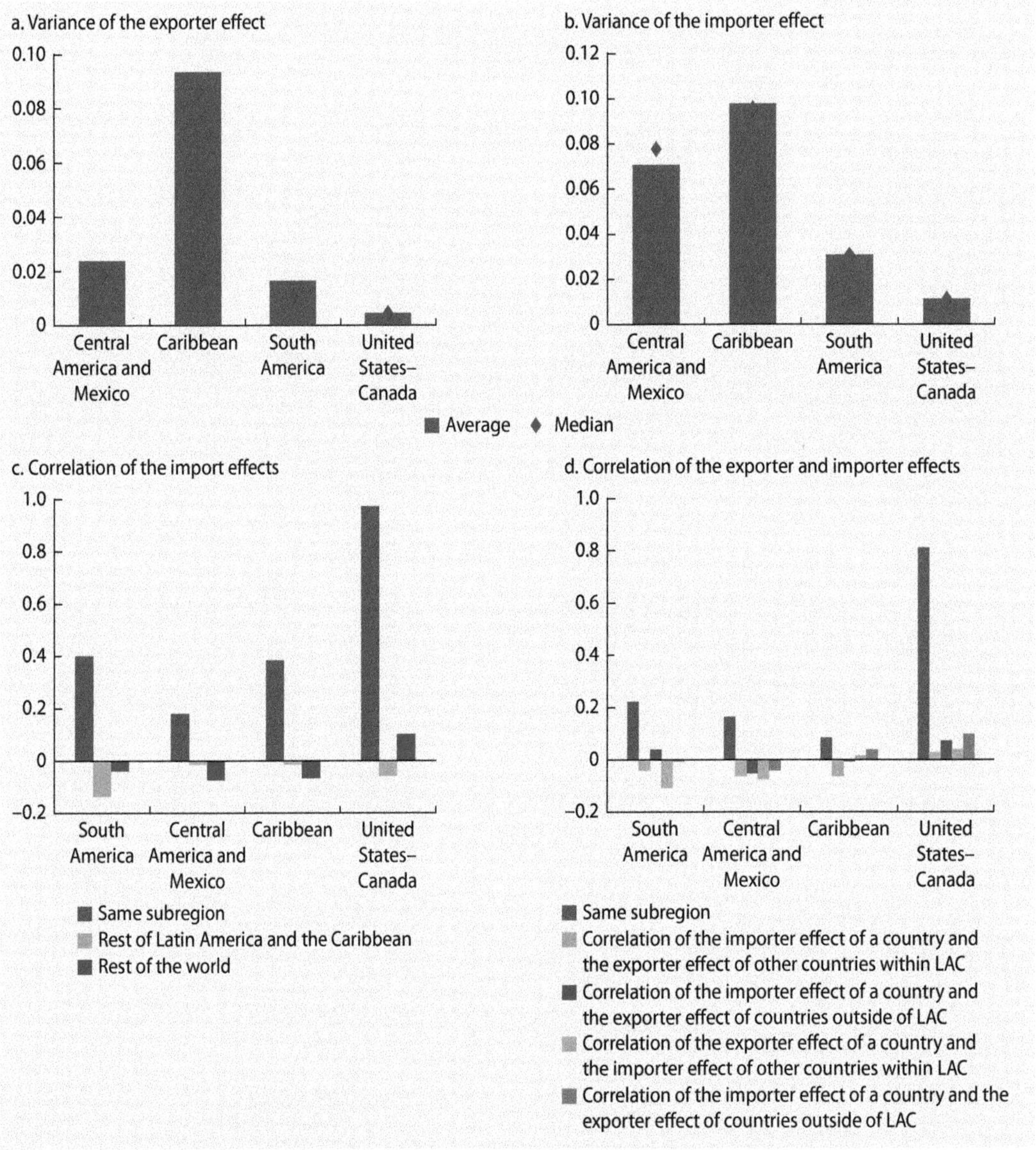

a. Variance of the exporter effect

b. Variance of the importer effect

■ Average ◆ Median

c. Correlation of the import effects

d. Correlation of the exporter and importer effects

■ Same subregion
■ Rest of Latin America and the Caribbean
■ Rest of the world

■ Same subregion
■ Correlation of the importer effect of a country and the exporter effect of other countries within LAC
■ Correlation of the importer effect of a country and the exporter effect of countries outside of LAC
■ Correlation of the exporter effect of a country and the importer effect of other countries within LAC
■ Correlation of the importer effect of a country and the exporter effect of countries outside of LAC

*Source:* World Bank calculations, following Bennett et al. 2016.
*Notes:* Exporter and importer effects are estimated by running a simple ordinary least squares (OLS) regression of sector-level trade data by year, controlling for sector and country fixed effect. Then, the year-by-year growth rate of the fixed effect is calculated. Finally, the variance of the growth rate is calculated for the 1990–2011 period. LAC = Latin America and the Caribbean; ROW = rest of world. See annex 1A for details on the regions.

so are exporter and importer fixed effects. In contrast, the correlations with other subregions are negative in most cases, albeit less so than with the rest of the world.

In sum, the alternative exercise suggests that deeper integration within subregions is likely to increase volatility, as import shocks are positively correlated within subregions in LAC, and so are export and import shocks. These patterns are accentuated by highly correlated terms of trade within subregions in LAC (figure 2.23). Integration across subregions in LAC may have more benefits in terms or reducing volatility, albeit less than integration with the rest of the world.

**FIGURE 2.23** **Average terms-of-trade growth correlations within subregions in LAC**

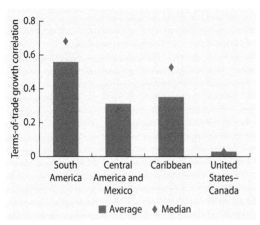

*Source:* World Bank calculations, using data from the World Development Indicators.
*Note:* Correlations are calculated at the country pair level and then aggregated by region. LAC = Latin America and the Caribbean. See annex 1A for details on the regions.

## In search of complementarities between the gains of regional and global integration

The evidence presented so far in the chapter shows that countries in LAC are too similar and invest too little in innovation and R&D, to achieve large gains from trade, which suggests that countries in LAC have to look beyond their immediate neighbors for efficiency, growth, and stability. Thus, there are tensions between preferential trade arrangements that provide incentives for intraregional trade, perhaps at the expense of trade with the rest of the world, and the realization that geography naturally favors intraregional trade. Why should LAC pursue an integration strategy that combines global and regional integration? The short answer is that there are important complementarities between regional integration and global integration that make LAC's international competitiveness and its ability to reach extraregional markets dependent on regional integration.

Indeed, however weak the evidence on the growth effects of regional trade preferences might be, there are several reasons why pursuing regional integration efforts could lead to more robust global integration. First, the impact of geography is unlikely to disappear any time soon. This implies that trade links with nearby countries will affect the global competitiveness of countries in the region. The link between regional trade and global competitiveness is most clearly illustrated in the case of "regionally traded goods." These are goods and services where the costs associated with distance are so high that they are typically only exchanged by neighboring countries and the policy-related barriers to trade are not import tariffs per se, but rather differences in regulatory schemes. For these goods and services, regional integration efforts are equivalent to global integration. Notable examples of these goods and services are electricity and land transportation. Hence, regional efforts to assure the quality and the efficient provision of these types of goods and services will be crucial for the growth and stability prospects of LAC and for the ability of the region to gain international competitiveness in sectors that use these regionally traded goods intensively.

Geography also appears to affect the ability of international economic interactions to facilitate the diffusion of knowledge and a country's ability to learn from the experience of its peers. As was discussed earlier, knowledge diffusion and learning can be stronger between nearby countries. The strength with which these channels affect a country's growth and competitiveness, however, will be affected by the stock of knowledge, the level of development, and the degree of global integration of its peers. For example, a country's likelihood to enter into and survive in third markets is higher when its current trading partners are actively exporting to those markets. This implies that a country's ability to learn from the experiences of its nearby partners depends on how open they are to global trade, which illustrates the complementarities between regional integration and global integration. Thus, the potential growth and competitiveness benefits that LAC countries can get from interacting with their neighbors will depend on regional efforts to invest in innovation and to integrate globally.

Coordinated regional efforts can also facilitate LAC's competitiveness in relation to the rest of the world, even if these efforts are not directly aimed at strengthening regional trade and factor market links. This point can be easily illustrated in the case of infrastructure and logistics, two areas where the region has a noticeable deficit. Domestic and regional policies that seek to improve the quality of LAC's infrastructure and connectivity can lower the costs associated with distance for all countries in the region, costs that rank among the highest in the world. Moreover, the potential for region-wide competitiveness gains is expected to be greater to the extent that these policies are implemented by a large number of countries in the region.

## Regionally traded goods and the benefits of regional integration

The evidence presented thus far has treated goods, or sectors, as if they were homogeneous. That is, the assumption has been that trade frictions are the same for all goods (sectors) and the pro-efficiency and pro-growth effects of trade are independent of the goods traded by a country. In the next two subsections we relax these assumptions. First, we study regional integration patterns for a particular class of goods, namely, regionally traded goods. These are goods and services whose nature is such that that they are typically traded with countries nearby. To the extent that these goods exhibit economies of scale, regional integration can increase the efficiency with which they are produced. The next chapter explores the potential role of trade policy as a tool to develop competitiveness in goods whose production may be desirable.

*Trade integration in regionally traded goods* One limitation of the approach followed in previous sections is the use of aggregated bilateral trade flows. This approach, which is widely used in the literature, has the caveat that it masks potential differences across products in

their sensitivity to distance. One noticeable exception to this approach is the work of Berthelon and Freund (2008), who estimate gravity equations for disaggregated product categories. The results shown by these authors indicate that there is indeed a great degree of variation across products in their elasticity to distance—the range of estimated elasticities goes from around zero to –3, and the distribution is centered approximately at –1.3.

The variability of the elasticity of trade flows with respect to distance suggests that some goods exhibit intrinsic characteristics that make it unlikely for these goods to be traded between distant partners. In the extreme, one would expect trade in these high-elasticity products among nonregional partners to be a low-probability event. For these goods, which are labeled regionally traded goods, efforts to integrate at the regional level are particularly important because they are almost equivalent to integration with the world. Hence, for these goods, there are no substitutes for regional integration.

The rest of this section delves deeper into LAC's standing in terms of these special types of goods. Particular attention is paid to regionally traded goods that have increasing returns to scale at the industry level because integration in these type of goods and services can result in competitiveness gains in the exporting economy as it exports at a bigger, more efficient, scale. Moreover, cost reductions in the production of regionally traded goods, which are typically important inputs in the production of other goods, can lead to competitiveness gains in other sectors because of input–output links.

Unfortunately, the analysis of regionally traded goods that follows excludes services. This is due to data limitations that prevent the analysis of services in the context of regionally traded goods. A first step toward overcoming these limitations is deferred to annex 2B, which presents a classification of regionally traded services and benchmarks LAC's performance in terms of regional integration in these services.

*Identifying regionally traded goods and their properties* Before benchmarking LAC's performance in terms of trade in regionally traded goods, this subsection deals with two important aspects of regionally traded goods. The first, and perhaps more basic, aspect has to do with the identification of such goods. The second has to do with their traits. In particular, it explores the extent to which these are differentiated goods that allow scope for potential quality upgrades relative to other producers and the prevalence of sectors with increasing returns to scale among regionally traded goods. Studying these traits can provide clues on whether integration in these goods can benefit the growth prospects of a country beyond the static gains from trade.

The analysis of regionally traded goods and services has to start with a methodology to identify such goods. The methodology used here follows the work of Berthelon and Freund (2008) and Artuc, Hillberry, and Pienknagura (2016) and estimates sectoral-level gravity equations to get the distance elasticities of trade in different sectors.[36] With these estimated elasticities, one can define regionally traded goods as goods that fall above the $x$th percentile of the distribution of elasticities. The analysis that follows defines regionally traded sectors as sectors falling in the top quartile of the distribution of distance elasticities (75th percentile of the distribution).

Table 2.4 presents a list of all sectors falling in the regionally traded goods category. Among these goods are (i) those in energy-related sectors, such as electricity and natural gas, for which production and distribution rely on large investments in infrastructure; (ii) perishable agricultural products and

**TABLE 2.4  List of regionally traded goods—merchandise goods**

| SITC Rev. 3 2 Digits | Description | Distance elasticity | Rauch classification |
|---|---|---|---|
| 35 | Electric current | $-\infty$ | Reference priced |
| 00 | Live animals other than animals of division 03 | −1.46 | Homogeneous |
| 24 | Cork and wood | −1.41 | Homogeneous |
| 4 | Cereals and cereal preparations | −1.32 | Homogeneous |
| 32 | Coal, coke, and briquettes | −1.28 | Reference priced |
| 64 | Paper, paperboard, and articles of paper pulp, of paper, or of paperboard | −1.26 | Reference priced |
| 06 | Sugars, sugar preparations, and honey | −1.21 | Homogeneous |
| 34 | Gas, natural and manufactured | −1.2 | Reference priced |
| 58 | Plastics in nonprimary forms | −1.11 | Reference priced |
| 57 | Plastics in primary forms | −1.11 | Reference priced |
| 02 | Dairy products and birds' eggs | −1.1 | Homogeneous |
| 82 | Furniture, and parts thereof; bedding, mattresses, mattress supports, cushions, and similar stuffed furnishings | −1.1 | Differentiated |
| 21 | Hides, skins, and furskins, raw | −1.09 | Differentiated |
| 43 | Animal or vegetable fats and oils, processed; waxes of animal or vegetable origin; inedible mixtures or preparations of animal or vegetable fats or oils, n.e.s. | −1.08 | Reference priced |
| 09 | Miscellaneous edible products and preparations | −1.08 | Differentiated |
| 67 | Iron and steel | −1.07 | Reference priced |
| 65 | Textile yarn, fabrics, made-up articles, n.e.s., and related products | −1.06 | Differentiated |

*Source:* World Bank calculations, using data from UN COMTRADE and following the approach proposed by Berthelon and Freund 2008 and Artuc, Hillberry, and Pienknagura 2016.
*Note:* Distance elasticities are the average of early industry-by-industry Poisson-Pseudo Maximum Likelihood (PPML) gravity estimations. The distance elasticity for trade in electric current cannot be estimated because of the low number of trade connections in this product. We interpret this as evidence of a very high distance elasticity. Rauch classifications capture the degree of differentiation of products in the sector. See Rauch (1999) for details.

livestock, such as cereals, live animals, and eggs; and (iii) heavy material, such as iron.

Turning to the attributes of these goods, regionally traded goods stand out as homogeneous goods. Table 2.4 presents a sectoral classification proposed by Rauch (1999), where sectors are divided into three groups: homogeneous, referenced price, and differentiated. Of the 17 sectors classified as regionally traded, only 4 fall in the differentiated category. Another way to highlight this point is presented in figure 2.24. The figure plots the relationship between the distance elasticity of each of the 67 SITC Rev 3, 2-digit sectors and the quality ladder of each sector.[37] In line with table 2.4, figure 2.24 shows that sectors that have a higher elasticity to distance have lower-quality ladder sizes (are less differentiated) compared to those with low distance elasticity.

In contrast, evidence suggests that, in proportional terms, the prevalence of sectors with increasing returns to scale (IRS) among regionally traded goods is similar to that of non-regionally traded goods. Based on estimations from Antweiler and Trefler (2002), 29 percent of the regionally traded sectors (5 out of 17) can be classified as having IRS, whereas 27 percent of non-regionally traded

goods are classified as having IRS.[38] Moreover, some of the regionally traded sectors with IRS, such as electricity and natural gas, are sectors that play important roles as inputs in other sectors. Hence, by allowing economies to gain market access and increase scale, regional integration can foster production and exports in IRS sectors as well as potential growth in other sectors using IRS sectors as inputs.

The role of integration as a tool helping countries to achieve a more efficient scale and gain competitiveness can be seen easily in a simple exercise. For each sector, an index, labeled PRODLF, is constructed following a similar methodology to that used in Hausmann, Hwang, and Rodrik (2007) to construct the PRODY index.[39] This index, the PRODLF, calculates the weighted average size of the labor force of countries exporting goods in sector $s$[40] and captures the extent to which a sector is exported by bigger countries, a potential indication that the sector is one with increasing returns to scale.[41] In fact, the PRODLF index appears to be closely associated with IRS—the PRODLF distribution of IRS sectors appears to be to the right of non-IRS sectors (table 2.5). Once the PRODLF is calculated, one can assess the

**FIGURE 2.24  Quality ladder size and distance elasticity**

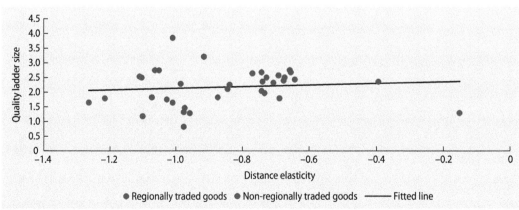

*Source:* World Bank calculations using data from Khandelwal 2010 and UN COMTRADE.
*Note:* Distance elasticities and quality ladder sizes are calculated using SITC Rev 3, at the 2-digit level. The analysis only includes sectors classified as differentiated according to the Rauch (1999) classification. Regionally traded sectors are sectors where the absolute value of the distance elasticity is above the 75th percentile of the distribution of distance elasticities in absolute values.

**TABLE 2.5    Distribution of the PRODLF indicator**

|  | Increasing returns to scale sectors | Non-increasing returns to scale sectors |
|---|---|---|
| 25th percentile | 19.50 | 13.69 |
| Median | 31.76 | 22.95 |
| 75th percentile | 40.72 | 38.81 |

*Source:* World Bank calculations from UN COMTRADE and Antweiler and Trefler 2003.
*Note:* Sectors are defined as the SITC Rev. 3 2-digit level. See text for details on variables.

extent to which a country's export basket is concentrated in goods typically produced by large countries (high PRODLF), which are also likely to have increasing returns, and how the weight carried by high-PRODLF sectors in total exports changes during periods of liberalization. In particular, one should examine changes in the average PRODLF weighted by country-specific trade weights (denoted EXPLF) around periods of liberalization for countries that liberalized their trade regimes in the 1990s, a restriction that is imposed to compare episodes of liberalization that occurred under similar global conditions.[42] The changes are evaluated between the five years after liberalization and the five prior to liberalization.

The results in figure 2.25 show that the countries that liberalized in the 1990s shifted their export baskets toward high-PROLF goods.[43] Of the 18 countries that liberalized in the 1990s, 17 experienced increases in their EXPLF, with an average increase in the index of 5 percent. In contrast, all countries experienced decreases in the implicit average size of their import baskets (IMPLFs). Moreover, differences in the change of countries' EXPLFs appear to be correlated with the size of the country—smaller countries experience more pronounced changes in their EXPLFs after liberalization compared to bigger countries. All this indicates that trade integration allows small countries to gain scale and shift their export patterns toward sectors typically produced by large countries.

The results presented above suggest that regional integration is unlikely to facilitate quality upgrades in regionally traded goods,

but it can lead to efficiency gains as countries that integrate can produce and export at a more efficient scale. Moreover, improvements in sectors related to energy can improve the competitiveness of other sectors through reductions in input costs, allowing countries to gain competitiveness in sectors that rely heavily on energy or energy-intensive inputs.

However, a region's ability to reap the benefits of regional integration through the mechanisms highlighted above hinges on the levels of integration observed for that region. Hence, the next section benchmarks integration in regionally traded goods across regions.

*Benchmarking integration in regionally traded sectors* Previous sections of this chapter have highlighted LAC's deficit in terms of regional integration, a deficit that appears related to the small size of economies and the long distances prevalent in the region. The question is: Do these conclusions apply to regionally traded sectors?

A preliminary look at the data does suggest that LAC stands behind other regions in terms of regional integration in these sectors. Trade in regionally traded sectors within countries in LAC accounts for a relatively low share of total trade in these sectors—intra-LAC trade stands at 40 percent of total flows (figure 2.26). In contrast, in regions such as the United States and Canada, EU15+, and EAP, the incidence of regional trade on total trade in regionally traded goods stands between 50 and 73 percent. Similar conclusions emerge when focusing on IRS regionally traded sectors—LAC's intraregional trade in

**FIGURE 2.25**   **Changes in the composition of export and import baskets around liberalization episodes in the 1990s**

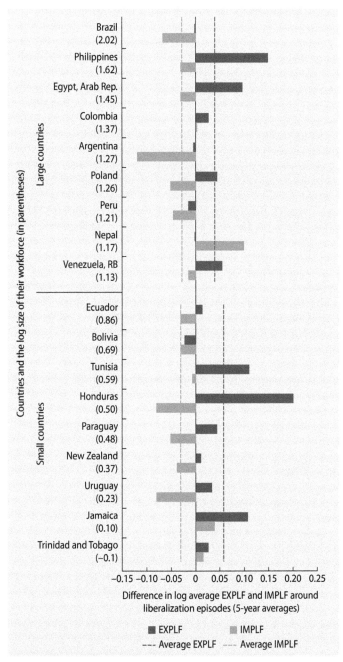

*Source:* World Bank calculations, using data from UN COMTRADE.
*Note:* Liberalization episodes are taken from Wacziarg and Welch 2008. EXPLF and IMPLF capture the trade-weighted average PRODLF of a country's export and import basket, respectively. The PRODLF is a product attribute that captures the size of the labor force of countries that have a revealed comparative advantage in a given product. A higher PRODLF implies that the product is typically exported by countries that are large in terms of their labor force. Hence, a positive change in the EXPLF implies that after the liberalization episode the country tilts its export basket toward goods typically exported by large countries. Similarly, a negative change in the IMPLF implies that after liberalization the country tilts its import basket toward goods that are typically exported by smaller countries.

these sectors ranks below what is observed in regions like EAP or EU15+.

To what extent do geography and size play a role in LAC's apparent low levels of regional integration in regionally traded sectors? Figure 2.27, which shows the results of a gravity estimation similar to the one presented in figure 2.3, suggests that LAC's intraregional trade in all regionally traded goods stands close to what size and geography predict. Indeed, the region's same-region dummy is positive but not significantly different from zero. Interestingly, the exercise also shows that regions like EU15+, ECA, and the United States and Canada, which topped the ranking in terms of the incidence of regional trade in regionally traded goods, have intraregional trade levels that exceed what standard gravity variables can explain. In part this contrasts with the results of the benchmark exercise presented in figure 2.3, where the relatively high incidence of intraregional trade in all sectors in regions like the United States and Canada, and to a lesser extent EU15+, was explained by gravity factors. Hence, in terms of regionally traded sectors, the overperformance of certain regions appears to be related to factors beyond gravity variables.

The patterns displayed in figure 2.27 are reinforced when looking at trade integration in regionally traded sectors with IRS. In most regions, intraregional trade in regionally traded goods with IRS exceeds what can be explained by gravity variables (figure 2.28). The exceptions are LAC, SSA, and MENA. In the case of LAC, intra-LAC trade stands close to what is predicted by standard gravity variables.

In sum, gravity forces appear to be behind LAC's relatively low levels intraregional integration in terms of distance-sensitive goods, labeled here as regionally traded goods. Moreover, these constraints can have repercussions in terms of the efficiency with which these goods are produced, as many of them display increasing returns to scale.

*Zooming into energy markets: The road ahead for further integration in LAC*   One important category of regionally traded goods

**FIGURE 2.26    Intraregional trade as a share of total trade in regionally traded goods**

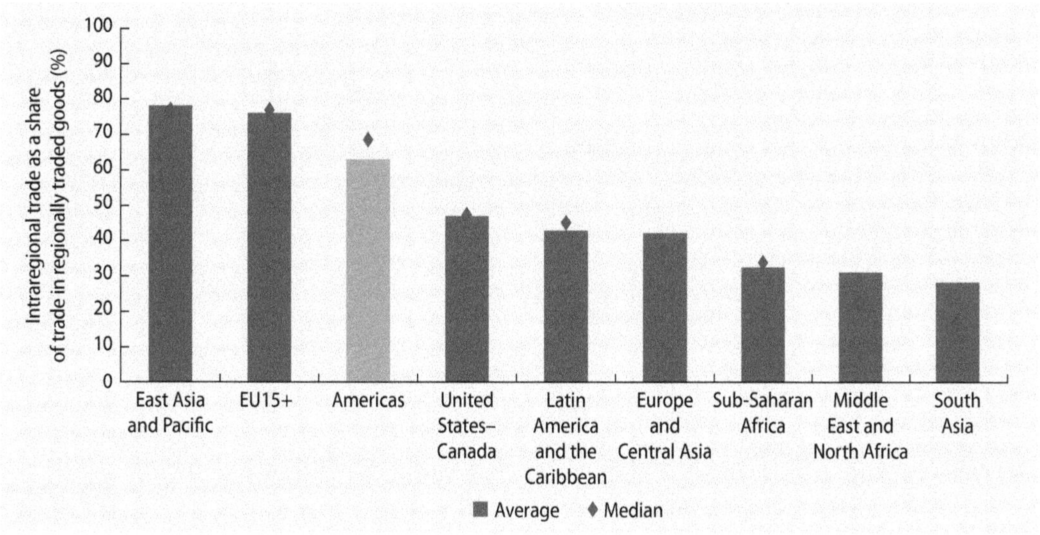

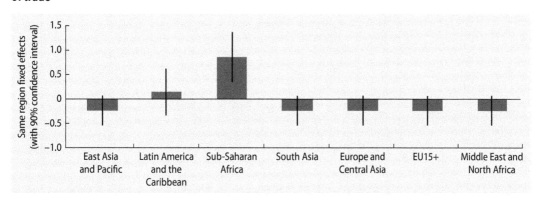

*Source:* World Bank calculations, using data from UN COMTRADE.
*Note:* Regionally traded goods are goods whose distance elasticity in a sector-by-sector gravity equation falls on the top quartile. Shares are calculated at the country level and then aggregated at the regional level. See annex 1A for a list of countries in each region.

**FIGURE 2.27    Benchmarking intraregional trade in regionally traded goods through a gravity model of trade**

*Source:* World Bank calculations, based on Artuc, Hillberry, and Pienknagura 2016.
*Note:* Bars represent the region-specific same-region dummies from a gravity equation similar to that estimated in figure 2.3. The estimation uses bilateral trade flows for regionally traded goods only. Lines plot 90 percent confidence intervals. See annex 1A for a list of countries in each region.

is energy, a sector that appears among the most regional of all. Indeed, a very high share of trade in electricity occurs between regional and contiguous neighbors (see figure 2.29). Moreover, this is a sector that displays

increasing returns to scale, which implies that economies can operate at a more efficient scale as they gain market access.

Indeed, in recent years there has been increased attention to the idea of regionally

**FIGURE 2.28** **Benchmarking intraregional trade in regionally traded goods with increasing returns to scale through a gravity model of trade**

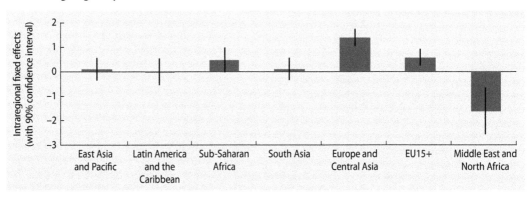

Source: World Bank calculations, based on Artuc, Hillberry, and Pienknagura 2016.
Notes: Bars represent the region-specific same-region dummies from a gravity equation similar to that estimated in figure 2.3 The estimation uses bilateral trade flows for regionally traded goods only. Lines plot 90 percent confidence intervals. See annex 1A for a list of countries in each region.

**FIGURE 2.29** **Intraregional trade in electricity**

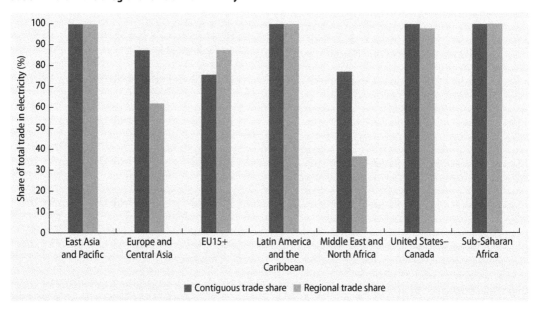

Source: World Bank calculations, using data from UN COMTRADE.
Note: Trade shares are calculated at the country level and then aggregated at the regional level. See annex 1A for a list of countries in each region.

integrating energy markets in LAC, particularly in the smaller economies of the region. Beyond the benefits from economies of scale, regional integration of electricity markets can also increase the stability of the grid by allowing countries to diversify their energy sources and achieve energy security. As an example, during the El Niño season countries reliant on hydroelectric power for their energy (those that experience shortages due to drought conditions) could access electricity generated from other countries based on natural gas reserves to fill shortfalls in the power system.[44] Furthermore, regional integration of power systems can help facilitate the transition to and investment in clean sources of energy by facilitating the use of such sources on a larger scale (as an example, clean geothermal energy from St. Kitts and Nevis currently underused because of the small population of the island could help power the rest of the Caribbean if a regional electric grid were in place).

The interest in integration in electricity markets has translated into clear efforts to achieve this goal. For example, beginning with NAFTA, Mexico has established several electrical connections with the United States and, with the liberalizing of the energy sector, plans for further integration in natural gas markets with the United States are under way (United States Department of Energy 2015). In Central America, the Central American Electrical Interconnection System (SIEPAC) has already made regional electrical grid integration a reality. The program facilitated the construction of electrical transmission lines from Guatemala to Panama, with proposed extensions to include Mexico and Colombia in the near future. In the Caribbean, integration efforts being discussed include the Eastern Caribbean Gas Pipeline, to carry natural gas from Trinidad and Tobago through the Caribbean as far north as Miami, and the implementation of a system of submarine electric cables connecting islands in the region (see Gerner and Hansen 2011). In South America, work is proceeding on the Andean Electric Interconnection system, a project backed by the Inter-American Development Bank (IDB), to connect the electric grids of Bolivia, Chile, Colombia, Ecuador, and Peru. Countries in Mercosur have begun to integrate electricity and energy markets, mainly though binational agreements and private activities. Much of the regional electric trade comes from the fact that Argentina, Brazil, Paraguay, and Uruguay share several large hydroelectric dams; but there are also important natural gas pipeline connections between Bolivia and Brazil and Argentina and Chile, as well as power line connections between northern Argentina and Brazil (Pineau, Hira, and Froshauer 2004).

Despite these efforts toward the integration of energy markets, significant barriers to further progress remain. These barriers arise partly from the gravity forces already highlighted—lackluster growth and a complex geography play against more robust integration in the region. Other forces acting as barriers to further integration and to the full use of these emerging integrated markets are the lack of homogeneous technical and regulatory standards and political constraints (see box 2.3). Hence, beyond growth and geography, the streamlining of the regulatory and

---

**BOX 2.3    Obstacles to integration in energy markets within LAC**

Despite efforts to achieve deeper integration of energy markets in LAC, there are still a number of obstacles in the region's path to fully benefit from these efforts. One such obstacle is the need for harmonization of national standards. One example of this is the Machala Zorritos power line between Ecuador and Peru, which was completed in 2004 but was inactive for many years because of an inability to negotiate commercial agreements and technical issues between the grids (Sauma et al. 2011).

Another is a lack of infrastructure and insufficient regional regulatory frameworks, of which countries in Mercosur are a good example. In theory, the region has large incentives for energy market integration because of the role of Brazil as a large potential importer of energy and diversity among the countries in terms of energy endowments and consumption patterns that can provide some level of energy security (Hira and Amaya 2003). In fact, integration has been led mainly by private investors

*(continued)*

and through binational treaties rather than through a truly regional approach—partly because of these strong incentives in the marketplace—and governments in the region have been slow to catch up. This process could potentially be made more efficient and comprehensive through a harmonization of regulatory standards and increased coordinated infrastructure investment that would facilitate greater energy connections among countries in the region.

Finally, there are political impediments to effective integration in the energy sector. For example, a recent analysis of the Regional Electric Market (MER for its Spanish acronym) and SIEPAC in Central America found that the potential of the system to attract private investment is limited by the

fact that most governments in the region will not allow more than 1 year of electricity transmission rights to be given at a time for political reasons (Development and Training Services 2015). Furthermore there appears to be a lack of consensus on the part of national actors in various Central American countries with regard to whether a regional energy market is in their best interest. This hesitation limits the potential for investing in increasing the network's capacity. Its existence has also created a free rider problem, allowing Nicaragua and Honduras to delay upgrading their national power lines and instead use the capacity of the SIEPAC regional line as a replacement for their own grids, reducing the overall impact of the regional integration system.

technical frameworks for energy production and distribution stands as a top priority in order for the region to accrue the benefits of integration in energy markets.

## Regional integration as a stepping-stone toward global integration

A first look at the potential for international integration to deliver high growth in LAC suggests that the region may benefit more from integration with nonregional partners. Successfully integrating with these partners depends on entry decisions of exporting firms and their survival in foreign markets.[45] Yet both these outcomes are difficult to attain. Only a small share of firms ever enter into export markets, and trade relations tend to be remarkably short-lived (see, among others, Bernard et al. 2007; Besedes and Prusa 2006; Eaton, Kortum, and Kramarz 2011; and Lederman 2010). Naturally, there are many factors that can act in favor of better entry and survival profiles with nonregional export markets and, as will be argued below, regional integration is one of these. The question then is: Can LAC use deeper regional integration as a stepping-stone toward

attaining higher levels of integration with the rest of the world?

Before answering this question, it is worth noting that low entry into new export markets and low survival are particularly evident among developing countries (Brenton, Pierola, and von Uexkull 2009). This is illustrated in figure 2.30, panels a and b, which show entry rates into new export markets and the average duration of these episodes by income groups. In particular, following Brenton, Saborowski, and von Uexkull (2010), the analysis identifies new entry episodes as episodes where a country exports a product to another country for the first time (see box 2.4 for details on the data and methodology).[46] The results show that average entry rates and the average duration of entry episodes are positively correlated with income levels.[47]

LAC is no exception to the patterns observed in other developing countries, especially regarding survival. The average survival of new entry episodes in LAC is 0.7 year. In contrast, in EU15+ and the United States and Canada, the average survival is 0.85 and 0.75 year, respectively. Looking at entry rates, the analysis conducted suggests that LAC has higher entry rates compared to the United States and Canada or to EU15+ countries. This may reflect the fact that, as suggested earlier in the chapter, LAC has more unexploited export markets relative to high-income countries. Despite this observation, LAC underperforms relative to other regions such as EAP and ECA.

One of the implications of low entry rates and survival in LAC is that the aggregate export growth of the region, and in turn its integration with international markets, is lower compared to what it could be, should these two outcomes improve. Hence, a clear understanding of the factors behind entry rates and survival is of first-order importance in LAC's quest for deeper global commercial ties.

The economics literature offers some guidance for identifying these factors. A first set of variables affecting survival and entry into export markets includes gravity variables. In particular, economic size increases survival after entry, geographic distance tends to decrease entry and survival rates, and variables like colonial ties and common language increase both these rates (Brenton, Saborowski, and von Uexkull 2010). A second set of variables includes actions taken by government agencies and incumbent exporters from the entrant's country of origin. Lederman, Olarreaga, and Zavala (2015) show that export-promotion agencies encourage entry into new export markets and survival upon entry. Fernandes and Tang (2014) and Wagner and Zhaler (2015) show that actions taken by incumbent exporting firms provide information to potential entrants, which in turn affect the latter's decision to enter new export markets. Similarly, Cadot et al. (2013) show that the probability of survival of an exporter from a given country in a new export market increases with the number of incumbent exporters from that country that are active in the export market. All this is interpreted as evidence that direct and indirect information acquisition by potential exporters from local agents fosters entry and survival in new export markets. Finally, the literature has identified exporting experience

FIGURE 2.30 **New entries into export markets, entry rates, and duration, by income group**

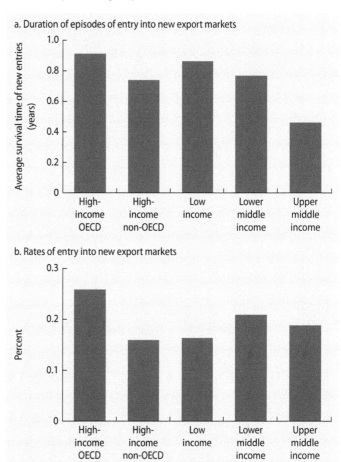

a. Duration of episodes of entry into new export markets

b. Rates of entry into new export markets

■ Average  ◆ Median

*Source:* World Bank calculations, using UN COMTRADE.
*Note:* See box 2.4 for details on the methodology used to identify episodes of entry into new export markets. OECD = Organisation for Economic Co-operation and Development.

as another factor favoring export survival (see Albornoz, Hallak, and Fanelli 2014).

There are a number of reasons why experience may affect survival and entry into export markets. One reason is that experience acts as a selection mechanism—it implies that a firm has been subject to international competition and survived. Hence, firms that export may represent a sample of the most efficient firms. Another possibility is that exporting experience may result in learning by exporting, making experienced exporters more efficient than inexperienced ones.

---

**BOX 2.4    Identifying new entries using bilateral trade data**

The goal of this section is to study the determinants of entry into export markets and survival upon entry. Crucial for this goal is identifying new entries. Ideally, an analysis of entry and survival would rely on exporter-level databases with entry decisions and observed survival upon entry. This is the case of the work of Cadot et al. (2013); Fernandes, Lederman, and Gutierrez-Rocha (2013); and Cebeci et al. (2012). However, the usefulness of such databases for the purpose of this analysis is constrained by two problems. First, country coverage is limited, which implies that conclusions would be specific to the set of countries in the sample. Second, time coverage is short, which makes it hard to identify episodes of new entries.

To overcome this problem, the analysis in this section uses bilateral product-level trade data. In particular, the analysis uses data from UN Comtrade, Revision 3, at the four-digit level from 1980 until 2011. It uses this time frame because data before 1980 are less reliable and coverage is less extensive (Berthelon and Freund 2008). The analysis identifies new entries as product–destination pairs to which an exporter country has not exported prior to year $t$ and to which it starts exporting in $t$. To minimize the risk of confusing episodes of reentry with episodes of new entries, the analysis considers only episodes of new entries from 1985 onward (it gives the new entry five years of information prior to the entry episode).

---

Finally, exporting experience may help exporting firms enter and succeed in new markets by allowing them to gain information about conditions in third markets from firms in their current export markets. In this sense, having experience in a given destination country may facilitate entry and survival in a third country where the destination country has trade links of its own (Morales, Sheu, and Zhaler 2014; Chaney 2011).

Two implications arise from the discussion of determinants of entry and survival. First, the characteristics of the markets in which an exporter currently operates may determine the likelihood of entry and survival in a new market. In particular, exporters that have established links with countries that have a large number of trade connections with the world or where competition is high are better suited to enter and survive in new export markets than those that have established links in countries with a small number of connections and where competition is low. Yet established partners are not random. Gravity forces suggest that exporters in a country will typically have a higher likelihood of having an established trade connection with nearby countries. All this indicates that the characteristics of nearby countries

may be an important factor determining a country's ability to integrate with the rest of world.

To dig deeper into the role of established partners as platforms to stronger global integration, table 2.6 presents the results of two sets of estimations. Columns (1) through (4) show the results of a linear probability model of entry into new export markets. Columns (5) through (8) show the results of a linear probability model of surviving more than one year after entry. Columns (1), (2), (5), and (6) test the role of experience and the characteristics of the markets in which a country has exporting experience in explaining entry and survival, respectively. In particular, for each country $i$, product $p$, and time $t$, the exercise constructs a dummy variable taking value 1 if the country has exported the product in the past. Then, the exercise identifies the set of countries to which country $i$ has exported product $p$ for five or more consecutive years immediately prior to $t$. This set of countries is called established partners, and the log trade-weighted average distance and the log trade-weighted average GDP per capita are calculated for the set of $i$'s established partners. Columns (1) and (5) control for product experience and the (trade-weighted) average

TABLE 2.6    **Determinants of entry and survival in new exporting markets**

| | Entry | | | | Survival | | | |
|---|---|---|---|---|---|---|---|---|
| | (1) | (2) | (3) | (4) | (5) | (6) | (7) | (8) |
| Previous exporting experience with product | 0.00343*** | 0.00348*** | 0.00397*** | 0.00391*** | 0.0604*** | 0.0609*** | 0.0626*** | 0.0618*** |
| | (0.000103) | (0.000103) | (0.000103) | (0.000103) | (0.00194) | (0.00194) | (0.00194) | (0.00194) |
| Network effect | | | 0.0299*** | 0.0289*** | | | 0.0429*** | 0.0373*** |
| | | | (0.000158) | (0.000158) | | | (0.00111) | (0.0011) |
| Trade-weighted average distance to established partners | 0.00248*** | | | 0.00144*** | 0.0146*** | | | 0.0127*** |
| | (0.0000123) | | | (0.0000127) | (0.000127) | | | (0.000139) |
| Trade-weighted average GDPpc of established partners | | 0.00188*** | 0.000940*** | | | 0.0108*** | 0.00889*** | |
| | | (0.0000105) | (0.0000109) | | | (0.000107) | (0.000118) | |
| Observations | 6,36,17,870 | 6,36,17,870 | 6,36,17,870 | 6,36,17,870 | 28,94,544 | 28,94,544 | 28,94,544 | 28,94,544 |
| R-squared | 0.198 | 0.198 | 0.199 | 0.199 | 0.3 | 0.3 | 0.3 | 0.301 |
| Product-year FE | YES | YES | YES | YES | YES | YES | YES | YES |
| Exporter-importer-year FE | YES | YES | YES | YES | YES | YES | YES | YES |

*Source:* World Bank calculations, based on data from UN COMTRADE; World Development Indicators, and Centre d'Études Prospectives et d'Informations Internationales (CEPII).
*Note:* FE = fixed effects. Columns correspond to different specifications. See text for variable definition. Standard errors are in parentheses and clustered at the destination level.
\*\*\* $p<0.01$, \*\* $p<0.05$, \* $p<0.1$.

distance with established partners; columns (2) and (6) control for product experience and the (trade-weighted) average GDP per capita of established partners. Columns (3) and (7) test the role of trade connections of established partners in the new entry market in determining entry and survival. In particular, a dummy variable labeled "in network" is created, where the dummy takes value 1 if the potential new market of country $i$ is an established partner of one or more of $i$'s established partners. This variable, "in network," is included in the regressions as a way to capture the network effect described above. Finally, columns (4) and (8) test the joint effect of all these variables.

The results in table 2.6 show that export experience increases the likelihood of entry into new export markets and survival in these markets. However, the characteristics of the set of countries in which the exporting country has experience do appear to affect the entry and survival probabilities. In particular, having established links with more distant and richer countries increases the likelihood of entry and survival (columns (1)

and (5), and (2) and (6), respectively).[48] Similarly, links between established partners and potential new markets increase a country's entry and survival probability (columns (3) and (7)). Moreover, both these channels appear to be operational because the inclusion of both network effects and the characteristics of established partners do not alter the significance of either one.

A number of messages emerge from the results in table 2.6. First, global integration appears to be a self-reinforcing process, in the sense that experience in farther markets facilitates entry into even farther markets. Moreover, as countries become more and more integrated with other highly integrated economies, they will have higher entry and survival probabilities in international markets. Hence, for countries that are highly integrated in the global economy, regional integration does not seem to play a big role in fostering global integration. However, at early stages of integration, where gravity forces suggest that a country's established partners will be mostly regional, regional integration can facilitate global integration.

Nevertheless, not all countries that are integrating into the global economy get an equal push from their regional partners. In this sense, LAC countries appear to be at a disadvantage relative to those in other regions, especially some ECA and EAP countries. First, countries in LAC have a lower GDP per capita and lower levels of competition than other developing regions like EAP and ECA (see Lederman et al. 2014). This means that LAC countries that export to other LAC countries have less scope for improvements triggered by competition and learning by exporting from their experience in regional markets than do those in other developing regions. This, in turn, gives LAC exporters a smaller edge in successfully entering and surviving in farther markets. Moreover, as was highlighted earlier in the chapter, LAC countries typically have fewer connections with international markets relative to other regions, minimizing the potential for network effects to operate. Having said this, there are still potential bright spots in the role that regional integration can play in LAC as large countries like Mexico and Brazil tend to have larger export networks relative to other countries in the region. This means that, by integrating with these two countries, other countries in the region may boost their chances of a more robust performance in new markets as they leverage on Brazil's and Mexico's established network.

## Conclusions

This chapter has assessed the potential growth and stability gains that LAC countries could attain from pursuing different integration strategies. The results show that the gains from pursuing regional integration at the expense of global integration appear to be small. In contrast, the region can benefit most from an integration strategy that exploits the complementarities between regional and global integration. The next two chapters look at the state of LAC's trade and factor integration policies. These two chapters examine the steps that need to be taken from a policy standpoint to seize what appear to be unexploited complementarities between regional and global integration. These steps constitute the renewal of LAC's OR strategy.

## Annex 2A. Estimating trade flows through gravity equations

The gravity trade model, despite having purely empirical origins, has become widely used and accepted in the trade literature. As an analogy of physical gravitational forces, the "attraction" (volume of trade) between two "objects" (countries) is proportional to their respective "masses" (demand and supply) and inversely proportional to the distance between them. Artuc, Hillberry, and Pienknagura (2016) depart from the standard OLS estimation of the gravity model and follow the PPML estimation strategy proposed by Santos-Silva and Tenreyro (2006).

PPML allows for zero trade in the estimation, circumventing the selection and bias brought forth by Helpman, Melitz, and Rubinstein (2008) that frequents OLS estimations where only positive trade flows are considered. When compared to the former, PPML does not rely on the validity of the often-unconvincing exclusion restriction found in a Heckman-style two-stage estimation.[49] In addition, Hillberry (2002) notes that Heckman-style estimators perform poorly in the context of highly disaggregated product levels because of the presence of a large proportion of zero trade flows.[50]

Additionally, as pointed out in Fally (2015), the PPML has desirable adding-up properties that pertain specifically to the benchmarking exercises carried out for this report. Specifically, fitted trade flows associated with dummy variables correspond exactly to the level of observed trade flows. For example, if one were to sum the excess trade associated with a regional dummy across all origins and destinations, it would be exactly equal to the excess trade associated with said regional dummy.

The baseline PPML specification presented in Artuc, Hillberry, and Pienknagura (2016) denotes the trade flow from country $i$

to country $j$ in sector $k$ at time $t$ as $x_{k,t}^{ij}$ and equate it to:

$$x_{k,t}^{ij} = exp(c_{k,t}^{i} + d_{k,t}^{j} + B_{k,t}' b^{ij}) + e_{t}^{ij}, \qquad (2A.1)$$

where $c_{k,t}^{i}$ and $d_{k,t}^{j}$ denote the origin fixed effect and the destination fixed effect for countries $i$ and $j$ respectively; $b^{ij}$ is a vector of bilateral variables (distance, common language, and colonial ties); $B_{k,t}$ is the coefficient vector; and $e_{k,t}^{ij}$ is the regression residual.

The bilateral variables included in the regression are standard in the gravity literature:

1. *Distance*: Defined as the logarithm of the distance (in kilometers) between origin and destination.
2. *Language*: Dummy variable defined as 1 if origin and destination share an official language.
3. *Colonial ties*: Dummy variable defined as 1 if origin and destination ever had a colonial link.

In order to obtain a benchmark regarding intraregional trade additional dummies were included in the estimation. The results shown in figure 2.3, panel a, include eight dummies (one for each region) that are equal to 1 if the origin and destination lie in said region. Note that these dummies are not region fixed effects, but capture intraregional trade that is not explained by either origin, destination, or gravity effects. Panel b and c of figure 2.3 present a more granular look at intraregional trade. In these cases, three subregional dummies take the place of the LAC dummy: South America (SA), Central America (CA), and the Caribbean (CB). In the estimation behind panel b, each subregional dummy is equal to 1 if the destination country belongs to the respective subregion, while the origin country is a member of the LAC region. Panel c, in turn, defines each subregional dummy equal to 1 if the exporting country forms part of the respective subregion and the importing country belongs to LAC.

Figure 2.4 follows an analogous estimation with a broader definition of region.

The United States and Canada are joined with LAC to form the "AMERICAS" macroregion; EU15+ and ECA form "EUROPE"; SAR and EAP form "ASIA"; and MENA and SSA are joined to form "AFRICA." In panels b and c the same subregion decomposition of intraregional trade is performed with the subregions of the AMERICAS macroregion defined as before but now including USA-CAN as a fourth subregion.

Note that, in figures 2.3 and 2.4, no distinction is made between sectors as the authors benchmark total trade. This is not the case in the estimation illustrated in figures 2.27 and 2.28. In order to benchmark intraregional trade in a particular set of goods (regionally traded goods in figure 2.27 and regionally traded goods with increasing returns to scale in figure 2.28), each of the eight regional dummies is interacted with a dummy corresponding to the set of goods in question. The resulting coefficients for each region capture the excess (or shortcoming) of intraregional trade, net of gravity effects in a particular set of goods.

## Annex 2B. Benchmarking intraregional trade in regionally traded services

In the case of services, the methodology used to identify regionally traded services differs from the one used for merchandise goods. The reason for this discrepancy stems from the poor quality of databases on bilateral trade flows, especially for regional trade in developing countries (see box 2.1). This limitation makes estimates of distance elasticities through gravity equations unreliable and in many cases unfeasible.[51] With this caveat in mind, an alternative classification scheme is pursued. Broadly speaking, this alternative approach ranks services in each country based on the intensity with which they are exported and imported to regional partners. The higher the intensity, the more regional the service is from the point of view of the country. Once these rankings are calculated, the methodology aggregates the information by product in various ways (12 ways in total). Finally, it ranks products according to the number of times the product is classified as regional based on the various aggregations.

More precisely, the methodology is implemented as follows:

1. First, four indexes are calculated for each country service combination. The first two are the share of total export and import values in service $s$ that country $i$ trades with its regional partners:

$$I_{1,i,s} = \frac{X_{i,s,j\in R}}{\sum_j X_{i,s,j}} \tag{2B.1}$$

$$I_{2,i,s} = \frac{M_{i,s,j\in R}}{\sum_j M_{i,s,j}} \tag{2B.2}$$

with $R$ being the set of regional partners of country $i$.

The other two indexes capture the number of regional partners that country $i$ exports and imports in service $s$, relative to the total number of partners with which it trades in that service:

$$I_{3,i,s} = \frac{N^X_{i,s,j\in R}}{\sum_j N^X_{i,s,j\in R}} \tag{2B.3}$$

$$I_{4,i,s} = \frac{N^X_{i,s,j\in R}}{\sum_j N^X_{i,s,j\in R}} \tag{2B.4}$$

2. Then, for each indicator and country, services are ranked, giving each service a number ranging from 1 to S (number of services in the service trade data). A ranking of 1 means that the service is the least regional in nature for that country, and a ranking of S means that the service is the most regional for that country.

3. The next step is to aggregate the data at the service level. To do so, the methodology uses three aggregation methods. The first calculates the average ranking that sector $s$ has across countries, the second calculates the median, and the third calculates the number of times the service falls in the 90th percentile of each index. This procedure gives a total of 12 rankings for each service.

4. The last step of the methodology aggregates the information of the 12 rankings. In particular, it counts the number of times a given service falls in the top quartile of the ranking. Table 2A.1 provides the ranking as well as the score of "regional propensity" that the methodology gives to each sector.

As a robustness check, the methodology was also applied to merchandise data, using the same sectors as in table 2.5. The results obtained show that the rankings emerging from the methodology described above match very closely those obtained from an estimation of the distance elasticity. This suggests

**TABLE 2A.1  Ranking of services in terms of their propensity to be regionally traded**

| BOP code | Description | Top quartile frequency |
|---|---|---|
| 249 | Construction services<br>• Construction abroad<br>• Construction in the compiling country | 10/12 |
| 214 | Other transport<br>• Space transport<br>• Rail transport<br>• Road transport<br>• Inland waterway transport | 9/12 |
| 287 | Personal, cultural, and recreational services<br>• Audiovisual and related services<br>• Other | 8/12 |

*(continued)*

**TABLE 2A.1    Ranking of services in terms of their propensity to be regionally traded** *(continued)*

| BOP code | Description | Top quartile frequency |
|---|---|---|
| 245 | Communications services<br>• Postal and courier services<br>• Telecommunications services | 7/12 |
| 236 | Travel<br>• Business travel<br>  ○ Expenditure by seasonal and border workers<br>  ○ Other<br>• Personal travel<br>  ○ Health-related expenditures<br>  ○ Education-related expenditures<br>  ○ Other | 5/12 |
| 260 | Financial services | 3/12 |
| 291 | Government services n.i.e.<br>• Embassies and consulates<br>• Military units and agencies<br>• Other | 2/12 |
| 262 | Computer and information services | 2/12 |
| 206-210 | Sea and air transport | 1/12 |
| 266 | Royalties and license fees | 1/12 |
| 253 | Insurance services<br>• Life insurance<br>• Freight insurance<br>• Other<br>• Reinsurance<br>• Auxiliary services | 0/12 |
| 268 | Other business services<br>• Merchanting and other trade-related services<br>• Operational leasing services<br>• Miscellaneous business, professional, and technical services<br>  ○ Legal, accounting, management consulting, and public relations<br>  ○ Advertising, market research<br>  ○ Research and development<br>  ○ Architectural, engineering, and other technical services<br>  ○ Agricultural, mining, and other on-site processing services<br>  ○ Other<br>  ○ Services between related enterprises | 0/12 |

*Source:* World Bank calculations, using International Monetary Fund Balance of Payments data.

that the proposed methodology provides one way to construct a classification of regionally traded services without facing the estimation challenges emerging from the relatively poor coverage of trade in service data.

Table 2A.1 provides the ranking of services in terms of their propensity to be regionally traded. At the top of the ranking stand construction and, and as anticipated earlier in the chapter, transport services. The technology that characterizes the delivery of these services, especially transport, is such that the supplier and the demander have to be close by in order for them to trade. For instance, it is unlikely that a Mexican trucking company exports trucking services to an Italian firm because there are no roads connecting the two countries.[52] In contrast, Mexican trucking companies are likely to export transport services to U.S. firms. Similar logic applies to construction because the delivery of the service requires movement of people and other factors of production and this entails costs that are likely to increase with distance. At the other extreme stand services such as business services or insurance services, where the delivery technology and the transactions associated with the provision of the service do not necessarily increase with distance. In such cases, information technologies allow countries to sidestep the difficulties of bringing together supply and demand.

Turning to the benchmarking of LAC's standing in terms of regional integration in regionally traded goods, the analysis takes a shortcut to overcome the unreliability of bilateral trade flows in services. In particular, it assumes that all services classified as regionally traded are traded with regional partners. Then it benchmarks a country's performance through a simple regression of the log of the trade value in regional traded services on log GDP and log size of the labor force. Figure 2A.1 plots both the actual value of the trade in regionally traded services and the predicted value from the regression.

**FIGURE 2A.1   Benchmarking trade in regionally traded services**

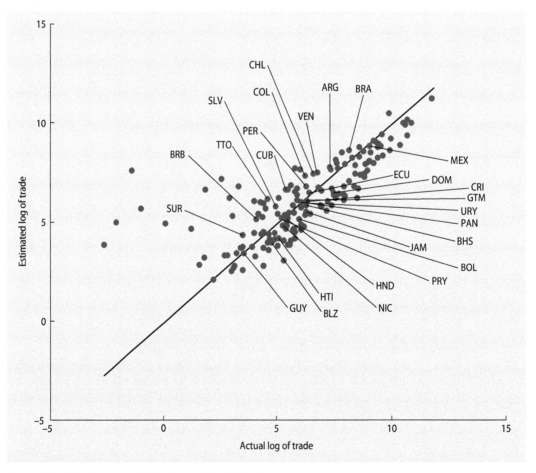

*Source:* World Bank calculations, using data from Francois and Pindyuk (2013)
*Note:* Estimated trade flows are calculated running a simple ordinary least squares (OLS) regression of log trade in regionally traded services on log GDP and log size of the labor force.

The results of figure 2A.1 show a great deal of heterogeneity within LAC in terms of trade in regionally traded services. Trade in regionally traded services in LAC-7 countries (that is, the seven largest LAC economies) typically stands below what their level of development and size would predict. A similar pattern emerges for commodity-exporting Caribbean countries like Trinidad and Tobago and Suriname. A second group of countries, comprising many Central American countries, some Caribbean economies, and smaller South American countries, displays levels of trade in regionally traded services that stand close to the levels predicted by the estimated equation. Finally, a handful of Caribbean countries like Belize, Guyana, Haiti, and Jamaica appear to have levels of trade in regionally traded services that stand above those predicted by the estimated equation.

## Notes

1. Baldwin and Venables (1995) and Vamvakidis (1998) observed that the literature has offered limited analyses of the effects of discriminatory trade liberalization on growth.
2. Annex 1A presents a detailed explanation of the regional classifications used throughout the report, along with the list of countries included in each region.
3. Other notable examples are the intraindustry trade models of Helpman and Krugman (1985, 1989) and the heterogeneous-firm models that generally reference Melitz (2003).
4. Chapter 3 reviews other arguments in favor of regional trade preferences, potentially at the expense of trade with the rest of the world, with the objective of gaining comparative advantage in products that are usually exported by high-income economies.
5. Regional trade flows are trade flows that occur between countries in the same region.
6. To be sure, the weight carried by overall intraregional trade flows has been following a declining trend over the past 25 years, falling from close to 50 percent of total trade in 1990 to slightly above 40 percent in 2014. This downward trend captures at least two important changes in the world economy since 1990. The first is the emergence of China on the global trade map since 2000 (see de la Torre et al. 2015). In fact, the Asian giant is quickly becoming an important trading partner of countries outside of Asia, such as Chile, Peru, and the United States. A second change is the strong wave of trade liberalization that took place in the 1990s among developing countries, which translated into a process of export market diversification tilted toward extraregional partners (see Sachs and Werner 1995; Wacziarg and Welch 2008; and Cadot, Carrère, and Strauss-Khan 2013).
7. The gravity model of trade was first used by Nobel laureate Jan Tinbergen in 1962. The author proposed an empirical relation between bilateral trade flows, economic size, and distance that follows the logic of Newton's law of gravity, which states that the force of attraction between two bodies is proportional to their mass and inversely proportional to the distance between them. In Tinbergen's model, economic size plays the role of mass and the geographic distance between two countries plays the role of the distance between the two objects.

   Originally, the gravity model was presented as an empirical relationship that provided a good description of bilateral trade patterns. Recent advances in the field of international trade have provided microeconomic foundations for the gravity model and have provided a better understanding of the implications of the relationship. Early papers using the gravity equation were reduced form estimations of the relationship that in many cases delivered misleading predictions (see Head and Mayer, 2014). This problem has been solved by the introduction of structural gravity equations derived from formal economic models (see Anderson 1979 or Eaton and Kortum 2002, among others). Importantly, structural gravity equations allow for the analysis of counterfactual policy experiments.
8. For example, Trefler (1995) finds that there is substantially less trade observed in the data compared to the levels predicted by the Heckscher-Ohlin (HO) model. The inability of traditional models to correctly predict trade patterns planted the seeds for new trade models that try to match features of the data, such as intraindustry trade between similarly endowed economies (see Krugman 1981) or the heterogeneity of firms in terms of their productivities (Melitz 2003), which are not usually incorporated in Ricardian or HO models.

9. Although trade flows are larger, trade over GDP may not be.

10. These costs may be linked to freight and insurance costs, or any other economic friction that increases the costs of international commerce even when not strictly related to geographic distance. The latter are often associated empirically with language differences, cultural differences, as well as trade taxes and nontariff barriers.

11. The Andean Pact changed its name to Andean Community in 1996. República Bolivariana de Venezuela is no longer a member.

12. The authors also include dummies for pairs of countries that are in the Asia-Pacific Economic Cooperation (APEC) bloc, the European Community, and the European Free Trade Association (EFTA).

13. The gravity specification used by Artuc, Hillberry, and Pienknagura (2016) controls for origin and destination fixed effects, colonial links, same language, and distance. The results presented in the chapter, which are based on the specification by Artuc, Hillberry, and Pienknagura (2016), use the average bilateral trade flows between 2004 and 2013 and include an FTA dummy as an additional control.

14. The collection of data on cross-border trade in services is notoriously difficult, in large part because of the intangible nature of services but also because of the high capacity needed to record such data. This is particularly true for developing countries.

15. However, when controlling for heterogeneous gravity effects, LAC's coefficient is statistically different from the positive coefficient displayed in panel a.

16. The positive distance elasticity seen in figure 2.6, panel b, refers to SAR's intraregional distance elasticity and stems from historic political tensions and mistrust between members of the region. This particular situation in SAR also explains the strong negative coefficient for SAR, both in the contiguous coefficient (panel b) and FTA coefficient (panel a).

17. The literature provides some evidence that domestic trading costs and the economic business environment are significant determinants of the volume of trade between countries. See, for example, Limao and Venables (2001); Wilson, Mann, and Otsuki (2003); Anderson and Marcouiller (2002); and Hoekman and Nicita (2011).

18. For more information, see http://www.doingbusiness.org.

19. Data on the quality of road and railway infrastructure are from the World Economic Forum's *Global Competitiveness Report 2013–14* (Schwab and Sala-i-Martin 2013). Data on road and railway density are from the World Bank's World Development Indicators.

20. The Liner Shipping Connectivity Index (LSCI) captures countries' level of integration in the liner shipping network. Liner shipping is typically used for general cargo on fixed trade routes and on fixed timetables. The higher the index, the easier it is to access a high-capacity and high-frequency global maritime freight transport system.

21. For discussions of access to liner shipping and port infrastructure in LAC, see, for example, Clark, Dollar, and Micco (2004) and ECLAC (2014).

22. Evans and Harrigan (2005) provide some evidence that the growing importance of speed in shipping to final markets has led to a resourcing of U.S. imports from Asia to Mexico and the Caribbean.

23. About two-thirds (in weight) of all air cargo in LAC travels by passenger aircraft. Air cargo statistics may therefore underestimate the importance of air transport for the cross-border flows of goods.

24. Revealed comparative advantage (RCA) is calculated in a similar way as Vollrath (1991). In particular, for each country and sector, RCA is calculated as $RCA_{i,s} = \ln((X_{i,s}/X_i)/(X_{W,s}/X_W)) - \ln((M_{i,s}/M_i)/(M_{W,s}/M_W))$, where $X_{i,s}$ are exports of country $i$ in sector $s$, $X_i$ are country $i$'s total exports, $X_{W,s}$ are world exports in sector $s$, $X_W$ are world exports, and $M$ stands for imports.

25. In Ricardian models of trade, sectors differ in their total factor productivity. In factor endowment models, sectors differ in their factor intensity.

26. For the Caribbean, the analysis of countries with a common border is limited to Belize, Dominican Republic, Guyana, Haiti, and Suriname because the other countries do not have land borders.

27. The calculation is such that the stock of R&D of country $i$ is

$$R\&D_i^T = R\&D_i^D + (1-\delta)\sum_{j=1}^{J} m_{i,j} R\&D_j^T$$

$$= \underbrace{R\&D_i^T}_{\text{Local}} + \underbrace{(1-\delta)\sum_{j=1}^{J} m_{i,j}\ R\&D_j^D}_{\text{First-order effect}}$$

$$+ \underbrace{(1-\delta)^2 \sum_{j=1}^{J} m_{i,j} \sum_{j'=1}^{J'} m_{j,j'}\ R\&D_{j'}^T}_{\text{Higher-order effects}}$$

where $R\&D_i^T$ is a country's total stock of R&D, $R\&D_i^D$ is the stock of R&D coming from own investments, $\delta$ is the depreciation of knowledge when it is transmitted across borders, and $m_{i,j}$ are import weights. The sum contains the first-order and second-order effects. The equation implies a system of equations that takes the following form:

$$R\&D^T = (I - (1 - \delta)M)R\&D^D$$

where $R\&D^T$, $R\&D^D$ are vectors, and M is a matrix whose $i,j$ element is $m_{i,j}$.

28. The tight link between trade and GDP volatility over the last 20 years to some extent is not surprising—trade has outpaced GDP over this period, which implies that in many countries it now carries a larger weight in GDP relative to the past. But this is not the end of the story. Trade over the past 20 years has fostered stronger and broader trade links across the board (de la Torre et al 2015). A consequence of this denser trade network is that country-specific factors explain a smaller share of a country's GDP growth variance compared to the contribution of global and regional factors (see Hevia and Servén 2016).

29. For example, Haddad et al. (2013) show that trade openness reduces volatility to the extent that countries are well diversified.

30. Trade policy may be used as a foreign policy tool or as a tool to control the effects of non-discriminatory trade policy on a country's income distribution (Baldwin 1989).

31. Hanson and Robertson (2008) argue that, when these importer and exporter dummies are allowed to vary by year, they can be interpreted as functions of structural parameters and country-specific variables that determine a country's export supply and import demand.

32. The four sectors are identified using a grouping of Leamer's (1995) sectoral classification. Leamer (1995) proposes a set of 10 industrial clusters. The distinguishing feature of each of these clusters is that the products included in each of them tend to be exported by countries that are similar in terms of their endowments of labor, land, and natural resources. The 10 broad clusters are petroleum, raw materials, forest products, tropical agriculture, animal products, cereals, labor-intensive goods, capital-intensive goods, machinery, and chemicals. Bennett et al. (2016) then group Leamer's industry clusters into four broad sectors: primary agricultural goods, nonagricultural primary sectors, labor-intensive manufacturing, and capital-intensive manufacturing. Primary agricultural sectors include Leamer's forest products, tropical agriculture, animal products, and cereals clusters. Nonagricultural primary sectors correspond to Leamer's chemical, petroleum, and raw materials clusters. Labor-intensive manufacturing sectors include Leamer's labor-intensive cluster, and capital-intensive sectors correspond to Leamer's capital-intensive and machinery clusters.

33. This is equivalent to assuming that the shares have no impact on the different terms affecting growth. This assumption may be violated if, as was explored in the previous section, regional integration affects a country's growth.

34. The fixed effects are obtained from the variation across sectoral exports.

35. Moreover, Bennett et al. (2016) show that many of the conclusions obtained in the analysis of bilateral trade flows regarding the contribution of global, country-specific, and sectoral factors on export growth volatility remain with the aggregate data.

36. Sectors at the SITC Rev. 3, 2-digit category. Under this definition there are a total of 67 sectors.

37. The estimated size of the quality ladder of each sector comes from the results presented in Khandelwal (2010).

38. The 2-digit SITC Rev 3 sectors with increasing returns are live animals (00); coal, coke, and brickets (32); gas, natural and manufactured (34); electric current (36); iron and steel (67).

39. The PRODY is an index that captures the trade-weighted average GDP per capita of countries exporting an export good.

40. The index is calculated as

$$PRODLF_s = \sum_{i=1}^{S} \frac{X_{is}/X_i}{\sum_{i'=1}^{S} X_{i's}/X_{i'}} LF_i$$

where *LF* is the size of the labor force of country *i*, $X_{is}$ are the exports of country *i* of sector *s*, and $X_i$ are total exports of country *i*.

41. Bigger countries are expected to produce at a more efficient scale, making them more competitive in international markets.

42. Episodes of liberalization come from Wacziarg and Welch (2008), who use the methodology proposed by Sachs and Warner (1995).

43. Given the analysis of episodes of liberalization occurring in the 1990s, PRODLFs are computed using average trade weights and labor force sizes for the 1985–90 period.

44. In fact, this is not just a theoretical case; during a drought in 2013, Panama imported electricity equivalent to the average monthly consumption of 100,000 families from the rest of Central America through the existing SIEPAC regional electric grid system to make up for power shortages caused by low reservoirs at hydroelectric plants (IDB 2013).

45. Fernandes, Lederman, and Gutierrez-Rocha (2013) study the impact of entrants and incumbent firms on the growth rates of a set of Latin American countries. The authors find that, during the expansion of the 2000s, incumbent firms contributed more to aggregate export growth. In contrast, entrants contributed more during the global financial crisis. This suggests that the contribution to export growth of entry and survival may vary along the business cycle.

46. Notice that, contrary to Brenton, Saborowski, and von Uexkell (2010), the analysis shown here uses a strict definition of entry. In particular, entry episodes are defined as entries that have been preceded by no previous trade relations at the exporter, importer, and product levels. Moreover, as in Brenton, Saborowski, and von Uexkell (2010), one-year interruptions are considered exits.

47. A similar exercise shows that entry rates and survival are typically lower in smaller economies, defined by the size of their labor force, than in bigger economies.

48. These results are robust to the inclusion of product-year fixed effects, which capture time-varying product characteristics such as global demand or technical changes, and exporter-importer-year fixed effects, which capture gravity variables like distance and also changes in country conditions in the importer and exporter country such as size.

49. The exclusion restriction requires a dependent variable that plays a role in the extensive margin of trade (that is, probability of trade) but has no part in the intensive margin (that is, the volume of trade, conditional on trade being positive).

50. Second-stage estimators depend on the inverse Mills ratio estimated in the first stage. If poorly estimated in the first stage, any bias due to misspecification could potentially do more harm than good in the second stage.

51. The estimation of the fixed effect in a gravity model requires a sufficient number of trading partners by country in order to identify the fixed effects.

52. Mexican firms can report exports of transport services to Italian firms, to the extent that Italian-owned firms operate in markets that are close to Mexico. However, the data suggest that this is not a common event.

## References

Agrawal, A., A. Galasso, and A. Oettl. 2014. "Roads and Innovation." CEPR Discussion Paper 10113, Centre for Economic Policy Research, London.

Albornoz, F., J. C. Hallak, and S. Fanelli. 2014. "Survival in Export Markets." Working Paper 112, Departamento de Economia, Universidad de San Andres, Argentina.

Anderson, J. E. 1979. "A Theoretical Foundation for the Gravity Equation." *American Economic Review* 69 (1): 106–16.

Anderson, J. E., and D. Marcouiller. 2002. "Insecurity and the Pattern of Trade: An Empirical Investigation." *Review of Economics and Statistics* 84: 342–52.

Antweiler, W., and D. Trefler. 2002. "Increasing Returns and All That: A View from Trade." *American Economic Review* 92 (1): 93–119.

Artuc, E., R. Hillberry, and S. Pienknagura. 2016. "Benchmarking Intra-regional Trade Flows." Background paper prepared for this report.

Bahar, D., and H. Rapoport, 2016. "Migration, Knowledge Diffusion and the Comparative Advantage of Nations." CESifo Working Paper No. 5769, CESifo, Munich.

Baldwin, R., 1989. "The Political Economy of Trade Policy." *Journal of Economic Perspectives* 3 (4): 119–35.

Baldwin, R. and A. Venables. 1995. "Regional Economic Integration." In Vol. 3 of *Handbook of International Economics*, edited by G. M. Grossman and K. Rogoff, 1597–1644. Amsterdam: Elsevier.

Bennett, F., D. Lederman, S. Pienknagura, and D. Rojas. 2016. "Trade Volatility in the 21st Century: Whose Fault Is It Anyway?" Policy Research Working Paper 7781, World Bank, Washington, DC.

Bernard, A. B., J.B. Jensen, S. J. Redding, and P. K. Schott. 2007. "Firms in International Trade." *Journal of Economic Perspectives* 21 (3): 105–30.

Berthelon, M., and C. Freund. 2008. "On the Conservation of Distance in International Trade." *Journal of International Economics* 75 (2): 310–20.

Besedes, T., and T. Prusa. 2006. "Ins, Outs, and the Duration of Trade." *Canadian Journal of Economics* 104 (1): 635–54.

Bravo-Ortega, C., A. P. Cusolito, and D. Lederman. 2016. "Faraway or Nearby? Domestic and International Spillovers in Patenting and Product Innovation." Policy Research Working Paper 7828. Washington, DC: World Bank.

Bravo-Ortega, Claudio, Ana P. Cusolito, and Daniel Lederman, 2016. "Faraway or Nearby? Domestic and International Spillovers in Patenting and Product Innovation." Policy Research Working Paper 7828, World Bank, Washington, DC.

Brenton, P., M. Pierola, and E. von Uexkull. 2009. "The Life and Death of Trade Flows: Understanding the Survival Rates of Developing-Country Exporters." In *Breaking into New Markets: Emerging Lessons for Export Diversification*, edited by Richard Newfarmer, William Shaw, and Peter Walkenhorst. Washington, DC: World Bank.

Brenton, P., C. Saborowski, and E. von Uexkull. 2010. "What Explains the Low Survival Rate of Developing Country Export Flows?" *The World Bank Economic Review*, 24 (3): 474–99.

Cadot, Olivier, Céline Carrère, and Vanessa Strauss-Kahn. 2013. "Trade Diversification, Income, And Growth: What Do We Know?" *Journal of Economic Surveys* 27 (4): 790–812.

Cadot, O., L. Iacovone, M. Pierola, and F. Rauch. 2013. "Success and Failure of African Exporters." *Journal of Development Economics* 101: 284–96.

Calderón, C. and L. Servén. 2010. "Infrastructure in Latin America." Policy Research Working Paper 5317, World Bank, Washington, DC.

Caselli, F., M. Koren, M. Lisicky, and S. Tenreyro. 2015. "Diversification through Trade," NBER Working Paper 21498, National Bureau of Economic Research, Cambridge, MA.

Cebeci, T., A. M. Fernandes, C. Freund, and M. Pierola. 2012. "Exporter Dynamics Database." Policy Research Working Paper 6229, World Bank, Washington, DC.

Chaney, T. 2011. "The Network Structure of International Trade." NBER Working Paper 16753, National Bureau of Economic Research, Cambridge, MA.

Clark, X., D. Dollar, and A. Micco. 2004. "Port Efficiency, Maritime Transport Costs, and Bilateral Trade." *Journal of Development Economics* 75 (2): 417–50.

Coe, D. T., and E. Helpman. 1995. "International R&D Spillovers." *European Economic Review* 39 (5): 859–87.

Corden, W. Max. 1997. *Trade Policy and Welfare, Second Edition.* Oxford, U.K.: Clarendon Press.

de la Torre, A., T. Didier, A. Ize, D. Lederman, and S. Schmukler. 2015. *Latin America and the Rising South: Changing World, Changing Priorities.* Washington, DC: World Bank.

di Giovanni, J., and A. Levchenko. 2009. "Trade Openness and Volatility." *The Review of Economics and Statistics* 91 (3): 558–85.

Development and Training Services Inc. 2015. "Evaluation of the Connecting the Americas 2022 Initiative." Analysis prepared for United States Department of State, Washington, DC.

Djankov, S., C. Freund, and C. Pham. 2010. "Trading on Time." *Review of Economics and Statistics* 92 (1): 166–73.

Ducret, C., and T. Notteboom. 2012. "The World Maritime Network of Container Shipping: Spatial Structure and Regional Dynamics." *Global Networks* 12 (3): 395–423.

ECLAC (Economic Comission for Latin America and the Caribbean). 2014. "Latin America and the Caribbean: Port System Evolutio, 1997–2013." *FAL Bulletin* 2 (330).

Eaton, J., and S. Kortum. 2002. "Technology, Geography, and Trade." *Econometrica* 70 (5): 1741–79.

Eaton, J., S. Kortum, and F. Kramarz. 2011. "An Anatomy of International Trade: Evidence from French Firms." *Econometrica* 79 (5): 1453–98.

Estevadeordal, A., and E. Talvi. 2016. "Towards a New Trans-American Partnership." Brookings Global Policy Brief, Brookings Institution, Washington, DC.

Evans, C. L., and J. Harrigan. 2005. "Distance, Time, and Specialization: Lean Retailing in General Equilibrium." *American Economic Review* 95 (1): 292–313.

Fally, T. 2015. "Structural Gravity and Fixed Effects." *Journal of International Economics* 97 (1): 76–85.

Fanelli, J. M. 2007. "Regional Agreements to Support Growth and Macro-Policy Coordination in Mercosur." G-24 Discussion Paper, United Nations Conference on Trade and Development (UNCTAD).

Fay, M., and M. Morrison. 2007. *Infrastructure in Latin America and the Caribbean: Recent Developments and Key Challenges.* Washington, DC: World Bank.

Fernandes, A. M., D. Lederman, and M. Gutierrez-Rocha. 2013. "Export Entrepreneurship and Trade Structure in Latin America During Good and Bad Times," Policy Research Working Paper 6413, World Bank, Washington, DC.

Fernandes, A., and H. Tang. 2014. "Learning to Export from Neighbors." *Journal of International Economics* 94 (1): 67–84.

Francois, J., and O. Pindyuk. 2013. "Consolidated Data on International Trade in Services," IIDE Discussion Papers 20130101, Institute for International and Development Economics.

Frankel, J., E. Stein, and S. Wei. 1995. "Trading Blocs in the Americas: The Natural, the Unnatural and the Super-Natural." *Journal of Development Economics* 47: 61–95.

Gavin, M., and R. Hausmann. 1998. "Growth with Equity: The Volatility Connection." In *Beyond Tradeoffs: Market Reforms and Equitable Growth in Latin America*, edited by Nancy Birdsall, Carol Graham, and Richard H. Sabot, 91–109. Washington, DC: Inter-American Development Bank and the Brookings Institution.

Gerner, F., and M. Hansen. 2011. "Caribbean Regional Electricity Supply Options." World Bank, Washington, DC.

Grossman, G. M., and E. Helpman. 1991. "Trade, Knowledge Spillovers, and Growth." *European Economic Review* 35 (2-3): 517–26.

Haddad, M., J. J. Lim, C. Pancaro, and C. Saborowski. 2013. "Trade Openness Reduces Volatility When Countries Are Well Diversified." *Canadian Journal of Economics* 46 (2): 765–90.

Hanson, G. H., and R. Robertson. 2008. "China and the Manufacturing Exports of Other Developing Countries." NBER Working Paper 14497, National Bureau of Economic Research, Cambridge, MA.

Hausmann, R., J. Hwang, and D. Rodrik. 2007. "What You Export Matters." *Journal of Economic Growth* 12 (1): 1–25, March.

Head, K., and T. Mayer. 2014. "Gravity Equations: Workhorse, Toolkit, and Cookbook." In Vol. 4 of *Handbook of International Economics*, edited by Gita Gopinath, Elhanan Helpman, and Kenneth Rogoff. Amsterdam: Elsevier.

Helpman, E., M. Melitz, and Y. Rubinstein. 2008. "Estimating Trade Flows: Trading Partners and Trading Volumes." *The Quarterly Journal of Economics* 123 (2): 441–87.

Helpman, E., and P. Krugman. 1985. *Market Structure and Foreign Trade.* Cambridge, MA: MIT Press.

———. 1989. *Trade Policy and Market Structure.* Cambridge, MA: MIT Press.

Hevia, C., and L. Servén. 2016. "International Business Cycles: Global or Regional?" Unpublished manuscript.

Hira, A., and L. Amaya, 2003. "Does Energy Integrate?" *Energy Policy* 31 (1): 185–99.

Hillberry, R. H. 2002. "Aggregation Bias, Compositional Change, and the Border Effect," *Canadian Journal of Economics* 35 (3): 517-30.

Hnatkovska, V., and N. Loayza. 2004. "Volatility and Growth." Policy Research Working Paper 3184, World Bank, Washington, DC.

Hoekman, B., and A. Nicita. 2011. "Trade Policy, Trade Costs, and Developing Country Trade." *World Development* 39 (12): 2069–79.

Hu, Y., and D. Zhu. 2009. "Empirical Analysis of the Worldwide Maritime Transportation Network." *Physics and Society* 388: 2061–71.

Hummels, D. 2007. "Transportation Costs and International Trade in the Second Era of Globalization." *Journal of Economic Perspectives* 21: 131–54.

IDB (Inter-American Development Bank). 2013. "Energy Integration in Central America: Full Steam Ahead." Available at http://www.iadb .org/en/news/webstories/2013-06-25/energy -integration-in-central-america,10494.html.

Jansen, M., C. Lennon, and R. Piermartini. 2016. "Income Volatility: Whom You Trade with Matters." *Review of World Economics* 152 (1): 127–46.

Khandelwal, A. 2010. "The Long and Short (of) Quality Ladders." *Review of Economic Studies* 77 (4): 1450–76.

Keller, W. 1998. "Are International R&D Spillovers Trade-Related? Analyzing Spillovers among Randomly Matched Trade

Partners." *European Economic Review* 42 (8): 1469–81.

Keller, W. 2002. "Geographic Localization of International Technology Diffusion." *American Economic Review* 92 (1): 120–42.

Koren, M., and S. Tenreyro. 2007. "Volatility and Development." *Quarterly Journal of Economics* 122 (1): 243–87.

Krugman, P. 1981. "Intraindustry Specialization and the Gains from Trade." *The Journal of Political Economy*, 89 (5): 959–73

Laursen, T., and S. Mahajan. 2005. "Volatility, Income Distribution, and Poverty." In *Managing Economic Volatility and Crises: A Practitioner's Guide*, edited by Joshua Aizenman and Brian Pinto, 101–136. New York: Cambridge University Press.

Leamer, E. 1995. "The Heckscher-Ohlin Model in Theory and Practice." Graham Lecture, Princeton Studies in International Finance No. 77, February.

Lederman, D. 2010. "An International Multilevel Analysis of Product Innovation." *Journal of International Business Studies* 41 (4): 606–19.

Lederman, D., and J. Lesniak. Forthcoming. *Economic Development with Limited Supplies of Labor: Common Challenges, Shared Solutions for Small Economies.* Washington, DC: World Bank.

Lederman, Daniel, and William F. Maloney. 2003. "Research and Development (R&D) and Development." Policy Research Working Paper 3024, World Bank, Washington, DC.

———. 2012. *Does What You Export Matter? In Search of Empirical Guidance for Industrial Policies.* Washington, DC: World Bank.

Lederman, D., J. Messina, S. Pienknagura, and J Rigolini. 2014. *Latin American Entrepreneurs: Many Firms but Little Innovation.* Washington, DC: World Bank.

Lederman, D., M. Olarreaga, and L. Zavala. 2015. "Export Promotion and Firm Entry into and Survival in Export Markets." Policy Research Working Paper 7400, World Bank, Washington, DC.

Lederman, D. and Ç. Özden. 2007. "Geopolitical Interests and Preferential Access to U.S. Markets." *Economics and Politics* 19 (2): 235–58.

Lederman, D., S. Pienknagura, and D. Rojas. 2015. "Latent Trade Diversification and Its Relevance for Macroeconomic Stability." Policy Research Working Paper 7332, World Bank, Washington, DC.

Levchenko, A., and J. Zhang. 2016. "The Evolution of Comparative Advantage: Measurement and Welfare Implications." *Journal of Monetary Economics* 78: 96–111.

Limão, N., and A. Venables. 2001. "Infrastructure, Geographical Disadvantage, Transport Costs, and Trade." *World Bank Economic Review* 15 (3): 451–79.

Lumenga-Neso, O., M. Olarreaga, and M. Schiff, 2005. "On 'Indirect' Trade-Related R&D Spillovers." *European Economic Review* 49: 1785–98.

Maritime International Secretariat Services. 2013. "Sustainable Development: IMO World Maritime Day 2013." http://www.ics-shipping .org/docs/default-source/resources/policy-tools /sustainable-development-imo-world -mari time-day-2013.pdf.

Melitz, M.J. 2003. "The Impact of Trade on Intra-industry Reallocations and Aggregate Industry Productivity." *Econometrica* 71 (6): 1695–1725.

Mesquita Moreira, M., J. Blyde, C. Volpe, and D. Molina. 2013. *Too Far to Export: Domestic Transport Costs and Regional Export Disparities in Latin America and the Caribbean.* Washington, DC: Inter-American Development Bank.

Mesquita Moreira, M., C. Volpe, and J. Blyde. 2008. *Unclogging the Arteries: The Impact of Transport Costs on Latin American and Caribbean Trade, Special Report on Integration and Trade.* Washington, DC: Inter-American Development Bank.

Morales, E., G. Sheu, and A. Zahler. 2014. "Gravity and Extended Gravity: Using Moment Inequalities to Estimate a Model of Export Entry." NBER Working Paper 19916, National Bureau of Economic Research, Cambridge, MA.

Notteboom, T. E. 2009. "Complementarity and Substitutability among Adjacent Gateway Ports." *Environment and Planning A* 41 (3): 743–62.

Pineau, P., A. Hira, and K. Froschauer. 2004. "Measuring International Electricity Integration: A Comparative Study of the Power Systems under the Nordic Council, MERCOSUR, and NAFTA." *Energy Policy* 32 (13): 1457–75.

Proudman, J., and S. Redding. 2000. "Evolving Patterns of International Trade." *Review of International Economics* 8 (3): 373–96.

Rauch, James E. 1999. "Networks versus Markets in International Trade." *Journal of International Economics* 48 (1): 7–35.

Ramey, G., and V. Ramey. 1995. "Cross-Country Evidence on the Link Between Volatility and Growth." *American Economic Review* 85: 1138–51.

Rodrigue, J. P., and C. Comtois. 2006. *The Geography of Transport Systems*. New York: Routledge.

Sachs, J. D., and A. Warner. 1995. "Economic Reform and the Process of Global Integration." *Brookings Papers on Economic Activity* 26 (1): 1–118.

Santos Silva, J. M. C., and S. Tenreyro. 2006. "The Log of Gravity." *The Review of Economics and Statistics* 88 (4): 641–58.

Sauma, E., S. Jerardino, C. Barria, R. Marambio, A. Brugman, and J. Mejia. 2011. "Electric Systems Integration in the Andes Community: Opportunities and Threats." *Energy Policy* 39 (2): 936–49.

Schwab, K., and X. Sala-i-Martin, eds. 2013. *The Global Competitiveness Report 2013–2014*. Geneva: Word Economic Forum.

Tinbergen, J. 1962. *Shaping the World Economy: Suggestions for an International Economic Policy*. New York: Twentieth Century Fund.

Trefler, D. 1995. "The Case of the Missing Trade and Other Mysteries." *American Economic Review* 85 (5): 1029–46.

United States Department of Energy. 2015. "Quadrennial Energy Review: Energy Transmission, Storage, and Distribution Infrastructure." United States Department of Energy, Washington, DC.

Vamvakidis, Athanasios. 1998. "Regional Integration and Economic Growth." *World Bank Economic Review* 12 (2): 251–70.

Vollrath, T. 1991. "A Theoretical Evaluation of Alternative Trade Intensity Measures of Revealed Comparative Advantage." *Review of World Economics* 127 (2): 265–80.

Wacziarg. R., and K. H. Welch. 2008. "Trade Liberalization and Growth: New Evidence." *The World Bank Economic Review* 22 (2): 187–231.

Wagner, R., and A. Zahler, 2015. "New Exports from Emerging Markets: Do Followers Benefit from Pioneers?" *Journal of Development Economics* 114: 203–23.

Wilson, J., C. Mann, and T. Otsuki. 2003. "Trade Facilitation and Economic Development: A New Approach to Quantifying the Impact." *World Bank Economic Review* 17 (3): 367–89.

World Bank. 2009. *World Development Report 2009: Reshaping Economic Geography*. Washington, DC: World Bank.

World Shipping Council. n.d. "Top 50 World Container Ports." http://www.worldship ping .org/about-the-industry/global-trade/top -50-world-container-ports.

# LAC's Trade Policy and Regional Integration | 3

## Introduction

The previous chapter established that Latin America and the Caribbean (LAC)[1] tends to trade according to what is predicted by geography, economic size, and other factors. While the evidence presented thus far suggests that much of this can be explained by geography (distance) and other characteristics (languages, culture, and religion) common across countries that might facilitate trade links, what role might LAC's formal trade policy play in these patterns? Is LAC's trade policy applied in a nondiscriminatory manner and thus relatively neutral? If so, this might tend to let these other economic and natural forces determine trade flows. On the other hand, if LAC's trade policy is not neutral, is it applied in a way that tends to reinforce LAC's already natural tendencies to trade with itself? Or can LAC's trade policy be interpreted as an attempt to aggressively reduce the barriers to trade with the rest of the world—that is, the barriers that tend to inhibit the flows of extraregional trade? If so, the region could be moving toward an open regionalism (OR), whereby natural economic forces enhance regional trade while commercial policies bring the region closer to the rest of the world.

These questions are important for LAC's OR agenda, particularly in light of the findings in the previous chapter, which argued that LAC is more likely to obtain efficiency (and dynamic) gains and macroeconomic stability by enhancing its trade with the rest of the world. In a few instances, however, regional integration could bring efficiency gains, particularly through the integration of regionally traded goods and services and for small economies. Moreover, a more open region can lead to larger gains from regional integration.

An assessment of the move toward OR, however, requires analyses of at least two different trade policies. This chapter begins by examining the LAC countries' nondiscriminatory, or most-favored-nation (MFN) tariff policy. In the absence of preferential trade arrangements, this is the trade policy facing any potential exporters to LAC—such as those in the rest of the world. It then turns to an examination of the less-than-MFN tariffs that LAC offers to selected partners through its preferential trade arrangements.

After characterizing the patterns behind LAC's application of these two tariff policies, the chapter then describes some of the research that has examined not only the intertemporal relationship between the two policies but also their determinants, so as to speak to policy implications. In addition, the chapter reviews existing and new evidence concerning the possibility that preferential treatment within the region could have had salutary effects on the structure of trade, as if regional preferences were industrial policies that change economic structures away from a potentially suboptimal market equilibrium. Finally, the chapter explores some of the challenges in the design of trade policy for LAC policy makers going forward, especially with regard to the problems arising from the proliferation of preferential trade agreements observed in countries in the region.

## LAC's tariff treatment of the rest of the world

As is well known, most of the world's customers and firms do not live, work, or produce their goods in LAC. Furthermore, and as will be documented below, most of the world has not signed preferential trade agreements with LAC. From the perspective of trade policy, how open then is LAC to trade with the rest of the world?

The starting point for this analysis is to focus on LAC's nondiscriminatory, or MFN, tariffs. These are the import tariffs that all countries not receiving tariff preferences from LAC would have to pay in order to export their goods into the LAC market.

To facilitate the analysis, this chapter splits LAC countries into three broad groups. The first split is based entirely on population; this is done in order to consider separately the trade policy for a set of 11 extremely small countries, defined as those having fewer than 1 million inhabitants (Group C countries). Amongst the rest of LAC with populations over 1 million, countries are then split into those with relatively high MFN tariffs (Group A) and those with relatively low MFN tariffs (Group B). The applied MFN tariff cutoff used to make the high/low distinction is 10 percent. The tariff characteristics of each group of countries are described in table 3.1.

The next sections seek to answer a number of questions about the pattern of LAC's tariff treatment of the world. To begin, how high are these applied tariffs? Is there much variation across countries? How constrained are countries by their multilateral (World Trade Organization [WTO]) trade agreement commitments—in other words, do

**TABLE 3.1　MFN *ad valorem* tariffs across LAC countries, 2014**

| Country | MFN applied rate, simple average | MFN binding rate, simple average | Binding coverage | Coverage of applied duties > 15 percent | Coverage of binding rates > 15 percent | Coverage of binding overhang > 15 percent | Maximum MFN applied rate |
|---|---|---|---|---|---|---|---|
| | (1) | (2) | (3) | (4) | (5) | (6) | (7) |
| **Group A: Population > 1 million and average applied MFN tariffs > 10 percent** | | | | | | | |
| Argentina | 13.6 | 31.8 | 100 | 36.5 | 97.8 | 71.1 | 35 |
| Bolivia | 11.6 | 40 | 100 | 20.1 | 100 | 94.3 | 40 |
| Brazil | 13.5 | 31.4 | 100 | 36.2 | 96.4 | 63.7 | 55 |
| Cuba | 10.6 | 21 | 31.5 | 9.5 | 13.8 | 73.4 | 30 |
| Ecuador | 11.9 | 21.7 | 100 | 36.4 | 71.7 | 44.4 | 86 |
| Paraguay | 10 | 33.5 | 100 | 29.8 | 94.9 | 88.7 | 30 |
| Uruguay | 10.5 | 31.5 | 100 | 34.5 | 98.2 | 79.8 | 35 |
| Venezuela, RB | 12.9 | 36.5 | 100 | 32.6 | 99.1 | 87.8 | 160 |

*(continued)*

**TABLE 3.1    MFN *ad valorem* tariffs across LAC countries, 2014** *(continued)*

| Country | MFN applied rate, simple average | MFN binding rate, simple average | Binding coverage | Coverage of applied duties > 15 percent | Coverage of binding rates > 15 percent | Coverage of binding overhang > 15 percent | Maximum MFN applied rate |
|---|---|---|---|---|---|---|---|
|  | (1) | (2) | (3) | (4) | (5) | (6) | (7) |
| **Group B: Population > 1 million and average applied MFN tariffs < 10 percent** | | | | | | | |
| Chile | 6 | 25.1 | 100 | 0 | 100 | 99.9 | 6 |
| Colombia | 5.8 | 42.1 | 100 | 2.1 | 97.9 | 97.8 | 98 |
| Costa Rica | 5.6 | 43.1 | 100 | 1.3 | 96 | 95.7 | 150 |
| Dominican Republic | 7.3 | 34 | 100 | 29.1 | 89.4 | 90.1 | 40 |
| El Salvador | 6 | 36.7 | 100 | 2.2 | 97.6 | 95.2 | 164 |
| Guatemala | 5.6 | 41.3 | 100 | 0.6 | 94 | 95.2 | 40 |
| Haiti | 4.8 | 18.7 | 89 | 4.3 | 52.8 | 46.6 | 58 |
| Honduras | 5.7 | 31.9 | 100 | 0.6 | 89.7 | 85.7 | 164 |
| Jamaica | 8.5 | 49.6 | 100 | 26.9 | 83.9 | 88.6 | 100 |
| Mexico | 7.5 | 36.1 | 100 | 15.7 | 98.7 | 95.9 | 150 |
| Nicaragua | 5.7 | 40.9 | 100 | 0.8 | 98 | 99.2 | 164 |
| Panama | 6.8 | 22.9 | 100 | 1 | 68.6 | 64.9 | 260 |
| Peru | 3.4 | 29.5 | 100 | 0 | 98 | 98.5 | 11 |
| **Group C: Population < 1 million** | | | | | | | |
| Antigua and Barbuda | 9.9 | 58.8 | 97.5 | 24.4 | 97.5 | 99.8 | 70 |
| Bahamas | 35.1 | – | – | 81.7 | – | – | 222 |
| Barbados | 10.7 | 78.3 | 97.5 | 24.2 | 97.5 | 98.4 | 141 |
| Belize | 11.6 | 58.2 | 97.6 | 26.1 | 97.6 | 98.5 | 110 |
| Dominica | 10 | 58.7 | 94.3 | 23.7 | 94.3 | 100 | 165 |
| Grenada | 10.4 | 56.6 | 100 | 24.7 | 99.8 | 96.7 | 40 |
| Guyana | 11.2 | 56.6 | 100 | 25 | 100 | 99 | 100 |
| St. Kitts and Nevis | 9.1 | 76 | 97.5 | 21.6 | 97.5 | 100 | 77 |
| St. Lucia | 8.4 | 62.4 | 99.6 | 24.4 | 99.6 | 100 | 70 |
| St. Vincent and the Grenadines | 10.2 | 62.9 | 99.7 | 24 | 99.7 | 100 | 74 |
| Suriname | 10.4 | 18 | 26.8 | 24.5 | 20.9 | 71 | 50 |

*Source:* WTO (2015), except column (6), which is computed by the World Bank from HS06 tariff data as the share of HS06 products with applied most-favored-nation (MFN) rates more than 15 percentage points below the binding rate.
*Note:* LAC = Latin America and the Caribbean.

governments have the policy space to further raise their applied tariffs if they desired? Then, within these countries, are tariffs set uniformly across sectors, and across products within a sector? Do governments vary them much over time?

## LAC countries with relatively high external tariffs

More than 300 million people in LAC live in countries with average applied MFN tariffs that are higher than 10 percent. The top third of table 3.1 characterizes a number of the main features of the tariffs for these countries.

For ease of discussion, consider an interpretation of the tariff data for Argentina and begin with information on the tariffs that Argentina actually *applies*. In 2014, Argentina's simple average applied MFN tariff was 13.6 percent. Again, the applied MFN tariff is the duty paid by all exporters that do not have some sort of preferential trade agreement with Argentina. In Argentina, 36.5 percent of imported products had an applied MFN tariff that is 15 percent or more, and the country's maximum applied tariff rate was 35 percent.

How do these applied tariffs compare with Argentina's actual *legal* commitments to exporters in the other 163 WTO member economies? Indeed, not all of the important information on this trade policy is captured by applied tariffs; the applied tariffs are not the legally binding commitments to trading partners under the WTO system.

Could Argentina raise its tariffs even further under WTO rules if it wanted to? The answer is yes, but it could not raise the tariffs to arbitrarily high levels.

First, Argentina has agreed to some upper limit for tariffs for 100 percent of the products that it might import. Although table 3.1 suggests that this is typical across countries in LAC, it is worth noting that even this most basic legal commitment is not universal; most countries in Sub-Saharan Africa, for example, have not taken on this basic WTO commitment.[2]

Nevertheless, although Argentina has agreed to universal tariff binding coverage for its imported products under the WTO, the average *level* of the tariff bindings—that is, the WTO legal commitment for each product above which Argentina promises not to raise its applied MFN tariff—remains high, at 31.8 percent. Put differently, on average Argentina could more than double its applied MFN tariffs from 2014 levels (from 13.6 to 31.8 percent) and still be within the legal promises it has made to trading partners under the WTO. From this perspective, Argentina continues to retain a tremendous amount of applied MFN tariff "policy space"—that is, its applied tariff levels as of 2014 were hardly constrained by what it has legally agreed to at the WTO.

How different is Argentina from the other Group A countries? Given that, through the Mercosur customs union, Argentina, Brazil, Paraguay, Uruguay, and República Bolivariana de Venezuela are committed to applying a common external tariff toward nonmembers (with numerous exceptions, however), the first expectation is that the four other countries' tariff characteristics in table 3.1 should mimic Argentina's tariffs. Brazil's, Argentina's, and República Bolivariana de Venezuela's tariffs are quite similar on average, but there is more than 3 percentage points of difference for Paraguay and Uruguay. This is the first clear evidence that these four countries are not engaged in a "pure" customs union that would have harmonized MFN applied tariffs for 100 percent of imported products. There is more evidence on this below, once additional trade policy instruments beyond tariffs are taken into account.

The average tariffs for Bolivia, Cuba, and Ecuador exhibit a number of additional differences. First, although their average applied MFN tariffs are similar—ranging from 10.6 to 12.9 percent—Cuba has bound the tariffs for only 31.5 percent of its imported products. Furthermore, Ecuador has much lower average tariff bindings than most of the other countries in LAC, at 21.7 percent. The term tariff binding "overhang" is defined as the difference between the binding rate and the applied rate—this is the amount by which a country can increase its applied MFN tariff while still not violating its WTO commitments. As such, Ecuador has much less tariff binding overhang (an average of 9.8 percentage points) and thus less policy space to increase applied MFN tariffs relative to most other LAC countries.

How do Group A's tariffs compare to those of the other major economies of the world—including many of Group A's peers in other regions? For comparison, figure 3.1 illustrates the average applied tariffs, average binding tariffs, and the difference between the two (the tariff binding overhang) for these countries relative to a selection of major non-LAC

**FIGURE 3.1    Simple average MFN applied tariffs and bindings for selected LAC countries vs. the rest of the world, 2014**

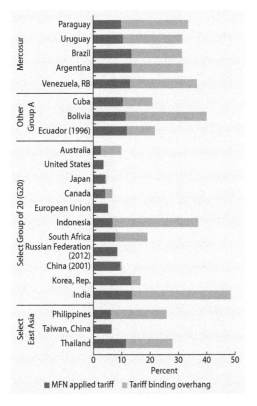

*Source:* World Bank construction, with data taken from WTO 2015.
*Note:* Year in parentheses indicates WTO accession year if 1996 or after; all other listed economies acceded to the WTO upon its inception in 1995. Economies in each group are ranked from low to high according to average applied MFN tariff in 2014.

countries. First note that the members of Mercosur, as expected, have applied tariffs and binding overhang that are close to one another but that do exhibit notable differences.

The high-income economies' applied MFN tariffs illustrated in figure 3.1, as well as their amount of tariff binding overhang, is two to four times less than the tariffs applied by the Group A countries. Average applied MFN tariffs range from 2.7 percent to 5.3 percent for Australia, Canada, the European Union (EU), Japan, and the United States. Furthermore, the EU, Japan, and the United States have zero tariff binding overhang: after decades of multilateral tariff negotiations taking place under the General Agreement on Tariffs and Trade (GATT)

between 1947 and 1994, their tariff bindings are not only low, but they have been negotiated down to the levels of their applied MFN rates. The result is that, unlike the LAC countries, the high-income economies have retained almost zero policy space to be able to raise their applied MFN tariffs.

How do Group A's tariffs compare to those of the other BRICS (Russian Federation, India, China, and South Africa) and other emerging economies? Although there are similarities with India, the tariffs for China, Indonesia, Russia, and South Africa are much different. Not only do the other BRICS have much lower average applied MFN tariffs, but China, Russia, and to a lesser extent even South Africa also have much less tariff binding overhang.[3] And even the smaller East Asian economies in figure 3.1—such as the Philippines; Taiwan, China; and Thailand—have lower average applied MFN tariffs than the Group A countries.

While Group A's applied MFN tariffs and tariff binding overhang are relatively high, are these tariffs uniformly applied across sectors? As figure 3.2 suggests, the answer to this question is no. Average applied MFN tariffs are relatively higher in sectors such as textiles and footwear—for example, Argentina's average tariffs for products in these sectors is 26 percent—as well as in agriculture, including products such as animals, vegetables, and processed foodstuffs. On the other hand, applied MFN tariffs are relatively lower in minerals, fuels, and chemicals. As will become apparent from the additional discussion below, some of this variation can be explained by countries imposing lower tariffs, on average, on goods in sectors dominated by intermediate inputs and higher tariffs on final goods, with potentially important implications for global value chains (GVCs).

Nevertheless, the clear patterns of the tariffs across these Group A countries—relatively high tariffs overall, significant tariff binding overhang, and substantial variation across sectors within a country's tariff structure—raise a number of questions both for research and for policy, some of which are addressed in more detail below.

**FIGURE 3.2    Simple average MFN applied tariffs and bindings for selected Group A countries, 2014, by sector**

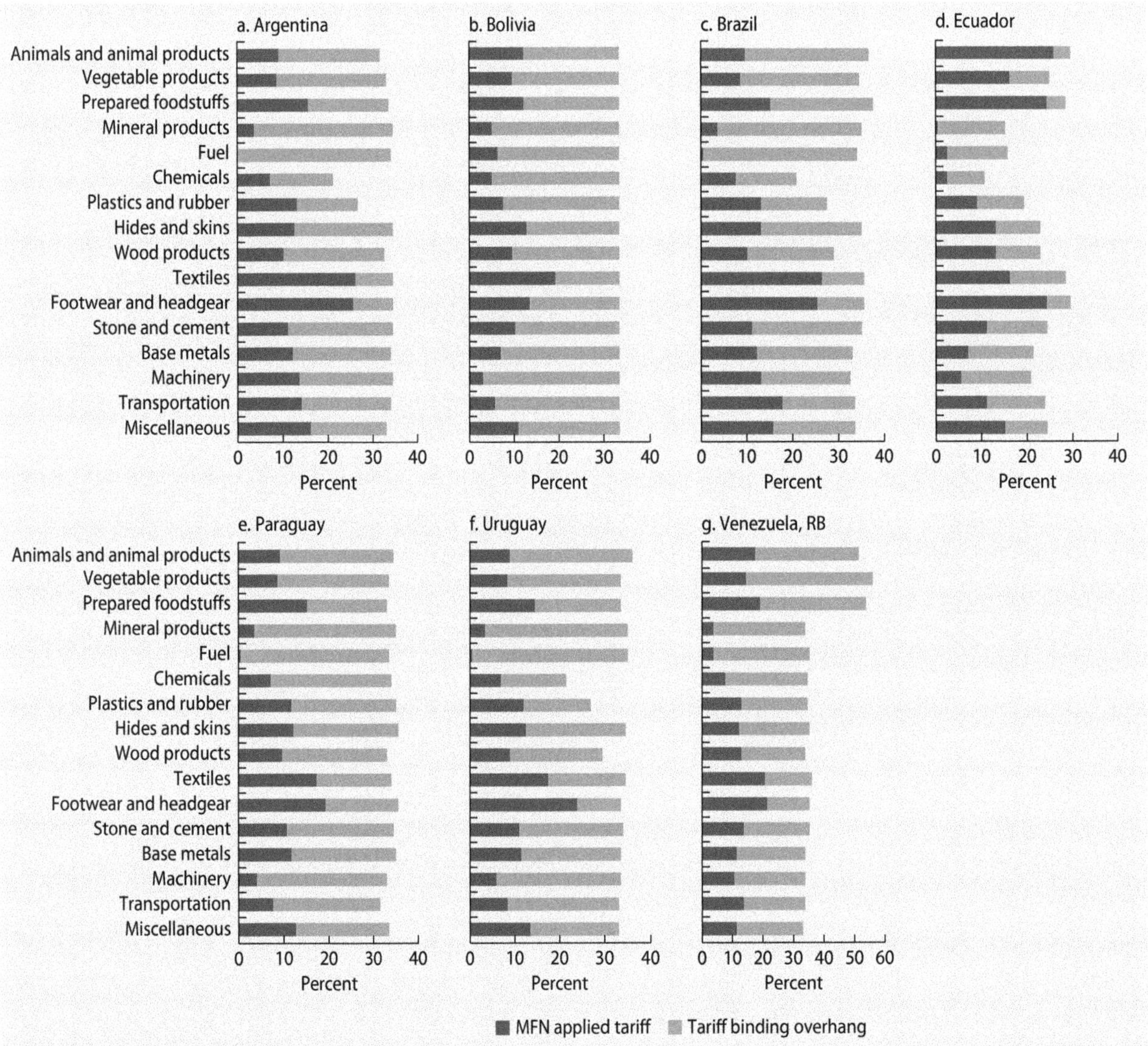

*Source:* World Bank construction, from tariff data at the HS-06 level from the International Trade Centre and the World Trade Organization. Data for Cuba not available.
*Note:* See annex 3A, table 3A.1, for industry definitions.

The fact that governments are not imposing tariffs uniformly across sectors and the existence of tariff policy space suggest that they are doing so by choice—that is, that their WTO commitments are not binding. However, this retention of substantial tariff binding overhang may also lead to unanticipated costs. Recent research by Handley and Limão (2015, 2016), for example, suggests

that eliminating overhang by reducing the level of tariff bindings—even without changing applied rates—can be used to reduce trade policy uncertainty and improve economic well-being.[4] The intuition is that the existence of tariff binding overhang implies that governments have an option to raise import tariffs without cost (that might arise via trading partner authorized retaliation), and that this uncertainty about future policy works to discourage investment and potential entry into international markets and to reduce overall economic welfare.

## LAC countries with relatively low external tariffs

The middle rows of table 3.1 describe the trade policy characteristics for a collection of 13 sizable LAC countries (Group B) with average applied tariffs of less than 10 percent in 2014. With the exception of Jamaica (8.5 percent), which is by far the smallest economy in this group, each of the Group B countries actually has average tariffs that are even lower—ranging from 3.4 percent (Peru) to only 7.5 percent (Mexico). Like the Group A countries, Group B countries have almost all (with the exception of Haiti) also taken on the commitment to bind 100 percent of their imported products at some upper limit under the WTO. On the other hand, with the exception of Haiti and Panama, these countries have even more tariff binding overhang—and thus applied MFN tariff policy space—than the Group A countries.

Regarding cross-sector tariff differences, as figure 3.3 illustrates, Group B countries also tend to have higher applied MFN tariffs in sectors like textiles, apparel, footwear, and agriculture. Notable exceptions are Chile—which has an applied rate of 6 percent for virtually all products—and Peru—which has much lower levels of import protection in agricultural products. Furthermore, most of the Group B countries tend to have substantial tariff binding overhang across sectors. Although the overall patterns of variation across sectors are quite similar between Group B and Group A countries, the main difference arises through the *levels* of applied MFN tariffs; Group B countries tend to apply tariffs that are much lower across the board.

Paradoxically, Group B actually has more tariff binding overhang precisely because it applies lower tariff rates. Interestingly, what makes the large tariff binding overhang less of a concern for the Group B countries is their particular pattern of free trade agreements (FTAs).

As is described in more detail in the section below, Group B's high tariff bindings are becoming a less and less relevant measure of the legal constraint for the tariff affecting their imports. For, with the exception of the Caribbean islands of Jamaica and Haiti, each of the other Group B countries has at least one other common characteristic: each also has an FTA in place with a major economy outside of the LAC region. This includes bilateral and reciprocal FTAs that Chile, Colombia, Mexico, Panama, and Peru have negotiated with the United States, as well as the multicountry Dominican Republic–Central American Free Trade Agreement (CAFTA-DR) with the United States. Many of these countries have also negotiated (or are in the process of negotiating) FTAs with the European Union and Japan. Applied MFN tariff policy space is not as worrisome for the Group B countries because, even if they were to raise their applied MFN tariffs to their binding levels, the existence of their FTAs with major economies of the world indicates that it would matter less and less for their import flows. We should note, however, that the Mercosur bloc is currently in the process of negotiating a trade agreement with the European Union, which is potentially good news if it were to be successfully implemented.

## Small economies in LAC

Although "small" LAC countries are defined here as those with populations of less than 1 million, it is worth noting that half of these countries actually have a population of 100,000 or less.[5] Furthermore, with the exceptions of Suriname and Guyana, these are Caribbean island economies that are primarily reliant on services trade (tourism) and, to a limited extent, agriculture.

In most of these countries, the lower rows of table 3.1 indicate that the average applied MFN tariff is 8–11 percent. Furthermore, only 25 percent of their tariffs are applied at rates greater than 15 percent. However, each country also continues to retain substantial tariff policy space through either extremely high tariff bindings or the small coverage of bound products (Suriname).

**FIGURE 3.3   Simple average MFN applied tariffs and bindings for selected Group B countries, 2014, by sector**

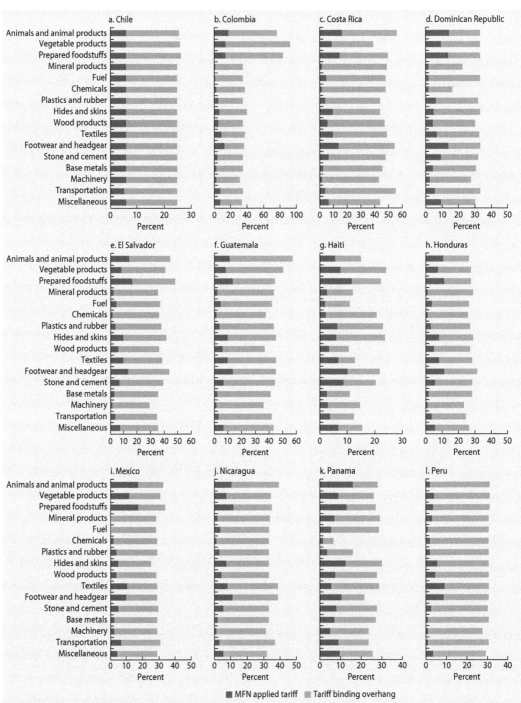

Source: World Bank construction, from tariff data at the HS-06 level from the International Trade Centre and the World Trade Organization.
Note: See annex 3A, table 3A.1, for industry definitions.

As figure 3.4 indicates, average applied MFN import tariffs are substantially higher in agriculture than in nonagricultural products for all of these countries. Across countries, average applied MFN tariffs for nonagricultural products were 7–10 percent.

Because these countries have such a limited domestic production capacity, especially for manufacturing industries, there is little efficiency distinction between the application of an import tariff and a consumption tax. Put differently, because many of these countries do not have the scale to produce domestically most of the goods in their tariff schedules, there is unlikely to be any domestic production *distortion* (efficiency loss) associated with the applied import tariff. Thus, although imposition of an import tariff will lead to a consumption distortion—this will be equivalent to the same-sized consumption tax—the tariff is not leading to the inefficient expansion of any domestic industry. Thus, if 7–10 percent is reasonable for an optimal consumption tax, it may be administratively efficient to collect this tax at the border rather than through each individual point of sale.

As highlighted by Corden (1997, chapter 4) the theoretical optimal level of import tariffs depends on the consumption- and production-side distortions that need to be balanced against the differential costs of raising revenues through other means. Our argument here is that, for very small economies, the production-side distortions are negligible and thus import tariffs could be superior to sales or income taxes, which require strong institutions or agencies to enforce them, in addition to customs agencies. Setting up such agencies and systems could be costly. Indeed, Lederman and Lesniak (2016) find that government current expenditures as a share of gross domestic product (GDP) systematically fall with the size of an economy's labor force, thus suggesting that there are economies of scale in the provision of public services more generally. However, this reasoning does not necessarily explain why import tariffs in LAC's smallest economies affect agricultural goods, which might in fact reflect a protectionist inclination.

**FIGURE 3.4** **Average applied MFN tariffs for LAC countries with populations of less than 1 million, 2014**

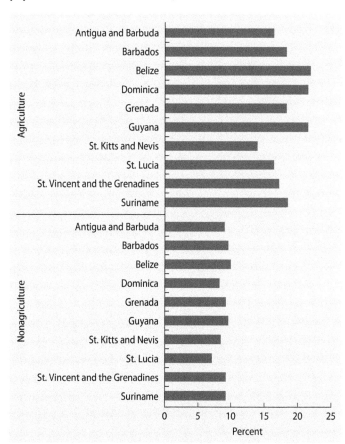

*Source:* World Bank construction, based on data taken from WTO 2015.
*Note:* Latin America and Caribbean (LAC) countries with populations of less than 1 million, excluding The Bahamas.

## LAC's tariff preferences

The previous section covered the benchmark trade policy—the MFN tariff—that LAC applies to imports from all WTO members, in the absence of any special tariff arrangements. However, LAC is also known for being heavily involved in FTAs. Because FTAs can result in an offering of lower-than-MFN tariffs to members, they also have the potential to influence the pattern of bilateral trade flows.

The next two sections characterize the basic patterns of tariff preferences that LAC countries offer to one another, and to countries outside of the region, under a web, or "spaghetti bowl," of FTAs that it has negotiated. The structure of the analysis follows the "large population" elements of the previous section; it analyzes first the Group A countries (with applied MFN tariffs of higher than 10 percent) and then the Group B countries (with applied MFN tariffs of lower than 10 percent).[6] It then describes implications of the trade policy patterns for trade flows.

## Tariff preference offerings by the high-MFN-tariff LAC countries

Consider first the Group A countries that have average applied MFN tariffs of 10 percent or more, as described in the previous section. Table 3.2 summarizes the state of their bilateral tariffs. Rows in the table characterize importing country tariff preference offerings, and columns in the table characterize exporting country receipt of potentially available tariff preference offerings.

Again, to interpret the data presented in table 3.2, consider Argentina, which had an average applied MFN tariff in 2014 of 13.6 percent. The first column indicates that Argentina has a lot of products for which it could potentially offer a bilateral tariff preference (relative to its applied MFN tariff rate); in 2014, 96.7 percent of Argentina's imported products had an applied MFN tariff that was greater than zero. Of those 96.7 percent of all imported products, Argentina offered a lower-than-MFN tariff preference to 100 percent (or nearly 100 percent) of these available products to all other exporters in Group A. Argentina also offered a lower-than-MFN tariff preference to nearly 100 percent of these available products to a few LAC exporters in Group B, including Chile, Colombia, and Peru, and slightly lower coverage to Mexico (87.8 percent of available products) and Panama (84.3 percent of available products). To all other exporters in Group B, it offered little to no bilateral tariff preferences. Finally, Argentina offered zero bilateral tariff preferences to the major non-LAC exporters—the European Union, Japan, and the United States.[7]

With a few minor exceptions, the pattern for the other Group A countries is comparable to Argentina in most critical ways.

First, most of the other Group A countries also have a substantial number of imported products for which it was possible for them to offer a tariff preference; this ranged from 87.6 percent of imported products in Uruguay to 96.8 percent in Brazil. The main exception is Ecuador, which had only 59.6 percent of imported products with applied MFN tariffs that were positive and thus for which it was possible to offer preferences.

Second, all of the Group A countries tend to have fairly universal coverage of bilateral tariff preference offerings to other Group A countries. Overall, of the 42 cells capturing bilateral (importer-exporter) pairings between Group A countries in the upper left quadrant of table 3.1, there are only four in which one country offered bilateral tariff preferences in less than 83.7 percent of all available products: Bolivia to Ecuador, Bolivia to República Bolivariana de Venezuela, Ecuador to Bolivia, and Ecuador to República Bolivariana de Venezuela.

Third, the Group A countries all tend to have much more limited preferential tariff offerings to the Group B countries in LAC than they do with each other. There are widespread preferences offered to Chile, Colombia, Mexico, and Peru, and slightly fewer preferences are offered to Panama. Finally, Group A countries have offered only a handful of bilateral tariff preferences to Group B countries in Central America.

Fourth, and finally, none of the Group A countries offered bilateral tariff preferences in 2014 to the major economies outside of LAC.

## Tariff preference offerings by the low-MFN LAC countries

Next, consider the bottom half of table 3.2 and the tariff preferences for the Group B countries in LAC that had applied MFN tariffs in 2014 that averaged less than 10 percent. For the countries for which the applied preferential tariff data are available, the highest average applied MFN tariff in 2014 was actually only 7.5 percent (Mexico).

First, it is striking, although not surprising, that the Group B countries have many fewer products for which they can offer any tariff preferences than do the Group A countries. In Peru, for example, only 48.1 percent of imported products in 2014 had an applied MFN tariff of greater than zero; this is less than half the number of products for which

**TABLE 3.2  LAC's imported products with available and granted bilateral tariff preferences, 2014**

Share of all HS06 products with applied bilateral tariff rate lower than the applied MFN tariff rate

| Policy-imposer | Available[a] | Group A exporters | | | | | | | Group B exporters | | | | | | | | | | | | Selected other exporters | | |
|---|---|---|---|---|---|---|---|---|---|---|---|---|---|---|---|---|---|---|---|---|---|---|---|
| | | ARG | BOL | BRA | ECU | PRY | URY | VEN | CHL | COL | CRI | DOM | GTM | HND | HTI | MEX | NIC | PAN | PER | SLV | USA | EUN | JPN |
| ARG | 96.7 | | 100 | 100 | 99.9 | 99.5 | 100 | 100 | 100 | 99.4 | 0 | 0 | 0 | 0 | 0 | 87.8 | 0.7 | 84.3 | 99.8 | 0 | 0 | 0 | 0 |
| BOL | 93.7 | 100 | | 100 | 66.5 | 100 | 100 | 61.5 | 64.5 | 61.5 | 0 | 0 | 0 | 0 | 0 | 98.9 | 0 | 61.2 | 1.7 | 0 | 0 | 0 | 0 |
| BRA | 96.8 | 99.9 | 99.9 | | 99.9 | 99.3 | 99.9 | 99.9 | 99.8 | 99.9 | 0 | 0 | 0 | 0 | 0 | 90.4 | 1 | 88 | 99.9 | 0 | 0 | 0 | 0 |
| ECU | 59.6 | 89.1 | 46.3 | 89.6 | | 88.6 | 83.7 | 39.6 | 97.7 | 39.6 | 0 | 0 | 0 | 0 | 0 | 39.8 | 0 | 38.9 | 1.2 | 0 | 0 | 0 | 0 |
| PRY | 89.2 | 99.8 | 99.9 | 99.8 | 97.9 | | 99.8 | 99.7 | 99.9 | 99.6 | 0 | 0 | 0 | 0 | 0 | 68 | 0 | 65.7 | 99.7 | 0 | 0 | 0 | 0 |
| URY | 87.6 | 99.8 | 99.9 | 99.8 | 95.5 | 99.4 | | 99.8 | 99.9 | 99.7 | 0 | 0 | 0 | 0 | 0 | 98.6 | 0 | 70.4 | 84.5 | 0 | 0 | 0 | 0 |
| VEN | 98.1 | 99.8 | 84.9 | 99.7 | 86.6 | 99.8 | 99.8 | | 98.4 | 89.9 | 6.5 | 0 | 6 | 6 | 20.3 | 83.3 | 6 | 83.4 | 0.9 | 0 | 0 | 0 | 0 |
| CHL | 99.8 | 100 | 100 | 100 | 99 | 100 | 100 | 99.4 | | 100 | 97 | 0 | 95.6 | 99.6 | 99.9 | 99.6 | 99.7 | 99.7 | 99.9 | 0 | 100 | 98.8 | 96.1 |
| COL | 54.2 | 99.1 | 77.3 | 98.7 | 77.3 | 99.6 | 99.4 | 83.6 | 100 | | 2.2 | 0 | 0.4 | 1.8 | 30.3 | 99.3 | 0.6 | 75.6 | 3.1 | 0 | 87.5 | 77.5 | 0 |
| CRI | 51.7 | 0 | 0 | 89.6 | 0 | 0 | 0 | 0 | 0 | 0 | | 99.6 | 99.8 | 99.8 | 0 | 0 | 99.8 | 98.1 | 90.7 | 99.8 | 98.6 | 75.4 | 0 |
| DOM | 46.6 | 0 | 0 | 0 | 0 | 0 | 0 | 0 | 0 | 0 | 31.1 | | 87.3 | 87.3 | 86.9 | 0 | 87.3 | 3 | 0 | 87.3 | 31.1 | 38.8 | 0 |
| GTM | 51.7 | 0 | 0 | 0 | 16.8 | 0 | 0 | 0 | 0 | 55.7 | 0 | 85.1 | | 100 | 0 | 0 | 100 | 97.5 | 0 | 100 | 99.2 | 75.8 | 0 |
| HND | 52.4 | 0 | 0 | 0 | 0 | 0 | 0 | 0 | 0 | 82.6 | 99.8 | 100 | 100 | | 0 | 0 | 100 | 72.1 | 0 | 100 | 99.8 | 77.3 | 0 |
| HTI | 55.7 | 0 | 0 | 0 | 0 | 0 | 0 | 0 | 0 | 0 | 0 | 0 | 0 | 0 | | 0 | 0 | 0 | 0 | 0 | 0 | 0 | 0 |
| MEX | 57.4 | 64.5 | 69.7 | 64.5 | 73 | 76.1 | 95.6 | 65.7 | 99.1 | 97.6 | 97.2 | 0 | 96 | 95.6 | 0 | | 99.5 | 66.7 | 86.8 | 0 | 100 | 92.5 | 87.8 |
| NIC | 51.9 | 0 | 0 | 0 | 0 | 0 | 0 | 0 | 0 | 0 | 98.5 | 98.5 | 100 | 100 | 0 | 0 | | 88.8 | 0 | 100 | 99.8 | 74 | 0 |
| PER | 48.1 | 99.6 | 9.6 | 99.6 | 11.2 | 99.8 | 74 | 1.5 | 99.8 | 1.5 | 79.6 | 0 | 0 | 0 | 0 | 81.9 | 0 | 0.6 | | 0 | 97.9 | 54.9 | 77.8 |
| SLV | 52.6 | 0 | 0 | 0 | 0 | 0 | 0 | 0 | 0 | 54.9 | 0.4 | 97.9 | 99.8 | 99.4 | 0 | 0 | 99.8 | 69.4 | 0 | | 99.2 | 75.3 | 0 |

*Source:* World Bank calculations, based on HS06 tariff data available from International Trade Centre.

*Note:* Rows are the importing (policy-imposing) countries, and columns are the exporting countries. Tariff preference offerings: data for Jamaica and Panama not available. See annex 3A, table 3A.2, for country acronyms. Dark gray is tariff preference offered in 70 percent or more of preference-possible products. Light grey is tariff preference offered for between 0 and 70 percent of preference possible products.

a. Available provides the share of HS06 products within the importing country with a non-zero applied most-favored-nation (MFN) tariff and thus for which a tariff preference is possible. Interpretation: in 2014, Argentina had preferences to offer in 96.7 percent of its HS06 products. It offered bilateral preferences to Bolivia in 100 percent of available products, whereas it offered bilateral preferences to Colombia in 99.4 percent of available products.

Brazil could offer a tariff preference. The exception in Group B is Chile, which, as was observed in figure 3.3, applied virtually all of its MFN tariffs at the uniform rate of 6 percent (but with numerous FTAs covering a significant portion of the world economy, as discussed below). Overall, the main point is that, because the Group B countries have so many more imported products with applied MFN tariffs that are equal to zero, they have far fewer tariff preferences to offer to any trading partner in the first place. Again, this reflects the potential trade-off between being open toward the global economy and the scope to grant trade preferences to selected partners, and Group B countries seem to be much more oriented toward an open trade approach than Group A.

This fact, then, begs the natural question: Are the Group B countries nevertheless still involved in many FTAs? On one hand, the relatively low applied MFN tariffs might predict that Group B countries would be less likely to be involved in FTAs. With so many MFN tariffs already at zero, and the bilateral tariff preference margin involved in any FTA thus relatively meaningless, why would trading partners go through the effort of negotiating an FTA with a Group B country? On the other hand, the fact that applied MFN tariffs for these Group B countries are so low and that so many products have applied MFN tariffs that have already reached zero may be *because of* their FTAs. Put differently, if the FTAs were the "building blocks" to multilateral liberalization, it may have been something about Group B's FTAs that catalyzed the application of low applied MFN tariffs. This latter possibility is one to which the analysis returns in the section below.

The lower half of table 3.2 reveals that Group B countries, despite their much lower applied MFN tariffs and fewer preferences to offer, nevertheless are involved in many FTAs. They grant tariff preferences for products for which it is possible to grant such preferences. They are also much more heterogeneous than the Group A countries in their offerings of bilateral tariff preferences, both toward other Group B countries and toward Group A countries.

Chile is at one extreme: with applied MFN tariffs that are greater than zero for 99.8 percent of its imported products, it has many products for which it could offer tariff preferences. Furthermore, Chile offers near universal coverage of bilateral tariff preferences to nine Group B countries and all seven Group A countries. Countries like Colombia, Mexico, and Peru are like Chile—although they have fewer products over which they can offer preferences, they tend to provide relatively comprehensive offerings of preferential tariffs to a wide range of LAC countries in both Group B and Group A.

Haiti is at the other extreme in Group B. Haiti offers zero preferences to all countries in Group B and Group A, even though 55.7 percent of its products have applied MFN tariffs that are greater than zero. However, this might be a case where there is a strong revenue motive to charge import duties if raising public revenues from other sources is costly or otherwise difficult to enforce. In addition, Haiti is a relatively small economy with a population of about 10 million people, of which only about 33 percent are of working age.

The Central American countries are between the two limiting cases. They are not as extreme as Haiti, because they do offer preferences to other Group B countries, especially other countries in Central America (through CAFTA-DR), but they are less likely to offer significant preferences to Group A countries.[8] A number of the Central American countries offer some significant preferences to other, non-CAFTA-DR countries in Group B—for example, Costa Rica offers preferences to Panama and Peru; the Dominican Republic offers preferences to Haiti; El Salvador, Guatemala, and Honduras offer preferences to Colombia and Panama; and Nicaragua offers preferences to Panama.

The main distinction between the Group B countries and the Group A countries is their willingness to extend tariff preferences to major economies outside of LAC. As the last three columns of table 3.2 document, with the exception of Haiti, all of the Group B countries offer significant tariff preferences to the United States and the European Union through FTAs (see box 3.1).[9]

## BOX 3.1    LAC's major extraregional free trade agreements

Beginning with the implementation of the North American Free Trade Agreement (NAFTA) between Mexico, Canada, and the United States in 1994, LAC has proceeded with fits and starts to sign and implement FTAs with major economies outside of the region. Table B3.1.1 lists the various FTAs that LAC countries have signed and implemented with the European Union, Japan, and the United States, as of the time of writing. Although not shown, Chile, Costa Rica, and Peru have also negotiated FTAs with China.

**TABLE B3.1.1    Selected major free trade agreements between LAC and non-LAC countries**

| LAC country | Non-LAC economy | Free trade agreement | In force |
|---|---|---|---|
| Mexico | United States[a] | North American Free Trade Agreement | 1994 |
| | EU | EU-Mexico Economic Partnership Agreement | 2000 |
| | Japan | Mexico–Japan Economic Partnership Agreement | 2005 |
| Chile | EU | Chile–European Union Free Trade Agreement | 2003 |
| | United States | United States–Chile Free Trade Agreement | 2004 |
| | Japan | Chile-Japan Free Trade Agreement | 2007 |
| El Salvador | United States | CAFTA-DR | 2006 |
| | EU | Central America–European Union Association Agreement | 2012 |
| Guatemala | United States | CAFTA-DR | 2006 |
| | EU | Central America–European Union Association Agreement | 2012 |
| Honduras | United States | CAFTA-DR | 2006 |
| | EU | Central America–European Union Association Agreement | 2012 |
| Nicaragua | United States | CAFTA-DR | 2006 |
| | EU | EU | 2012 |
| Dominican Republic | United States | CAFTA-DR | 2007 |
| | EU | EU Economic Partnership Agreement with CARIFORUM States | 2008[b] |
| Costa Rica | United States | CAFTA-DR | 2009 |
| | EU | Central America–European Union Association Agreement | 2012 |
| Peru | United States | United States–Peru Free Trade Agreement | 2009 |
| | Japan | Peru-Japan Economic Partnership Agreement | 2012 |
| | EU | Trade Agreement between the European Union and Colombia and Peru | 2013[b] |
| Colombia | United States | United States–Colombia Trade Promotion Agreement | 2012 |
| | EU | Trade Agreement between the European Union and Colombia and Peru | 2013[b] |
| Panama | United States | US-Panama Free Trade Agreement | 2012 |
| | EU | Central America–European Union Association Agreement | 2012 |

*Source:* Compiled from SICE 2016.
*Note:* CAFTA-DR = Dominican Republic–Central America Free Trade Agreement; EU = European Union; LAC = Latin America and the Caribbean.
a. NAFTA also includes Canada.
b. Provisionally applied, according also to data from European Union website on free trade agreements (FTAs).

Furthermore, Chile, Mexico, and Peru have gone even further as they also signed and have begun implementation of FTAs with Japan and, as of the time of writing this report, were also in the process of forming deeper trade ties with the United States and Japan through the Trans-Pacific Partnership (TPP) negotiations (see box 3.2).

---

**BOX 3.2    LAC and the Trans-Pacific Partnership**

The Trans-Pacific Partnership (TPP) is a megaregional trade agreement signed on February 4, 2016, in Auckland, New Zealand, by 12 economies that circle the Pacific Rim. Three of the 12 countries are from LAC—Chile, Mexico, and Peru—and the other nine TPP members include the Australia, Brunei, Canada, Japan, Malaysia, New Zealand, Singapore, the United States, and Vietnam. Overall, the countries involved in the agreement account for nearly 40 percent of world GDP and nearly 25 percent of world exports. As of the time of writing, the signed agreement had not yet been legally implemented by all member countries and thus had not entered into force.

Many of the countries involved in the TPP already have FTAs with one another and have reduced applied tariffs bilaterally to zero on nearly all products—for example, Chile, Mexico, and Peru already have FTAs with Canada, Japan, and the United States. With the exception of a few products in certain countries, the TPP would eventually lead to zero import tariffs on internal trade between its members.

The TPP's main innovations entail new rules. The agreement is an attempt to coordinate, rationalize, and sometimes harmonize the establishment of standards and different "behind-the-border" policies. The objective is to reduce the scope of such measures to create significant nontariff barriers to trade.

The agreement contains some updating to rules found in earlier FTAs. Sometimes the update arises as a modification to the rules constraining permissible forms of behavior by TPP countries relative to the rules of earlier FTAs. In other instances, the update takes "soft law" provisions found in earlier FTAs and makes them enforceable under the TPP, so that countries are permitted to bring a trade dispute to the agreement's formal dispute settlement provisions that could result in trade sanctions for failures to comply. Examples of TPP rules that would become subject to TPP dispute settlement include government procurement, electronic commerce,

state-owned enterprises (SOEs), labor, environment, and transparency and anticorruption.

The agreement also contains some completely new rules not found in prior FTAs. However, these newest TPP rules are in the form of soft law and are themselves so new that violations would not yet be enforceable through TPP dispute settlement. Examples include rules on temporary entry for businesspersons, small and medium-sized enterprises (SMEs), competition policy, and regulatory coherence. Regulatory coherence involves a first attempt to facilitate transparency and sharing of best practices amongst domestic regulators across countries as they conduct cost-benefit analyses and regulatory impact assessments to justify and structure new policies on product standards applying to public (animal, plant, or human) health, consumer protection, worker standards, or environmental standards.

For the three LAC countries involved—because each of them already has FTAs with the other major economies of the TPP—there are likely to be only relatively small gains arising through the standard economic channel of tariff cuts.[a] Through this channel, there are also thus only relatively small negative effects facing all of the LAC countries excluded from the newfound tariff preferences inherent in the TPP. There would likely be some tariff preference erosion as TPP countries Malaysia and Vietnam receive new tariff preferences into the U.S. market in products like apparel and electronics. However, this may take some time to develop because the TPP's relatively restrictive rules of origin—and the yarn-forward rule in particular—imply that TPP members' supply chains will need to alter their input sourcing strategies so as to take advantage of many of the new tariff preferences. (See discussion of rules of origins further below.)

The economic models that seek to predict and quantify the potential impact of TPP suggest that the largest potential economic effects of the agreement may arise through its reductions of nontariff

*(continued)*

## BOX 3.2 LAC and the Trans-Pacific Partnership *(continued)*

barriers. It is possible that the gains from the TPP could be sizable if the agreement is successful at inducing more economic efficiency through international cooperation over standards. Indeed, a number of models predict that the main impact of a TPP-induced reduction of nontariff barriers on third country nonmembers will be positive. This arises from the assumption that TPP countries' currently applied nontariff barriers reduce imports from TPP members and nonmembers alike, and, when they are reduced under the TPP, they will be reduced in relation to imports from all countries of the world. This is quite different from the case of bilateral (preferential) reductions of applied tariffs.[b]

However, the size of the gains arising from reductions of nontariff barriers should be interpreted with some caution because data on nontariff barriers to trade are sparse, such barriers are difficult to measure even where data are available, and the trade liberalization associated with new rules governing them are hard to predict. Analysts suggest a wide range of estimates as to how large nontariff barriers are in the first place and how much they can possibly be reduced through trade agreements like TPP.

Finally, for all of the nonmembers of the agreement, a critical long-run aspect of the TPP may be that its final chapter includes provisions for accession. For LAC countries interested in additional international cooperation beyond the WTO and their preexisting regional agreements, TPP accession is a potential path that would allow for additional tariff liberalization compared to a relatively large group of partners, many of which the Group A countries do not yet have trade agreements with. However, acceding countries most likely will also need to adopt a number of these new behind-the-border provisions affecting nontariff barriers to trade. But, before TPP can be expanded, it has to be implemented by the current signatories. At the time of writing, the future of TPP remained murky.

a. Examples of computable general equilibrium (CGE) or quantitative modeling exercises illustrating some of the predictions of the TPP on trade flows and economic welfare include Petri and Plummer (2016), PIIE (2016), World Bank (2016), Cerdeiro (2016), and USITC (2016). Schott and Cimino-Isaacs (2016) present an in-depth (and largely qualitative) analysis interpreting many of the new legal provisions found in the TPP agreement from an economic perspective.
b. That is, these models assume that liberalization of nontariff barriers will be different from tariffs in that they will take place on a nondiscriminatory (MFN) basis, thus positively creating market access for TPP outsiders as well.

## Implications: LAC's tariff preferences, intraregional trade, and the challenges ahead

Overall, the Group A countries' trade policies tend to be more insular than those of the Group B countries. Because the Group A countries have more products for which it is possible to give tariff preferences and higher applied MFN tariffs, they have many more products with tariff preference margins that are potentially more economically meaningful. As Viner (1950) first noted when defining the economic inefficiency concept of trade diversion, large tariff preference margins are likely to induce switching from efficient foreign producers in one trading partner to inefficient foreign producers in another trading partner. The implication being that the economy that offers the preferences will lose the tariff revenues but will not benefit from a substantial reduction of imported-goods prices.

The Group A countries' policies are insular in that they tend to have relatively comprehensive preferential trade agreements with each other. They only rarely extend tariff preferences to other (Group B) countries in LAC, and they do not extend them at all to the major economies outside of LAC.

On the other hand, the Group B countries have fewer products over which to offer tariff preferences. Furthermore, when they do offer tariff preferences, their tariff preference margins tend to be smaller because their applied MFN tariffs are relatively low. Combining this with the fact that the Group B countries also have FTAs with countries beyond LAC—including the United States, the European Union, and increasingly Japan—there is also less potential scope for Group B countries to have trade diversion arising toward inefficient foreign suppliers within LAC.

In putting these phenomena together, it appears as if neither Group A nor Group B countries have constructed their applied tariff policies in a manner that would tend to push back against the natural tendency (because of geography, as well as attributes common to countries across the region) to trade excessively within the region. If anything, the Group A countries have applied tariff policies that even tend to exacerbate the incentives for intraregional trade; they have relatively high applied tariffs toward countries outside of the region, and they have very low applied tariffs toward only selected countries within the region. In contrast, the Group B countries have policies that tend to be more neutral in their overall application. Their relatively low applied MFN tariffs present less potential for distortions to arise in the first place because of any selectivity of FTAs; furthermore, the increasingly *extraregional* spread of their FTAs beyond LAC serves to level the tariff playing field between exporters in LAC and exporters outside of the region that are seeking to trade with LAC countries.

Finally, these patterns are consistent with explanations behind the "FTA trade elasticity puzzle" identified by Limão (forthcoming) in his most recent survey of the research literature on preferential trade agreements. That survey concludes that the increase in bilateral trade between FTA members arising after FTA implementation is extremely large relative to what would be expected by the impact of the FTA tariff cuts alone. Possible explanations include that FTAs increase the trade elasticity with respect to tariffs and/or they reduce *relative* trade costs (for members relative to nonmembers) through channels well beyond tariffs. Especially across the Group A countries in LAC, there has been a substantial amount of selective regional integration taking place to the detriment of integration with the rest of the world. The Group A countries continue to apply high MFN tariffs to imports from the rest of the world—and they are very high relative to the tariffs applied bilaterally to other Group A countries—and this contributes to large flows of intraregional trade, some of which may be imports diverted away from more efficient, but nonpreferential, foreign suppliers from outside of the region. This said, below we explore the possibility that such high preferences might be efficient in the same sense that industrial policies could be efficient if they help an economy move toward a pattern of specialization that somehow allows an economy to exploit dynamic gains that are not permitted by market signals.

## How did LAC's trade policy arrive at this point?

The analysis of the MFN and preferential tariff information in the previous two sections lends support to the idea that there really exist two categories in the contemporary landscape of LAC trade policy. The first group has relatively high external MFN tariffs and involvement in FTAs that offer deep tariff preferences but that limit these tariff preferences in potentially worrisome (economic trade diversion) ways to other LAC countries. The second group of countries has relatively lower applied MFN tariffs; furthermore, even the level of the MFN tariff is overstated, given that these countries not only have FTAs with LAC countries but also have implemented FTAs with at least one (if not more) major non-LAC economy.

This section turns to recent economic research to address the question of how LAC arrived at this pattern of tariff policies. It uses two complementary approaches to provide contributing inputs to address this question. First, it revisits the question of whether LAC's FTAs are "building blocks" or "stumbling blocks" to external (applied MFN) tariff liberalization facing countries outside of the region. Second, it addresses whether the pattern of LAC's granting of tariff preferences is related to its participation in GVCs.

## LAC's FTAs over the longer run: Building blocks or stumbling blocks?

In a seminal study examining the intertemporal relationship between preferential and MFN tariffs in LAC over the 1990–2001 period, Estevadeordal, Freund, and Ornelas (2008) found economically and statistically significant evidence of a "building block" relationship for LAC countries involved in FTAs. That is, as the LAC countries cut tariffs bilaterally under FTAs, they tended to follow those bilateral tariff cuts with applied MFN tariff cuts toward the rest of the world. It is important to note both the sources of these underlying results as well as their limitations.

First, the building block results for LAC during 1990–2001 were found for the countries that adopted FTAs during that period. However, the FTAs that LAC adopted during the 1990s were mostly limited to other LAC countries. The only exception was Mexico's North American Free Trade Agreement (NAFTA) participation with Canada and the United States. Second, Estevadeordal, Freund, and Ornelas (2008) also found no evidence of any building block effect of preferential tariff liberalization for the countries that became involved in *customs unions* during the period.

What has happened to these countries' applied MFN tariffs since 2001? Figure 3.5 presents suggestive evidence of a potentially new type of building block effect arising in the 2000s for the Group B countries, and no effect for the Group A countries.

Consider first the Group B countries illustrated in figure 3.5. The figure plots three different pieces of information for each Group B country: (i) the average applied MFN tariff in 1995, (ii) the average applied MFN tariff for the country five years prior to its FTA with the United States going into force, and (iii) the average applied MFN tariff in 2014.[10] Recall that, in the 1990s, the evidence from Estevadeordal, Freund, and Ornelas (2008) for many of these countries was that they implemented FTAs with other LAC countries and these FTAs served as building blocks to external, applied MFN tariff liberalization. With the exception of Chile, each of the countries' first major extraregional FTA was with the United States. With the exception of Mexico, each of the countries' first major extraregional FTAs did not arise until well after 2001.

FIGURE 3.5 **Average applied MFN tariffs: In 1995, five years prior to U.S. FTA, and in 2014**

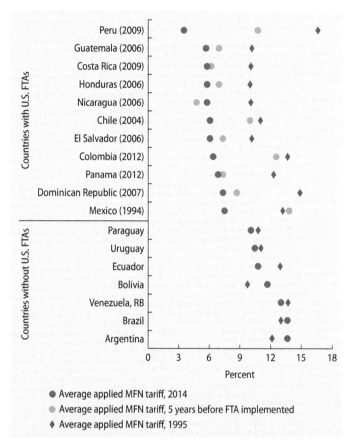

● Average applied MFN tariff, 2014
◐ Average applied MFN tariff, 5 years before FTA implemented
◆ Average applied MFN tariff, 1995

*Source:* World Bank construction, based on data from World Trade Organization and World Development Indicators.
*Note:* Mexico's 1989 data replaced with 1991, Panama's and Dominican Republic's 1995 data replaced with 1997. In parentheses are the year the country implemented the free trade agreement (FTA) with the United States. Countries in each group ranked from low to high according to average applied MFN tariff in 2014.

Figure 3.5 illustrates that applied MFN tariffs for many of the Group B countries declined substantially between 1995 and 2014. Across the 11 countries, the mean (median) average applied MFN tariff reduction was 5.0 (6.0) percentage points. Furthermore, tariffs for almost every Group B country continued to fall after it formed an FTA with the United States. The mean (median) average applied MFN tariff reduction that took place during the period between the FTA and 2014 was 2.6 (1.2) percentage points. This is at least broadly consistent with the Group B's extraregional FTAs serving as an additional building block to their reaching the relatively low applied MFN tariffs in effect as of 2014.[11]

Next consider the Group A countries illustrated in figure 3.5. Again, these countries have not signed or implemented an FTA with the United States. For most of these countries, their average applied MFN tariffs are virtually unchanged over this twenty-year period: the mean tariff change across countries is zero. For Ecuador, average applied tariffs went down slightly with its WTO accession process, but for other countries, such as Argentina and Bolivia, average applied MFN tariffs were actually higher in 2014 than they were in 1995.

What else may explain the lack of a continued building block effect for the countries in Group A in the period since 2001, aside from not forming extraregional FTAs with the United States or other countries outside of LAC? In follow-up work to the Estevadeordal, Freund, and Ornelas (2008) study, Bown and Tovar (forthcoming) reexamine the evidence for Argentina and Brazil over 1990–2001 and provide an additional potential contributing explanation. In particular, they develop more comprehensive measures of these countries' import policy beyond applied tariffs by also including application of these countries' temporary trade barrier (TTB) policies of antidumping and safeguards.[12] They find that the customs union period for Argentina and Brazil exhibited evidence of a "stumbling block" effect in which any internal liberalization was actually accompanied by an offsetting increase in external trade barriers toward the rest of the world. Even for the period in which Mercosur was a free trade area, inclusion of the TTB policies in the estimation for Argentina and Brazil makes any potential building block–effect evidence for these two countries disappear.

Some of the Bown-Tovar evidence can be understood through a simple examination of how Argentina and Brazil applied their import-restricting TTBs during the 1990–2001 period. First, Argentina and Brazil did not coordinate their use of TTBs against third countries, even during the customs union period of 1995–2001. In other words, each country applied its own new import restrictions through TTB policies independently against different trading partners and over different imported products. This lack of policy coordination, of course, calls into question the extent to which the two countries really have been engaged in a common external trade policy beginning in their customs union period.[13] Second, and perhaps even more surprising, Argentina imposed a number of new antidumping restrictions against imports from Brazil over 1990–2001. These new internal border barriers, of course, call into question the extent to which these two economies even have a free trade area. The failure to fully complete an internal free trade area may help explain why Mercosur failed to trigger the same sort of building block effect of subsequent external tariff liberalization that arose for the Group B countries in LAC, including after 2001.

## Are LAC's tariff preference offerings affected by its role in global supply chains?

A second potential explanation for the continuation of the regional "bias" in LAC's tariff preferences could be related to its participation in international supply chains. In a recent study of 14 high-income and emerging economies over the period 1995–2009, for example, Blanchard, Bown, and Johnson (2016) find that importing countries tend to offer greater tariff preferences to trading partners whose exports embody more of the importing country's own domestic value added (DVA).[14] Thus, one explanation of why some LAC countries may be limiting their tariff preference offerings to regional partners is because their supply chain links are only regional. In fact, previous research reported in de la Torre et al. (2015) highlighted the fact that South America has never obtained significant contribution to GVCs related to the automobile, apparel-textile, and electronics industries. As of 2012, South America contributed less to these GVCs than did almost all other subregions, surpassing only Sub-Saharan Africa's contribution. In contrast, Central America, the Caribbean, and Mexico were important contributors to global trade in these industries, falling behind only Eastern Europe and East Asia (see de la Torre et al. 2015, figure O.16, p. 19). Annex 3A provides additional comparative snapshots of LAC's patterns of participation in GVCs, evidence that further supports the contention that GVC participation is low in South America, and that for LAC as a whole North America remains, by far, the largest destination of LAC exports and the largest source of imports related to these three GVCs.

To explore the relationship between trade in GVCs and commercial policies in LAC, at least informally, consider first the predictions of the trade policy decision for a country like Brazil that would arise within the Blanchard-Bown-Johnson framework. Their model and

empirical results suggests that one reason why Brazil is more likely to offer a tariff preference to Mexico—relative to offering a tariff preference to the United States—is because the final goods that Mexico produces contain more intermediate inputs (for example, parts and components) produced and exported from Brazil than do the final goods that the United States produces. In such an example, Brazil offers Mexico a lower tariff than it offers the United States because this tariff preference stimulates bilateral imports from Mexico, and some of the benefits of those stimulated imports of final goods are passed back to Brazil's suppliers of intermediate inputs through international supply chains.

Figure 3.6 presents suggestive evidence from 2004 data for 15 LAC countries of this

**FIGURE 3.6    LAC's domestic value added as a share of foreign production across regions**

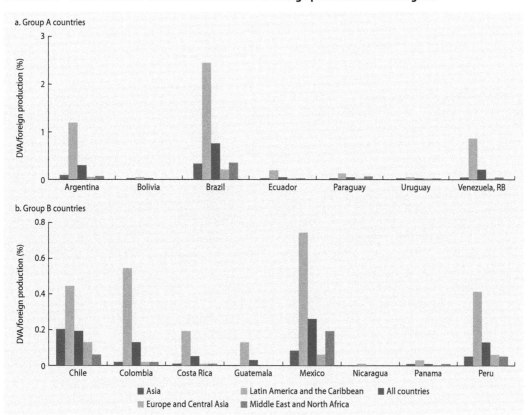

*Source:* World Bank construction, from GTAP data in 2004.
*Note:* Fifteen Latin American countries' domestic value added (DVA) as a share of foreign production (reported as percent) for countries in that region, averaged across 14 manufacturing sectors. For example, Brazil's DVA as a share of the value of production across countries in LAC is 2.4 percent. See annex 1A for a list of countries in each region.

as a potential contributing explanation.[15] To interpret the figure, consider the data for Brazil. Brazil's DVA—for example, Brazilian-produced parts and component inputs—as a share of the value of another country's local production averages to 2.4 percent for the production of LAC countries. On the other hand, Brazil's DVA as a share of local production across all countries of the world is only 0.75 percent. Thus Brazil's DVA share of local production is 3.3 times higher for countries in LAC than it is for all countries.

This pattern is consistent for each LAC country. Each of the 15 LAC countries shown in figure 3.6 has much more of its DVA embedded in other LAC countries' local production than in the production of countries in the rest of the world. Without making too much of it, there is also suggestive evidence that the difference between a country's DVA embodied in other LAC countries' production and that embodied in production in the rest of the world is on average slightly larger for the Group A countries than for those in Group B.[16] And, as has been observed earlier, many of the Group B countries subsequently went off to sign and implement new extraregional FTAs after 2004 that the Group A countries have not: the Group A countries have tended to rely only on deep intra-LAC preferences.

Of course, becoming more involved in global supply chains also means that LAC countries may need to import more parts and components from outside of LAC. This would similarly allow non-LAC countries to have more of their DVA embodied in LAC exports, and thus have an incentive to offer their own lower tariffs to LAC countries as well, perhaps through FTAs.

Figure 3.7 highlights one potential specific policy action that a number of LAC countries could take to improve their global competitiveness, namely, lowering their import tariffs on intermediate inputs. The figure illustrates each country's average applied tariff in 2014 by sector, where products in each sector are split on the basis of whether they are intermediate inputs or final goods. The figure illustrates the tariffs for four Group A countries

(Bolivia, Brazil, Ecuador, and República Bolivariana de Venezuela) and for three Group B countries (Chile, Mexico, and Peru).

The first noteworthy point from figure 3.7 is that there is evidence of tariff escalation—defined as the difference between the tariffs applied on final goods and the tariffs applied on intermediate inputs—across all countries in LAC, with the exception of Chile (which has uniform tariffs of 6 percent). However, the second and more striking point to note is that there is evidence that much more tariff escalation is taking place in the Group B countries. Whereas Group B countries have lower average applied MFN tariffs on imported *final* goods than the Group A countries, nevertheless they have *significantly lower* average applied MFN tariffs on imported intermediate inputs. The clear implication is that one way for the Group A countries to become more globally competitive and to further involve themselves in extraregional supply chains would be to focus on cutting their applied MFN tariffs on imported intermediate inputs.

## The challenge of rules of origin and the regional "spaghetti bowl" effect

FTAs are an integral part of today's global trade architecture. Moreover, their presence has been on the rise, especially in recent decades. In the early 1980s, the average country in the world granted tariff preferences to approximately 6 partners. In the early 2000s that number doubled, and by 2011 it had reached 28 countries. LAC countries are no exception to this pattern. In the early 1980s, the average LAC country granted preferences to about 6 countries; by 2010 that number had increased to 23.

Although FTAs are an important factor behind the decrease in applied tariffs observed around the world and, as a result, foster trade, their proliferation has brought upon the so-called spaghetti bowl effect. The spaghetti bowl effect refers to the complication that arises from the application of rules to determine the national source of a product and whether imported products receive MFN

**FIGURE 3.7    LAC's imported products with available and granted bilateral tariff preferences, 2014**

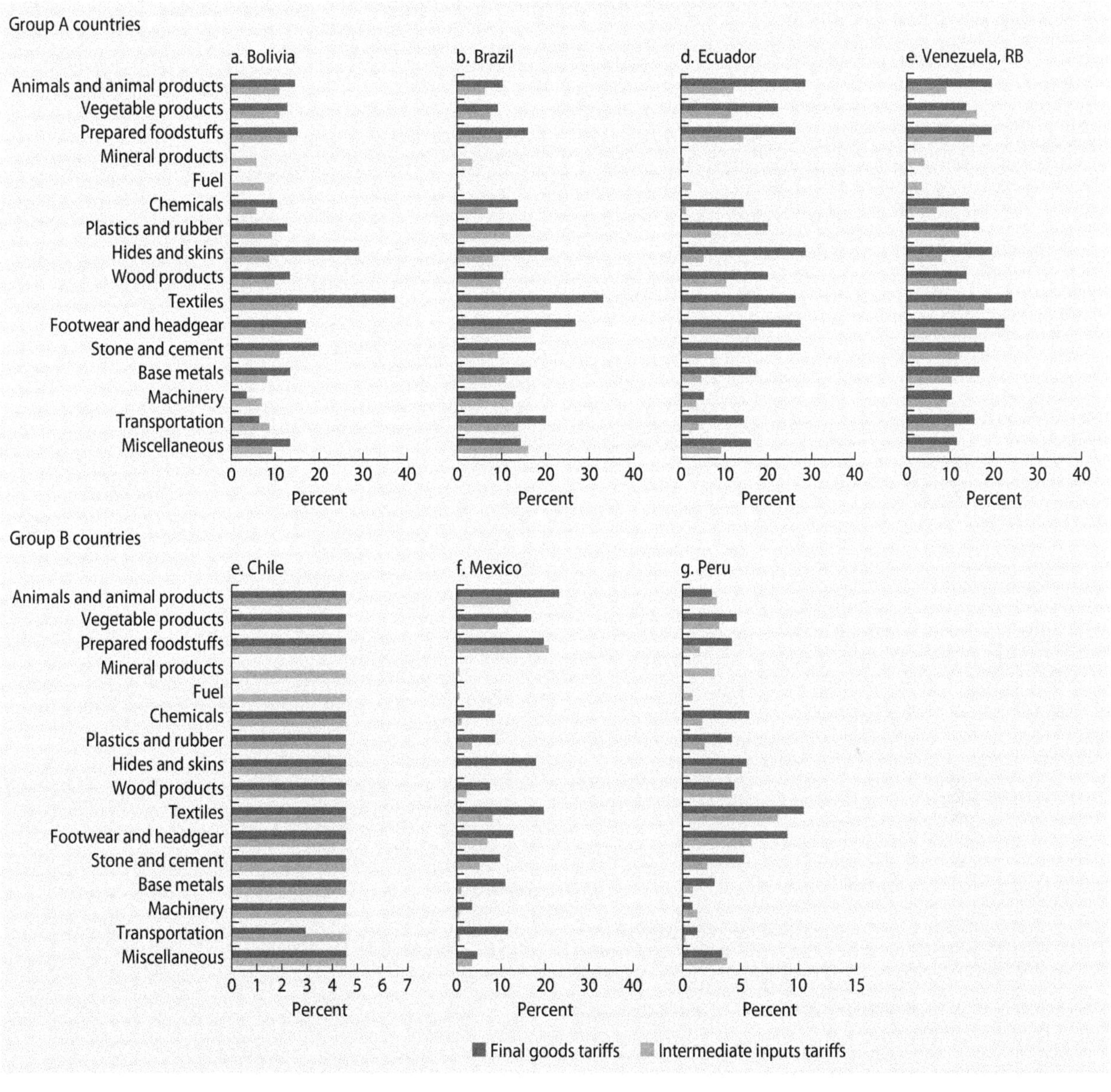

Source: World Bank construction, from applied MFN tariff data at the HS-06 level from the International Trade Centre.
Note: End-use categories for each HS06 product taken from the BEC, with mixed use goods dropped. See annex 3A, table 3A.1, for industry acronyms. Brazil, Bolivia, Ecuador, and República Bolivariana de Venezuela are examples of Group A countries; Chile, Mexico, and Peru are examples of Group B countries.

treatment or preferential treatment. These rules, known as rules of origin (RoOs), are explicitly designed to build a commercial policy fence around goods that are produced within the countries that constitute an FTA. Box 3.3 provides an analytical discussion of how RoOs are de facto trade barriers imposed by all of an FTA's signatories.

Furthermore, RoOs can impose hefty administrative and compliance costs on exporting firms, costs that are aggravated by the fact that each FTA establishes its own RoOs. Some take the form of minimum value-added content from the country in the FTA, some rely on identifying the country of manufacturing and processing, and some

## BOX 3.3    Rules of origin and export protection for FTA partners: The basic analytical framework

The text presented here aims to clarify how rules of origin (RoOs) can act as a protectionist device whereby the structure of production of one of the FTA partners determines the profitability of exporting firms.

Consider a Mexican firm deciding whether to export apparel products to the United States under the NAFTA preferences. Its expected profits can be formally written as follows:

$$\pi_A^{Mex} = P_A^{US} - P_T^{US}\alpha q - P_T^{W}(1-\alpha)q, \qquad \text{(B3.3.1)}$$

where $\pi$ represents the expected profits for this firm. If the firm sells the product in the U.S. market, it will receive revenues per unit of apparel equal to the U.S. price $(P_A^{US})$ for that article. On the cost side, the firm will have to pay the U.S. price for the necessary textile inputs. This cost has three components: (i) the unit price of textiles in the United States $(P_T^{US})$ if the firm decides to use U.S. components (which is likely because of the low-cost textile source within NAFTA); (ii) the resulting unit cost, which is the product of this price times the cost share of U.S. textile inputs $(\alpha)$ times the textile cost share relative to the value of apparel that is determined by the production technology $(q)$; and (iii) minus the cost of using textile inputs from other sources that might be cheaper than U.S. parts $(P_T^{W}(1-\alpha)q)$.

The relevant U.S. prices, world prices, and the technological parameter can be defined as follows:

$$P_A^{US} = (1+t_A^{US})P_A^{W}$$
$$P_T^{US} = (1+t_T^{US})P_T^{W} \qquad \text{(B3.3.2)}$$
$$q < 1$$

where $t_A^{US}$ is the ad valorem U.S. import tariff (equivalent) on apparel and $t_A^{US}$ is the corresponding U.S. tax on textile imports. To simplify, let world prices of apparel and textile inputs be equal to unity:

$$P_T^{W} = P_A^{W} = 1 \qquad \text{(B3.3.3)}$$

Then,

$$\pi_A^{Mex} = (1+t_A^{US}) - q[\alpha(1+t_T^{US}) + (1-\alpha)] \qquad \text{(B3.3.4)}$$

The RoOs determine $\alpha$, which is the share of textile inputs that must come from regional sources in order for the export of apparel to be eligible for NAFTA preferential treatment. In the specific case of textile and apparel products, the NAFTA RoOs

imply $\alpha = 1$ because of the yarn-forward rule, which says that apparel must be made from yarn originating in NAFTA countries. Thus, the profits for Mexican firms wishing to penetrate the U.S. market under the NAFTA preferences can be rewritten as follows:

$$\pi_A^{Mex} = (1+t_A^{US}) - q(1+t_T^{US}) \qquad \text{(B3.3.5)}$$

This formula shows that for exports under NAFTA preferences, Mexican firms' profits will be determined exclusively by U.S. tariffs on apparel and textiles and the technological parameter, which we can safely assume is constant in this case because it is unlikely that technological change in the apparel industry can reduce the amount of cloth used per unit of apparel. The fact that Mexican apparel profits are determined by U.S. tariff structure is the key result from Krueger (1993).

Alternatively, firms can choose not to use the NAFTA preferences. In this case, firms face the following profit condition:

$$\pi_A^{Mex} = 1 - q(1+t_T^{Mex}) \qquad \text{(B3.3.6)}$$

That is, the firm that decides not to use the NAFTA preferences for apparel exports will receive the world price minus the costs of textile inputs, which in this case depend solely on Mexico's textile import tariffs (and implicitly on the world price of textiles, which we have set equal to 1). Hence the decision to actually use the NAFTA preferences will depend on whether profits from using the preferences as defined in equation (B3.3.5) are greater than or at least equal to the profits from not relying on the preferences as defined in equation (B3.3.6). Thus, it is easy to show that the apparel preferential margin, which equals the U.S. tariff when all intra-NAFTA trade enters duty free, needs to be greater than or equal to the product of the textile cost share in production times the difference between the U.S. and Mexican textile tariffs:

$$t_A^{US} > q(t_T^{US} - t_T^{Mex}) \qquad \text{(B3.3.7)}$$

The analysis presented in the main text of this chapter discusses possible explanations for why the use of the NAFTA preferences in apparel exports from Mexico to the United States is relatively low, given that the extent of the preferential treatment under NAFTA has been quite high. The framework presented here indicates that there are three key parameters, which are those in equation (B3.3.7).

*Source:* Lederman, Maloney, and Servén 2005, 121–23, based on the framework proposed by Krueger 1993.

apply the tariff shift rule (Estevadeordal and Talvi 2016). As a result, the increasing number of FTAs, and the complex network of RoOs that arises from that increase, can accentuate the uncertainty faced by firms seeking to invest in foreign countries and can deter foreign direct investment (FDI) into a country. This kind of uncertainty is more prominent for firms that are involved in GVCs because their inputs will travel through a number of FTAs and will be subject to multiple tariff structures.

Hence, one prominent challenge for trade policy going forward will be to harmonize RoOs as a way to mitigate the adverse effects of the spaghetti bowl effect. For example, Estevadeordal and Talvi (2016) propose a Trans-American Partnership that allows for full accumulation of RoOs within the Americas. This, in turn, would help LAC attain higher dividends from its existing FTAs, by allowing firms to use materials from other countries without deterring preferential access. While this kind of proposal may face political pushback, its potential region-wide economic payoffs should not be ignored.

## The role of regional trade preferences as industrial policy

As discussed in chapter 2, one of the presumed benefits of trade integration is that it can foster efficiency gains and higher growth. Some of these efficiency and pro-growth effects operate through imports. For example, imports can facilitate knowledge diffusion and give local producers access to high-quality inputs, which can enhance growth and innovation among local firms. Imports can also exert competitive pressure on local producers, which in turn can have two effects. On the one hand, it can push local producers to innovate and improve the quality of their goods. On the other hand, it may push inefficient firms out of the market and reallocate resources toward efficient firms.

These efficiency and pro-growth effects notwithstanding, some view import competition as a potential drag on a country's growth.

The argument supporting this claim is as follows. In the extreme, when all local producers of goods facing import competition are too inefficient, the effect of competition is such that it can end up wiping out local production of these goods. Moreover, if the displacement of local production occurs in sectors that are more amenable to growth relative to those where the country has a comparative advantage, and toward which factors of production are reallocated, then import competition can end up hurting growth.[17] This idea lies at the heart of arguments in favor of protecting certain strategic industries, especially in the manufacturing sector, through industrial policies such as the import substitution (IS) strategies, which were widespread in LAC until the late 1980s.

Yet, even for advocates of industrial policies such as IS, protectionism alone cannot guarantee the development of key sectors because many of these sectors display scale economies and learning by doing. For these reasons, some regard regional integration as a means of achieving scale economies at the regional level behind protection from competition from extraregional partners. As economies prevent competition from high-quality imports and integrate with countries of similar levels of development, their local producers can become more competitive through learning by doing and by attaining a more efficient scale of production.[18] This process yields more efficient local producers who, in the medium term, should grow and become enabled to cope with foreign competition.

The above discussion raises a number of questions. Is there evidence of an adverse effect of import competition on growth in developing countries? Are countries pursuing commercial policies targeted toward specific strategic sectors? Are countries leveraging regional integration to gain competitiveness in strategic sectors? If they are doing so, is this translating into quality improvements and competitiveness in developing countries? The rest of this section tackles these questions.

The potentially heterogeneous effects of import competition on firm growth are highlighted in the work of Aghion et al. (2005)

and Acemoglu, Aghion, and Zilibotti (2006). In particular, these authors highlight that the effect of competition on growth may depend on initial levels of competition in the local economy and its initial level of development. Import competition may harm growth in countries that have too much competition to begin with or that are too far from the technological frontier. In these cases, limiting import competition may be the optimal policy from the point of view of growth. Amiti and Khandelwal (2013) dig deeper into the link between growth, competition, and initial level of development by studying the process of quality upgrading of Indian exports. The authors find that low import tariffs foster quality upgrades only in sectors where the initial quality was already high.

The findings of Amiti and Khandelwal (2013) can be expanded by exploring the link between the quality of imports and export quality growth in a global sample. This is precisely the exercise pursued in table 3.3, which reports regression results of the yearly (log) difference of the quality of exports of country $i$ in product $j$ on the (weighted) average quality of imports in $t–1$, the log level of export quality in $t–1$, and country-time and

product-time fixed effects. Because the exercise studies the effect of import quality in a given product on the growth of the quality of exports of the same product, one can interpret higher quality of imports as harsher import competition. The results in column (1) of table 3.3 show that, on average, countries that import higher-quality varieties of product $j$ experience a more rapid process of quality upgrading in that product. At the same time, the results show convergence; countries that have lower initial levels of quality experience faster growth of quality.[19] Column (2) explores whether the effect of the quality of imports on export quality growth varies with the initial quality of exports. The results found are in line with the findings of Amiti and Khandelwal (2013); countries with higher initial levels of export quality benefit more from the quality of imports (interpreted as harsher import competition).[20]

The results in table 3.3 suggest that the protection of certain industries may foster quality upgrades in LAC exports. But is there evidence that countries in the region are leveraging regional preferential agreements to achieve this goal? One attempt to answer this question is found in Moncarz,

**TABLE 3.3   Quality upgrade and import quality**

| Dependent variable | Log difference of export quality | | | |
|---|---|---|---|---|
| | (1) | (2) | (3) | (4) |
| Trade-weighted (log) quality of imports | 0.0450*** | 0.0727*** | 0.0657*** | 0.130*** |
| | (0.00227) | (0.00314) | (0.00186) | (0.00256) |
| Log initial quality | −0.234*** | −0.220*** | −0.131*** | −0.104*** |
| | (0.00158) | (0.00194) | (0.00121) | (0.00142) |
| Trade-weighted (log) quality of imports x log initial quality | | 0.0526*** | | 0.143*** |
| | | (0.00411) | | (0.00391) |
| Constant | −0.113*** | −0.106*** | −0.0116*** | −0.00538*** |
| | (0.0107) | (0.0107) | (0.000338) | (0.000377) |
| Observations | 151,249 | 151,249 | 151,249 | 151,249 |
| R-squared | 0.226 | 0.227 | 0.075 | 0.083 |
| Year FE | NO | NO | YES | YES |
| Exporter-year FE | YES | YES | NO | NO |
| Product-year FE | YES | YES | NO | NO |

*Source:* World Bank calculations, based on data from UN COMTRADE and the International Monetary Fund Diversification Toolkit.
*Note:* FE = fixed effects. Columns correspond to specifications. Standard errors in parentheses. *** $p < 0.01$, ** $p < 0.05$, * $p < 0.1$.

Olarreaga, and Vaillant (2016). The authors explore the effect of regional preferences in specific sectors in Mercosur on intra-Mercosur trade in those sectors. More specifically, they construct a measure of trade intensity within Mercosur and find that in the case of Brazil it is higher in sectors that are typically produced by high-income countries and have high intra-Mercosur preferences. The authors argue that, although this could be interpreted as Mercosur's allowing Brazil to pursue industrial policy objectives, the costs of this has fallen on the shoulders of other members. Moreover, the evidence indicates that Brazil has not experienced gains in global competitiveness in these goods.

The rest of this section expands the exercise by Moncarz, Olarreaga, and Vaillant

(2016) to explore the effects of regional FTAs on the patterns of revealed comparative advantage (RCA) of member countries. As in Moncarz, Olarreaga, and Vaillant (2016), in order to have a full picture of whether regional trade agreements (RTAs) help develop infant industries that would otherwise be concentrated in high-income economies, the exercise looks beyond trade intensity within RTAs. For instance, if the hypothesis that regional protection helps countries gain competitiveness in protected sectors is valid, one would expect countries in the RTA to experience positive changes in the patterns of RCA in these sectors.

Table 3.4 explores the impact of protection through tariffs and preferences with

**TABLE 3.4    Revealed comparative advantage, tariffs, and preferences**

| | MERCOSUR | NAFTA | CAFTA | ANDINA | MERCOSUR | NAFTA | CAFTA | ANDINA |
|---|---|---|---|---|---|---|---|---|
| | (1) | (2) | (3) | (4) | (5) | (6) | (7) | (8) |
| PRODY | 0.119 | 0.115* | −0.189*** | −0.259** | −0.0738 | −0.0180 | −0.180*** | −0.343*** |
| | (0.123) | (0.0687) | (0.0614) | (0.110) | (0.124) | (0.128) | (0.0577) | (0.0992) |
| Initial RCA | −0.0997** | −0.230*** | −0.413*** | −0.206*** | −0.163*** | −0.190** | −0.373*** | −0.241*** |
| | (0.0493) | (0.0381) | (0.0267) | (0.0494) | (0.0499) | (0.0762) | (0.0253) | (0.0423) |
| Preferences | 0.0492 | 0.257* | −0.133** | −0.159** | | | | |
| | (0.0659) | (0.143) | (0.0668) | (0.0696) | | | | |
| Preferences x PRODY | −0.00640 | −0.0319* | 0.0160** | 0.0162** | | | | |
| | (0.00722) | (0.0166) | (0.00748) | (0.00773) | | | | |
| Preferences x initial RCA | −0.00781** | −0.0186** | 0.00969*** | −0.00459 | | | | |
| | (0.00315) | (0.00867) | (0.00263) | (0.00376) | | | | |
| Median applied tariffs | | | | | −0.0589 | −0.0409 | −0.0722 | −0.213*** |
| | | | | | (0.0642) | (0.0577) | (0.0548) | (0.0631) |
| Median applied tariffs x PRODY | | | | | 0.00644 | 0.00343 | 0.00805 | 0.0215*** |
| | | | | | (0.00703) | (0.00654) | (0.00615) | (0.00700) |
| Median applied tariffs x Initial RCA | | | | | −0.00351 | −0.00445 | 0.00453** | −0.00102 |
| | | | | | (0.00308) | (0.00405) | (0.00223) | (0.00322) |
| Constant | −1.213 | −1.163* | 1.058* | 1.912* | 0.420 | 0.154 | 1.055* | 2.688*** |
| | (1.136) | (0.628) | (0.577) | (1.015) | (1.140) | (1.151) | (0.538) | (0.904) |
| Observations | 1,178 | 390 | 1,602 | 1,404 | 1,178 | 390 | 1,602 | 1,404 |
| R-squared | 0.114 | 0.209 | 0.230 | 0.194 | 0.111 | 0.203 | 0.226 | 0.201 |
| Country FE | YES | YES | YES | YES | YES | YES | YES | YES |

*Source:* World Bank calculations, based on data from UN COMTRADE, World Development Indicators, International Monetary Fund Diversification Toolkit, and UN TRAINS Tariff data.

*Note:* PRODY = a variable; RCA = revealed comparative advantage. Mercosur includes Argentina, Brazil, Paraguay, and Uruguay. NAFTA includes Mexico. CAFTA includes Costa Rica, Dominican Republic, Guatemala, Honduras, Nicaragua, and El Salvador. Andean Comm. includes Bolivia, Colombia, Ecuador, Peru, and República Bolivarian de Venezuela. Preferences are calculated as the average across preferential partners of the difference between the median applied tariff by the importing country and the preferential tariff. Standard deviations in parentheses. *** p<0.01, ** p<0.05, * p<0.1.

regional partners on a country's RCA. Columns (1)–(4) examine the effect of preferences and columns (5)–(8) explore the effect of protection. The first thing to notice is that across RTAs there is evidence of convergence in RCAs: sectors that have lower initial RCA tend to experience positive changes.[21] This is consistent with Levchenko and Zhang (2016), who document that there is convergence of RCAs across countries over time. Moreover, preferences appear to facilitate convergence in Mercosur and NAFTA, evidenced by the negative interaction of initial RCA and preferences. CAFTA preferences appear to lower a bit the convergence coefficient, whereas for the Andean Community, the coefficient is not significant. Looking at the interaction of preferences and the implicit GDP per capita of the countries that export a given good intensively (the PRODY variable), the results suggest that preferences fostered RCA increases in countries in the Andean Community and CAFTA, but they did not in NAFTA or Mercosur.[22] In contrast, when looking at protection, high tariffs appear to foster RCA increases in high-PRODY goods only in the Andean community. This suggests that, if anything, protection of strategic sectors led to RCA increases only in countries of the Andean Community.

In sum, the evidence regarding the role of RTAs in LAC as a tool to achieve IP objectives is mixed. On the one hand, protection and preferences granted by some RTA partners in LAC do appear to increase export intensity in goods typically produced by high-income economies. However, there is limited evidence that preferences and protection translate into gains in global RCA.

## Conclusions

In a nutshell, the evidence presented in this chapter indicates that the LAC region is not yet at a point in which it could be said that it practices OR that would bring efficiency gains; it is clear that MFN tariffs tend to be high and, more starkly, their tariff overhangs (defined as the difference between the applied MFN tariffs and their bound tariffs with the

WTO) are relatively high even when compared to emerging economies of East Asia. To be sure, there is notable heterogeneity within LAC, with a subgroup of countries appearing to have more open trade policies toward the rest of world in the form of both FTAs and lower MFN tariffs. In addition, within the region there is a glaringly incomplete regional integration agenda that could bring the North of the region closer to South America. Some of the smallest economies, however, seem to be a bit too open with the world, given that they tend to offer tariff preferences to various countries, which might have created unnecessary fiscal pressures in economies that are so highly specialized that import tariffs are unlikely to have distortionary effects on domestic production.

Finally, the evidence in favor of using preferential tariff treatment as a form of industrial policy is tenuous at best, because there is no evidence that, if tariff preferences were to be removed after decades of being in place, any structural effects would survive the test of competition with the rest of world. This is a necessary condition for concluding that preferential tariffs that shifted trade patterns in favor of goods and sectors that are intensively exported by high-income economies were successful in allowing so-called infant industries to mature to the point that they could survive without regional protectionism. It is also noteworthy that the most protected economies under the highest preferential margins are those that are the least integrated into GVCs. More research is surely needed on these issues, but these are the most cautious plausible conclusions that can be derived from the existing evidence.

## Annex 3A. Comparative snapshots of LAC's participation in global value chains

GVCs are classically characterized by lead firms that coordinate production networks. The coordination of activities required to operate dispersed production requires governance structures, which mediate the activities of multiple firms in a network with a lead firm at the center (Milberg and Winkler 2011). Some analyses of GVCs essentially view all trade as GVC-oriented, especially those analyses that focus on tracking global flows of value added through input-output methods (Mattoo, Wang, and Wei 2013). In this view, a country that does nothing but export crude oil or metallic ores may have a high degree of GVC participation of a sort because these crude materials are eventually transformed into sophisticated goods or parts of other goods in some other country.[23] However, links with lead firms of the sort leading to technology transfer or deeper interactions with final markets may be more likely to take place when countries are engaged in the middle or later stages of the production process.

The GVCs in vehicles, electronics, apparel, footwear, and textiles are characterized by a lead-firm network structure, and have been much studied. The similarities and differences in the organization of these five GVCs are a useful entry point into an understanding of GVCs, or, as they are sometimes called, "global supply chains"[24] (USITC 2011). They have been used to analyze the response of developing-country GVC participants in the crisis of 2008–09 (Cattaneo, Gereffi, and Staritz 2010). These five sectors differ in the methods used to coordinate activity over long distances, and in the extent to which they tend to be coordinated by traditional manufacturers (autos), owners of brand names with strong research capabilities (electronics), or buyers of final products working with global middlemen (apparel, footwear, and textiles). The share of total global merchandise exports accounted for by these five GVCs has fluctuated between about 14 percent and 28 percent since 1990.[25]

This study uses a modified version of the definition of the three classic GVCs in Sturgeon and Memedovic (2011). In their approach, products are classified as belonging to one of the three GVCs—namely, apparel and footwear, electronics, and autos—based on a combination of expert opinion and their position in the United Nations Statistical Division's Broad Economic Categories (BEC), which help to distinguish between intermediate and final goods. This leads to a list of over 400 traded goods, identified in the SITC Rev. 3 classification at the four-digit or five-digit level. Each of the GVCs is then divided into two subsectors to reflect intermediate and final goods (for example, intermediate electronics and final electronics), making six GVC sectors all told. For the purposes of this analysis of LAC, the Sturgeon and Memedovic categories are modified in three ways. First, the footwear sector, both intermediate and final, is separated from apparel, making eight categories instead of six. Second, the definition of the autos sector, which originally included only passenger motor vehicles and motorcycles, is broadened so as to encompass other road vehicles (for example, trucks, buses, and trailers). Finally, a fifth category comprising final textiles is also added.

LAC is the third-most-specialized region of the world in GVC exports, even though its overall GVC export share is only about one-half of those corresponding to South Asia (SAR) and East Asia and Pacific (EAP), which are at the top this ranking (slightly above 20 percent for LAC, nearly 40 percent for SAR and EAP. LAC's overall GVC export share is based on its strength as one of the most specialized regions in both final and intermediate autos, together with Europe and Central Asia (ECA) and North America, which both have a similar GVC specialization profile, and for which overall GVC export shares are also close to 20 percent (figure 3A.1). By contrast, East Asia is specialized in electronics, and SAR in final and intermediate apparel.

As previously noted, we consider "GVC imports" to be intermediate imports only because imports of final goods tend to be destined for consumption. In comparing imports in our focus sectors, LAC exhibits a slightly larger share of imports of GVC intermediates than does East Asia, even though the composition of such GVC imports is different between the two regions, with a leading role for autos followed by electronics in LAC, and the

**FIGURE 3A.1    GVC and non-GVC exports by each region to the world, 2014**

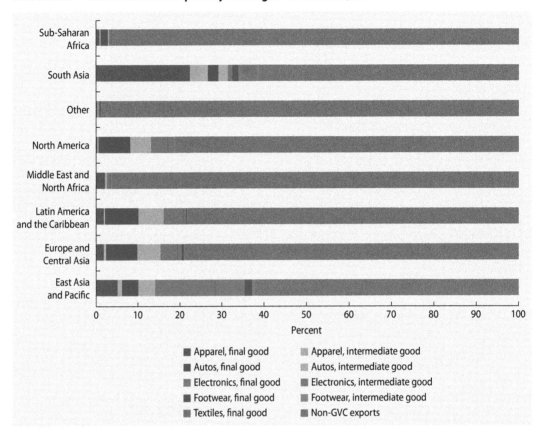

*Source:* World Bank calculations, based on UN COMTRADE and World Bank data.
*Note:* "Other" category comprises Free Zones, Neutral Zone, Special Categories, Unspecified, French Southern Territories, British territories, and U.S. Pacific Islands. See annex 1A for a list of countries in each region.

opposite for East Asia. In both regions, apparel comes third, well behind (figure 3A.2).

LAC GVC trade in intermediates is more integrated with North America than with any other region in the world, both as its main export destination and import source (figures 3A.3 and 3A.4). As an import source, North America is by a large margin LAC's main GVC partner, followed by EAP in the second position, ECA in the third, and with LAC itself coming fourth. In terms of LAC's exports of GVC intermediates, North America comes first again by a large margin, but now exports destined to within LAC are the second largest, followed far behind by ECA and EAP. Such pattern evidences not only a high integration of LAC with North America in GVC intermediates, but also a marked dependence on extraregionally sourced inputs and a relatively low capacity to compete globally in this segment. Autos and electronics are the most important GVC intermediate imports for LAC, whereas in the case of exports, autos are overwhelmingly the most important category.

The profile of LAC's integration into GVC intermediate goods' trade contrasts sharply with the picture that emerges in the case of EAP, which is heavily integrated with itself. This is especially so not only as an import source for GVC intermediates (where intraregional imports are by far predominant) but also as a destination for them, where a similar pattern is observed (figures 3A.5 and 3A.6).

**FIGURE 3A.2    GVC intermediate imports by each region of the world, 2014**

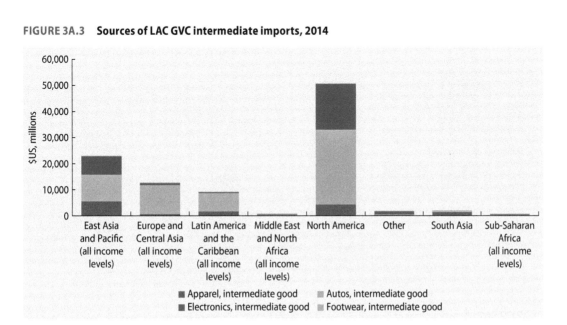

Source: World Bank calculations, based on UN COMTRADE and World Bank data.
Note: "Other" category comprises Free Zones, Neutral Zone, Special Categories, Unspecified, French Southern Territories, British territories, and U.S. Pacific Islands. See annex 1A for a list of countries in each region.

**FIGURE 3A.3    Sources of LAC GVC intermediate imports, 2014**

Source: World Bank calculations, based on UN COMTRADE and World Bank data.
Note: See annex 1A for a list of countries in each region.

FIGURE 3A.4 **Destinations for LAC GVC intermediate exports, 2014**

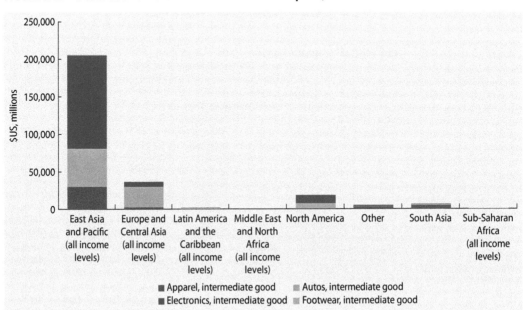

*Source:* World Bank calculations, based on UN COMTRADE and World Bank data.
*Note:* See annex 1A for a list of countries in each region.

FIGURE 3A.5 **Destination of East Asia GVC intermediate imports, 2014**

*Source:* World Bank calculations, based on UN COMTRADE and World Bank data.
*Note:* See annex 1A for a list of countries in each region.

**FIGURE 3A.6    Sources of East Asia GVC intermediate imports, 2014**

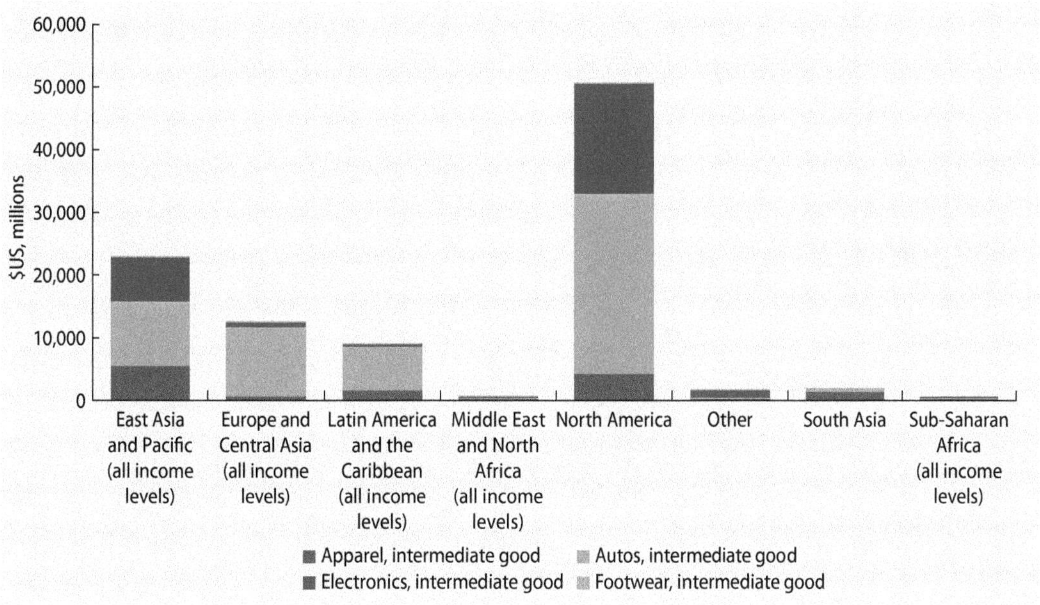

Source: World Bank calculations, based on UN COMTRADE and World Bank data.
Note: See annex 1A for a list of countries in each region.

**TABLE 3A.1    Industry classification used in the analysis**

| Acronym | Industry | Harmonized system 2-digit (HS02) section |
|---------|----------|------------------------------------------|
| ANIM | Animal products, live animals | 01-05 |
| VEGE | Vegetable products | 06-15 |
| FOOD | Prepared foodstuffs, beverages, spirits, vinegar, tobacco products, edible fats | 16-24 |
| MINE | Mineral products | 25-26 |
| FUEL | Mineral fuels | 27 |
| CHEM | Chemicals | 28-38 |
| PLAS | Plastics and rubber | 39-40 |
| HIDE | Hides, skins, leather, etc. | 41-43 |
| WOOD | Wood and articles of wood, pulp and paper | 44-49 |
| TEXT | Textiles, fibres, apparel, etc. | 50-63 |
| FOOT | Footwear, headgear, umbrellas, feathers, etc. | 64-67 |
| STON | Stone, cement, plaster, ceramics, glassware, pearls, etc. | 68-71 |
| META | Base metals and articles of base metal | 72-83 |
| MACH | Machinery, mechanical appliances, electrical equipment | 84-85 |
| TRAN | Transportation: vehicles, aircraft, vessels | 86-89 |
| MISC | Miscellaneous | 90-97 |

**TABLE 3A.2    Country and economy classifications used in the analysis**

| Acronym | Country | Acronym | Country | Acronym | Country |
|---------|---------|---------|---------|---------|---------|
| ARG | Argentina | ECU | Ecuador | PAN | Panama |
| ATG | Antigua and Barbuda | EUN | European Union | PER | Peru |
| AUS | Australia | GRD | Grenada | PHL | Philippines |
| BLZ | Belize | GTM | Guatemala | PRY | Paraguay |
| BOL | Bolivia | GUY | Guyana | RUS | Russian Federation |
| BRA | Brazil | HND | Honduras | SLV | El Salvador |
| BRB | Barbados | HTI | Haiti | SUR | Suriname |
| CAN | Canada | IDN | Indonesia | THA | Thailand |
| CHL | Chile | IND | India | TWN | Taiwan, China |
| CHN | China | JPN | Japan | URY | Uruguay |
| COL | Colombia | KNA | St. Kitts and Nevis | USA | United States |
| CRI | Costa Rica | KOR | Korea, Rep. | VCT | St. Vincent and the Grenadines |
| CUB | Cuba | LCA | St. Lucia | VEN | Venezuela, RB |
| DMA | Dominica | MEX | Mexico | ZAF | South Africa |
| DOM | Dominican Republic | NIC | Nicaragua | | |

Another interesting contrast between the pattern of GVC inputs integration in LAC and EAP lies in the fact that, whereas the former region is relatively more diversified in terms of import sources and has one overwhelmingly main export destination (North America), EAP is highly concentrated in terms of import sources (being its own main import source), and much more diversified when it comes to export destinations. This may be interpreted as a signal of LAC's heavy dependence on imported inputs and relatively low competitiveness as an exporter of them, with the exception of the particular situation with North America, which is to a large extent explained by Mexico. By contrast, East Asia appears very much self-sufficient in terms of procuring itself most of the intermediate inputs it needs for the development of its GVCs, and at the same time quite competitive as a global source of such goods, as evidenced by its non-negligible exports of GVC intermediates to every region in the world.

East Asia is perhaps the only region of the world that is truly a powerhouse in all of our focus GVCs: autos, apparel, electronics, and footwear. East Asia sends to itself 58 percent of its exports of intermediate electronics, 45 percent of them in the case of apparel, 37 percent of footwear, and 33 percent in the case of autos. LAC's imports from itself are only comparably high in the case of apparel (66 percent) and footwear (35 percent), but are relatively low when it comes to the quantitatively more important categories of autos (12 percent) and electronics (6 percent). EAP is the second largest source of electronics parts and components imports for LAC and is the main one by a large margin for North America and SAR. Similarly, LAC, SAR, North America, and Sub-Saharan Africa all tend to import footwear parts and components from East Asia. East Asia itself is largely self-reliant on GVC intermediates, with a majority of both its exports and imports consisting of intraregional trade, and other intermediates being sourced within national boundaries.[26]

## Notes

1. Annex 1A presents a detailed explanation of the regional classifications used throughout the report, along with the list of countries included in each region.

2. Bown (2015) provides an assessment of the tariffs for the 25 WTO member countries that have bound less than one-third of their non-agricultural import products, for example. For the tariff and other trade policy characteristics of the Group of 20 (G20) economies more broadly, see Bown and Crowley (forthcoming).

3. As Bown (2015) notes, economies that went through a rigorous WTO accession process after 1996 (see again Ecuador)—including China; Taiwan, China; and Russia—were granted entry with a much less permissible tariff binding overhang. In figure 3.2, Russia has still not fully phased in its applied MFN tariff reductions; by 2014 its average applied MFN tariff (8.4 percent) was still above its average binding level (7.6 percent).

4. Handley and Limão (2015) develop a dynamic, heterogeneous firms model with sunk costs of exporting and provide structural estimates of the effect of policy uncertainty on firm entry following Portugal's accession to the European Community in 1986. Their evidence suggests that the trade policy reform removed uncertainty about future EC policies and subsequently accounted for a large fraction of the observed Portuguese exporting firms' entry and sales. Handley and Limão (2016) extend the approach in order to study Chinese firm-level exports to the United States around the 2001 accession of China to the WTO. They found that WTO accession reduces trade policy uncertainty facing exporters, which leads to increased investment in export entry and technology upgrading, and that this, in turn, expanded trade flows and real income for U.S. consumers.

5. As noted by Lederman and Lesniak (forthcoming), economic size is a strong correlate of various economic outcomes, including the ratio of international trade flows over GDP and the level of export diversification (proxied by the number of exported goods and services, as well as the number of export destinations). However, the authors show that it is difficult to discern discrete changes in the relationship between labor force size and these economic variables. Consequently, any threshold level of population as a proxy for economic size is subjective. Lederman and Lesniak (forthcoming) analyze the performance of LAC countries with fewer than 4 million workers, defined as the population that is 15–64 years old. Here, the threshold of 1 million inhabitants covers the smallest economies in the region, which produce and export very few goods or services, and thus import tariffs are probably economically equivalent to a sales tax.

6. Bilateral tariff preference data from 2014 for all LAC countries is not available; notably missing are Panama, Jamaica, and all of the Group C countries. The data were generously made available by the United Nations International Trade Centre.

7. Although not noted here, some LAC countries offer tariff preferences for a handful of products to other developing countries outside of the region under what are referred to as "Partial Scope Agreements" such as the Global System of Trade Preferences (GSTP). For a discussion, see Bown and Crowley, forthcoming.

8. Exceptions include Guatemala, which offers some preferences to Ecuador, and Costa Rica, which offers some preferences to Brazil.

9. In the last three columns, the explanation behind why the coverage is significantly less than 100 percent is because the FTA between the United States or EU and the Group B country of interest had not yet been fully phased in by 2014.

10. The five-year period is chosen to proxy for the point in time at which the country decided it wanted to form an FTA with United States. The exact point in time at which negotiations on successful FTAs began varies across countries and FTAs.

11. This is roughly consistent with the pattern of results for the CAFTA countries in the 2000s studied by Tovar (2012).

12. Antidumping and safeguards are import-restricting policies that apply to only a well-defined set of products—that is, not an entire sector—and that countries can apply against selective trading partners. They are thus much more targeted and discretionary than tariffs.

13. This is reinforced even through a simple examination of the applied MFN tariff data. Table 3.1 and figures 3.1 and 3.2 have also illustrated some substantial differences across Mercosur countries as to their applied MFN tariffs on outsiders.

14. There are no formal regression estimates shown here because, unfortunately, the only two LAC countries available in the World Input-Output Database from which the Blanchard, Bown, and Johnson (2016) study draws are Brazil and Mexico. Cross-sectional estimates on a larger sample of 69 countries overall, 15 of which are from LAC, using GTAP data for 2004 gives a qualitative pattern of results similar to those in Blanchard, Bown, and Johnson (2016), albeit using different estimation techniques—that is, the Blanchard, Bown, and Johnson (2016) study uses a number of different forms of instrumental variables estimation to address potential endogeneity concerns between value added and tariffs.

15. This largely predates the wave of the LAC Group B countries' extraregional FTAs because all of LAC's Group B FTAs with the United States were implemented after 2004, with the exception of Mexico (1994) and Chile (2004). Chile's FTA with the EU was implemented in 2003.

16. In particular, consider the ratio of DVA to foreign production taking place in LAC relative to DVA to foreign production taking place in all countries. In parentheses, for the Group A countries, these are Argentina (3.9), Bolivia (5.0), Brazil (3.3), Ecuador (3.8), Paraguay (2.4), Uruguay (2.5), and República Bolivariana de Venezuela (4.0). For the Group B countries, these are Chile (2.3), Colombia (4.2), Costa Rica (3.8), Guatemala (4.3), Mexico (2.8), Panama (3.0), and Peru (3.2).

17. The debate on whether what a country produces and exports matters for growth is a long-standing one. In its most recent incarnation, work by Ricardo Hausmann, Hwang, and Rodrik (2007) has provided some evidence of a positive correlation between certain attributes of the goods a country produces and its growth rate. Among these attributes stand their connectivity to other sectors of the economy and the PRODY, which captures the average income per capita of the countries that export the good (Hausmann, Hwang, and Rodrik 2007). However, Lederman and Maloney (2012) suggest that other factors, such as the structure of trade or the way countries produce their goods, may be more important determinants of growth.

18. This is the so-called infant industry argument. Examples of this type of reasoning can be found as early as the 18th century in the United States, when then–secretary of the Treasury Alexander Hamilton promoted levying protective duties on imported manufactured goods from Europe as a way to foster the development of the U.S. manufacturing sector and help the transition from an agrarian to an industrial economy. A similar argument was made in LAC in the 1960s, influenced by the ideas of prominent Argentinean economist Raúl Prebisch.

19. One problem of the fixed-effects estimation presented in column (1) is that the coefficient on the initial quality has a downward bias. Hence, although the estimated coefficient is negative, the true coefficient could in fact be positive. To check that there is indeed convergence (negative coefficient of the initial level), column (3) shows the coefficient of an ordinary least squares (OLS) regression with just time fixed effects (no country- or product-specific fixed effects), where the coefficient has an upward bias. The fact that the coefficient of lagged quality is still negative in column (3) is reassuring; the "true" value of the coefficient is expected to be negative.

20. Column (4) shows a similar specification to that in (2) running a pooled OLS regression. The sign of the coefficients are the same as in (2), which reaffirms the signs of the coefficients in (2).

21. The convergence coefficient and the interaction are expected to have downward biases because of the inclusion of the fixed effect in an OLS estimation. However, the same coefficients are obtained in a pooled estimation, which is expected to have an upward bias, suggesting that there is indeed convergence of RCAs.

22. The PRODY is an index that captures the trade-weighted average GDP per capita of a country exporting an export good.

23. In particular, exporters of primary products experience the sort of GVC participation described as "forward links" in international input-output databases. Countries that export final goods requiring large amounts of imported intermediate goods are said to experience "backward links."

24. The terminology in this area is not entirely standardized. "Value chains" connotes the coordination of the production of complex goods over many countries, emphasizing the role of lead firms, which are usually multinational. "Supply chains" suggests a focus on the physical movement of goods necessary to make value chains happen, and can also be

used to describe the transactions used in connecting global buyers and sellers of simple goods such as agricultural products.

25. World Bank staff calculations. The weight of classic GVC trade in total merchandise trade tends to be higher when the price of oil is low, and vice versa.

26. East Asia also runs a trade surplus with other regions of the world in terms of GVC intermediate goods, with about $4.1 trillion of exports vs. $2.5 trillion of imports in 2013.

# References

Acemoglu, D., P. Aghion, and F. Zilibotti, 2006. "Distance to Frontier, Selection, and Economic Growth." *Journal of the European Economic Association* 4 (1): 37–74.

Aghion, P., N. Bloom, R. Blundell, R. Griffith, and P. Howitt. 2005. "Competition and Innovation: An Inverted-U Relationship." *The Quarterly Journal of Economics* 120 (2): 701–28.

Amiti, M., and A. Khandelwal. 2013. "Import Competition and Quality Upgrading." *The Review of Economics and Statistics* 95 (2): 476–90.

Blanchard, Emily J., Chad P. Bown, and Robert C. Johnson. 2016. "Global Supply Chains and Trade Policy." Policy Research Working Paper 7536, World Bank, Washington, DC.

Bown, Chad P. 2015. "What's Left for the WTO?" Policy Research Working Paper 7502, World Bank, Washington, DC.

Bown, Chad P., and Meredith A. Crowley. Forthcoming. "The Empirical Landscape of Trade Policy," In Kyle Bagwell and Robert W. Staiger, eds., *The Handbook of Commercial Policy*. Amsterdam: Elsevier.

Bown, Chad P., and Patricia Tovar. Forthcoming. "Preferential Liberalization, Antidumping, and Safeguards: Stumbling Block Evidence from MERCOSUR," *Economics & Politics*.

Cattaneo, Olivier, Gary Gereffi, and Cornelia Staritz. 2010. *Global Value Chains in a Postcrisis World: A Development Perspective.* Washington, DC: World Bank.

Cerdeiro, Diego A. 2016. "Estimating the Effects of the Trans-Pacific Partnership (TPP) on Latin America and the Caribbean (LAC)." IMF Working Paper No. 16/101, International Monetary Fund, Washington, DC.

Corden, W. Max. 1997. *Trade Policy and Welfare, Second Edition.* Oxford, U.K.: Clarendon Press.

De la Torre, Augusto, Tatiana Didier, Alain Ize, Daniel Lederman, and Sergio L. Schmukler. 2015. *Latin America and the Rising South: Changing World, Changing Priorities.* World Bank Latin American and Caribbean Studies. Washington, DC: World Bank.

Estevadeordal, Antoni, Caroline Freund, and Emanuel Ornelas. 2008. "Does Regionalism Affect Trade Liberalization Toward Nonmembers?" *Quarterly Journal of Economics* 123 (4): 1532–75.

Estevadeordal, A., and E. Talvi. 2016. "Towards a New Trans-American Partnership." Brookings Global Policy Brief, Brookings Institution, Washington, DC.

Handley, Kyle, and Nuno Limão. 2015. "Trade and Investment under Policy Uncertainty: Theory and Firm Evidence." *American Economic Journal: Economic Policy* 7 (4): 189–222.

Handley, Kyle, and Nuno Limão. 2016. "Policy Uncertainty, Trade and Welfare: Theory and Evidence for China and the U.S." Mimeograph, University of Maryland, March. Available at http://terpconnect.umd.edu/~limao/tpu_submitted.pdf.

Krueger, Anne. 1993. "Free Trade Agreements as Protectionist Devices: Rules of Origin." NBER Working Paper 4352, National Bureau of Economic Research, Cambridge, MA.

Lederman, D., and J. Lesniak. Forthcoming. *Economic Development with Limited Supplies of Labor: Common Challenges, Shared Solutions for Small Economies.* Washington, DC: World Bank.

Lederman, Daniel, William F. Maloney, and Luis Servén. 2005. *Lessons from NAFTA for Latin America and the Caribbean.* Washington, DC: Stanford University Press and the World Bank.

Lederman, Daniel, and William Maloney. 2012. *Does What You Export Matter? In Search of Empirical Guidance for Industrial Policies.* Latin American Development Series. Washington, DC: World Bank.

Levchenko, Andrei, and Jing Zhang. 2016. "The Evolution of Comparative Advantage: Measurement and Welfare Implications." *Journal of Monetary Economics* 78: 96–111.

Limão, Nuno. Forthcoming. "Preferential Trade Agreements." In *The Handbook of Commercial Policy*, edited by Kyle Bagwell and Robert W. Staiger. Amsterdam: Elsevier.

Mattoo, Aaditya, Zhi Wang, and Shang-Jin Wei. 2013. *Trade in Value Added: Developing New*

*Measures of Cross-Border Trade*. Washington, DC: World Bank.

Milberg, William, and Deborah Winkler. 2011. "Economic and Social Upgrading in Global Production Networks: Problems of Theory and Measurement." *International Labour Review* 150 (3-4): 341–65.

Moncarz, P., M. Olarreaga, and M. Vaillant. 2016. "Regionalism as Industrial Policy; Evidence from MERCOSUR." *Review of Development Economics* 20 (1): 359–73.

Petri, Peter A., and Michael G. Plummer. 2016. "The Economic Effects of the Trans-Pacific Partnership: New Estimates." Peterson Institute for International Economics Working Paper 16-2, Washington, DC, January.

PIIE (Peterson Institute for International Economics). 2016. *Assessing the Trans-Pacific Partnership, Volume 1: Market Access and Sectoral Issues*. Peterson Institute for International Economics Briefing 16-1, Washington, DC, February.

SICE (Sistema de Informacion sobre Comercio Exterior). 2016. "Foreign Trade Information System." Organization of American States, available at http://www.sice.oas.org/agreements _e.asp, last accessed March 7.

Schott, Jeffrey J., and Cathleen Cimino-Isaacs, eds. 2016. *Assessing the Trans-Pacific Partnership, Volume 2: Innovations in Trading Rules*. PIIE Briefing 16–4. Washington, DC: Peterson Institute for International Economics.

Sturgeon, Timothy J., and Olga Memedovic. 2011. "Mapping Global Value Chains: Intermediate Goods Trade and Structural Change in the World Economy." UNIDO Development Policy and Strategy Research Branch Working Paper 05/2010. United Nations Industrial Development Organization, Vienna.

Tovar, Patricia. 2012. "Preferential Trade Agreements and Unilateral Liberalization: Evidence from CAFTA." *World Trade Review* 11 (4): 591–619.

USITC (U.S. International Trade Commission). 2011. *The Economic Effects of Significant U.S. Import Restraints: Seventh Update 2011, Special Topic: Global Supply Chains*. USITC Publication 4253, Washington, DC: USITC, August.

———. 2016. *Trans-Pacific Partnership Agreement: Likely Impact on the U.S. Economy and on Specific Industry Sectors*. USITC Publication Number 4607, Washington, DC: USITC, May.

Viner, Jacob. 1950. *The Customs Union Issue*. Washington, DC: Carnegie Endowment for International Peace.

World Bank. 2016. "Potential Macroeconomic Implications of the Trans-Pacific Partnership." Chapter 4 in *Global Economic Prospects*, 219–36. Washington, DC: World Bank.

WTO (World Trade Organization). 2015. *World Tariff Profiles 2015*. Geneva: World Trade Organization.

# In Search of Growth and Stability through Factor Market Integration

4

## Introduction

An important part of the renewal of the open regionalism (OR) agenda focuses on factor markets. Although many trade agreements in Latin America and the Caribbean (LAC) already include chapters that facilitate the movement of factors of production, policies pursuing factor market integration are typically overshadowed by the emphasis put on tariffs.[1] This chapter presents evidence illustrating how LAC would benefit from putting factor market integration front and center in its OR agenda.

A simple decomposition of gross domestic product (GDP) suggests that its components—generally represented in economics as labor, capital, materials, and technology—are affected by gravity and proximity. Frankel and Romer (1999) and Norguer and Siscart (2005) suggest that countries that are closer and larger will trade more, and trade leads to growth. Proximity is important for factor markets as well. Understanding economic integration, therefore, requires that we pay particular attention to the integration of factor markets. Factor market integration in particular can have important macroeconomic consequences (see, for example,

Schäfer and Steger 2014). Most studies of factor market integration focus on labor or capital markets. In this chapter, we focus specifically on labor and capital market integration by drawing upon both the academic literature and new research.

Understanding labor market integration is important for several reasons. The lack of labor market integration may imply that resources are not efficiently allocated across countries. When people migrate they bring ideas with them that could contribute to productivity growth. Labor market integration may also mitigate macroeconomic shocks by allowing shocks to dissipate across borders. Studying labor market integration can uncover how global integration—such as financial flows or migration—affects wages. For example, Bloom and Noor (1995) show that the sharp increase in international trade significantly contributed to the sharp increase in labor market integration among East and Southeast Asian countries from the 1980s to 1991. Ben-David (1993) and Michaels (2008), find similar results using data ranging from U.S. states to income differentials within the European Economic Community.

Comparable research for other regions, such as LAC, is rare.

Capital market integration (CMI) is important for several reasons. International CMI can expand domestic credit. Expanding credit allows productive investments that would otherwise not be possible, thus raising productivity (Bonfiglioli 2008). At the same time, expanding credit allows for a diversification of investment projects that might otherwise be so similar as to face similar shocks (Acemoglu and Zilibotti 1997; Eichengreen and Mussa 1998). Foreign investment may bring in new products, processes, or managerial expertise that may spill over to the domestic economy (Kose et al. 2009). Foreign investment may also increase competition, which would increase the incentive to improve productivity in domestic firms.

In addition to its effect on credit and competition, CMI may also improve the domestic financial system in several ways. Domestic banks may either learn about or be motivated to adopt procedures that meet international standards when faced with exposure to foreign capital markets (Levine 1996; Levine and Zervos 1998; Chinn and Ito 2006; and Baltagi, Demitiades, and Law 2009). The presence of foreign banks could also motivate the government to improve regulation or, at least, diminish the power of the government to favor certain domestic banks (Gourinchas and Jeanne 2009). Foreign bank presence may also contribute to the stabilization of domestic credit when domestic banks experience negative shocks (Galindo, Micco, and Powell 2004). Foreign banks can draw from parent institutions to effectively smooth the effects of domestic shocks.

On the other side, however, CMI can increase the economy's exposure to foreign shocks and, in some cases, amplify domestic shocks. Morgan and Strahan (2003) illustrate this dichotomy and show that foreign banks may reallocate their portfolios in response to domestic risk. Furthermore, Galindo, Micco, and Powell (2004) show that foreign shocks can affect the behavior of a foreign bank's host country. Whether, on balance, CMI is

positive or negative (that is, whether the benefits of increased growth outweigh the increased risk through foreign exposure) is still open for debate.

In this chapter, we present the results from recent and ongoing research that applies various empirical approaches to analyze factor market integration in LAC. In the first section, we describe these approaches by defining three measures of factor market integration. The results of this section highlight the common themes present in studies of both labor and capital markets. The next section reviews the labor market integration literature through the lens of these three measures. The following section applies the three measures to capital market integration. The results, summarized in the last section, suggest that factor market integration within LAC is modest. Factor market integration is stronger with the North than within LAC, which sets LAC apart from other regions of the world. There may be gains from encouraging additional factor market integration in the region.

## Three measures of factor market integration

In this section, we present three measures of integration: long-run price convergence, short-run responsiveness to shocks, and finally capital flows and migration. They capture the different concepts of integration and have been applied to different contexts and situations. Each is discussed in turn.

### Measure 1: Price convergence (long run)

One of the most common and perhaps intuitive (at least to economists) measures of economic integration is price convergence. The idea of price convergence is that two markets can be considered integrated if the prices of goods sold in those markets are identical. The main reason why this idea is so pervasive is that one of the core aims of economic exchange is to take advantage of price differences. Buying where prices are low and selling where prices are high creates returns for those who link these markets, but this activity also eventually affects the markets themselves by causing prices to equalize. Thus, it is not surprising that price convergence as a measure of market integration is found throughout a wide range of economic literature. Two widely cited studies, McCallum (1995) and Engel and Rogers (1996), use output prices as a measure of international market integration. Other examples include Berkowitz and DeJong (2003) and Knetter and Slaughter (2001), who analyze international macroeconomic integration. Studies of particular markets often apply the same concept. Dawson and Dey (2002); Mohanty, Peterson, and Smith (1996); Ghosh (2003); and Mohanty and Langley (2003) are all examples of studies that apply the idea of price convergence to study the degree of integration in agricultural markets.

Income per capita may be considered a particular price in an economy. As such, the extent of actual economic integration may be measured by analyzing the convergence of income levels. Examining income convergence helps put LAC in context and motivates the focus on factor market integration. It also suggests that evaluating economic integration begins with understanding these income gaps, which is where we now turn.

Using GDP per capita (valued in purchasing power parity [PPP]) data in constant (2011) dollars from the World Development Indicators for 169 countries, figure 4.1 shows the standard deviation and mean pairwise differences for all the world's countries. An increase indicates divergence, whereas a fall indicates convergence. The dispersion increases until the 2008 financial crisis. The rise and fall follow business cycles, suggesting that the higher-income countries pulled ahead during the boom period, and then fell back during the crisis. There is little evidence here of long-run convergence.

Using GDP per capita data for 28 LAC countries covering the period 1990–2013, figure 4.2 illustrates both the standard deviation and the average value of the absolute value of the pairwise (log) difference over

**FIGURE 4.1   Comparing the mean pairwise differentials and standard deviation of GDP per capita over time, all available countries**

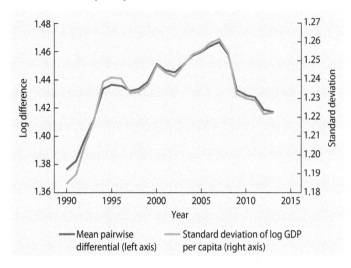

*Source:* World Bank calculations, using data from the World Development Indicators.

**FIGURE 4.2   Comparing the mean pairwise differentials and standard deviation of GDP per capita over time, LAC countries**

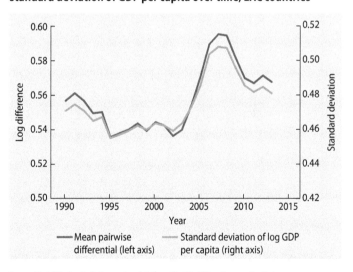

*Source:* World Bank calculations, using data from the World Development Indicators.

time.[2] As in figure 4.1, figure 4.2 shows clear business cycle patterns over the 24-year period. Also as in figure 4.1, little evidence of convergence emerges; the average log difference and the standard deviation are nearly identical in 2013 and 1990.

The lack of evidence of integration over this period may be due to the fact that capital and labor shares vary across countries and that labor and capital may exhibit different degrees of integration. Guerriero (2012) constructs estimates of the labor share of income for 89 countries and demonstrates that the labor share of income varies widely across country, time, and definition. In general, however, her results show that the labor share of income in LAC is generally much lower (on average across different measures) than in developed countries. For example, for the latest year available (between 2005 and 2010 and varying for different countries), Argentina's labor share of income ranged from about 35 percent to 55 percent (depending on definition), Chile's ranged from 45 percent to 65 percent, and Mexico's ranged from 35 percent to 60 percent. In contrast, the labor shares of France ranged from 75 percent to 81 percent, Germany's ranged from 65 percent to 80 percent, and shares in the United States ranged from about 70 percent to nearly 85 percent. Guerriero (2012) also shows that the labor shares change over time. Although in most countries labor shares are falling, LAC countries exhibit more heterogeneity depending on the time period and country. The time series of labor shares varies across countries as well. For example, Mexico has exhibited generally falling shares since the Peso Crisis, whereas Chile's labor share rose from the late 1980s until the middle of the 2000s. The variation across countries and across time suggests that GDP per capita may not be the most accurate measure of labor market integration or wage convergence, which motivates our focus on specific factor markets.

## Measure 2: Responsiveness to shocks in neighboring countries (short run)

One interesting point of debate that emerges from several studies is the possibility that price convergence is not necessary for markets to be considered integrated. Even when prices do not completely converge, the debate surrounding purchasing power parity[3] suggests that barriers to trade inhibit complete price convergence, but

prices may still move together across markets over time. Paul, Miljkovic, and Ipe (2001) apply cointegration procedures that capture the co-movement of prices of different levels to gasoline markets in the United States; and Mohanty, Peterson, and Smith (1996), Ghosh (2003), and Mohanty and Langley (2003) are examples that apply cointegration measures to agricultural markets. The key lesson for our study is that it is important to distinguish between long-run integration (as evidenced with price convergence) and short-run integration (as evidenced by the responsiveness to short-run shocks).

To motivate a measure of short-run economic integration, consider an economy composed of two countries ("A" and "B"). While this approach could apply to any factor or good with a price, we continue our focus on income and therefore use labor as a representative factor. Using labor here helps introduce and motivate mechanisms of integration. If labor in the two countries is a price substitute, an increase in the wages of workers in Country A increases the demand for workers in Country B. At this point we remain very general and allow wages to be related through trade, capital flows, migration, or other forces. If, for example, capital flows between the two regions are somewhat slow to react, the lagged Country B wage would affect the demand for labor in Country A. A general form that captures these assumptions is:

$$L_t^{dA} = \delta_0 + \delta_1 w_{t-1}^B - \delta_2 \left[ w_t^A - \gamma w_{t-1}^A \right] + \delta_3 \quad (4.1)$$

where $L^{dA}$ is labor demand in Country A, $W^A$ is the natural log of the Country A wage, and $W^B$ is the natural log of the Country B wage. The parameter $\gamma$ captures the responsiveness of demand to lagged wages, and $\delta_3$ is a term to capture random factors affecting labor demand. The subscript $t$ represents time.

Rising wages in Country B attract workers from Country A. If workers migrate quickly from one region to another, the supply of

Country A labor is responsive to wage levels in both regions. A general form that captures these assumptions is:

$$L_t^{sA} = \sigma_0 + \sigma_1 w_{t-1}^B - \sigma_2 \left[ w_t^A - \varphi w_{t-1}^A \right] + \sigma_3 \quad (4.2)$$

The variable $L^s$ represents labor supply. The parameter $\varphi$ captures the responsiveness of supply to lagged wages, and $\sigma_3$ is a random term. The coefficients $\delta_1$ and $\sigma_1$ capture the cost of migration to demanders and suppliers of labor, respectively. In the presence of exogenous costs, an equilibrium differential separates regional wages. Wages may temporarily deviate from their equilibrium values, but they will eventually return. Equating supply and demand, equilibrium is:

$$\begin{aligned} &\delta_0 + \delta_1 w_{t-1}^B - \delta_2 \left[ w_t^A - \gamma w_{t-1}^A \right] + \delta_3 \\ &= \sigma_0 + \sigma_1 w_{t-1}^B - \sigma_2 \left[ w_t^A - \varphi w_{t-1}^A \right] + \sigma_3 \end{aligned} \quad (4.3)$$

Solving (4.3) for the current Country A wage produces an expression in terms of the lagged Country A wage and the current and lagged Country B wage:

$$\begin{aligned} w_t^A =& \frac{\delta_0 - \sigma_0}{\delta_2 + \sigma_2} + \frac{\delta_{3j} - \sigma_{3j}}{\delta_2 + \sigma_2} + \frac{\gamma \delta_2 - \varphi \sigma_2}{\delta_2 + \sigma_2} w_{t-1}^A \\ &+ \frac{\sigma_1}{\delta_2 + \sigma_2} w_t^B + \frac{\delta_1}{\delta_2 + \sigma_2} w_{t-1}^B, \end{aligned} \quad (4.4)$$

which can be rewritten as

$$w_t^A = a_0 + a_1 w_{t-1}^A + e_1 w_t^B + e_2 w_{t-1}^B. \quad (4.5)$$

Hendry and Ericsson (1991) show that long-run homogeneity between $W^A$ and $W^B$ implies that the sum of $a_1$, $e_1$, and $e_2$ equals 1. Thus, a differenced form of (4.5) is:

$$\Delta w_t^A = \alpha_0 + \alpha_1 \Delta w_t^B + \alpha_2 \left( w^A - w^B \right)_{t-1} + \mu_t \quad (4.6)$$

This equation describes a short-run measure of economic integration that can be used to estimate the responsiveness to shocks from another country (represented by the alpha 1 parameter) and the speed at which the wages, when shocked, return to

the equilibrium differential (the alpha 2 parameter). Stronger responses to shocks (larger alpha 1 parameters) and faster convergence speeds (more negative alpha 2 parameters) imply deeper integration.

To illustrate, table 4.1 shows the results from estimating (4.6) using the same GDP per capita data described above for LAC. As expected, table 4.1 shows that the estimated coefficient on the first term is positive and the lagged difference terms are negative. These results suggest that on average the effects of shocks in an average country on another average country are not large and that there is very little evidence of global integration.

The model can be easily augmented with gravity variables (for example,. distance and borders) to explore the relative transmission of shocks across countries that are nearby or share borders, relative to the rest of the world. Borders and distance are expected to affect integration in intuitive ways, and the empirical results match expectations. The estimates from the border dummy variable suggest that bordering countries have strongly correlated shocks and faster convergence. This is consistent with the results in chapter 1, which emphasizes the geographic clustering of economic performance. The transmission of shocks across bordering countries is about four times that of other countries. Using the inverse of the log distance between countries as weights generates stronger results. The rate of convergence for countries that share a border is an order of magnitude larger than that of noncontiguous country pairs.

LAC is commonly compared to East Asia and the Pacific (EAP). Table 4.2 adds regional controls for EAP and LAC. The rest of the countries of the world make up the omitted (reference) category. According to the results in table 4.2, LAC countries are both more responsive to shocks and exhibit more rapid convergence back to the equilibrium differential than the EAP countries, which suggests that LAC countries may be more integrated, even if we do not observe long-run convergence in GDP per capita.

**TABLE 4.1  Model of shocks across borders in log GDP per capita, 169 countries with border interaction terms**

| Variables | (1)<br>Unweighted | (2)<br>Weighted | (3)<br>Unweighted | (4)<br>Weighted |
|---|---|---|---|---|
| Change in partner's log GDP per capita (Country B) | 0.067***<br>(0.001) | 0.071***<br>(0.001) | 0.063***<br>(0.001) | 0.066***<br>(0.001) |
| Change x border | | | 0.187***<br>(0.009) | 0.191***<br>(0.008) |
| Lagged difference | −0.000<br>(0.000) | −0.000<br>(0.000) | −0.000<br>(0.000) | −0.000<br>(0.000) |
| Lagged difference x border | | | −0.003***<br>(0.001) | −0.003***<br>(0.001) |
| Constant | 0.017***<br>(0.000) | 0.017***<br>(0.000) | 0.017***<br>(0.000) | 0.017***<br>(0.000) |
| Observations | 592,480 | 592,480 | 592,480 | 592,480 |
| R-squared | 0.004 | 0.005 | 0.005 | 0.006 |

*Note:* In column (3), the sum (standard error) of the change and the border interaction effect is 0.250 (0.009). The sum of the lagged difference and interaction effect is −0.0032 (0.0007). In column (4), the sum (standard error) of the change and the border interaction effect is 0.257 (0.008). The sum of the lagged difference and interaction effect is −0.0028 (0.0006). The main contiguous effect is included but not reported. Standard errors in parentheses. *** $p < 0.01$, ** $p < 0.05$, * $p < 0.1$.

**TABLE 4.2  Model of shocks across borders in log GDP per capita, 169 countries with regional interaction terms**

| Variables | (1)<br>Unweighted | (2)<br>Weighted | (3)<br>Unweighted | (4)<br>Weighted |
|---|---|---|---|---|
| East Asia and Pacific (EAP) | 0.006***<br>(0.001) | 0.006***<br>(0.001) | 0.006***<br>(0.001) | 0.006***<br>(0.001) |
| Latin America (LAC) | 0.000<br>(0.001) | 0.000<br>(0.001) | 0.000<br>(0.001) | 0.000<br>(0.001) |
| Change in partner's log GDP per capita (Country B) | 0.066***<br>(0.001) | 0.070***<br>(0.001) | 0.066***<br>(0.001) | 0.070***<br>(0.001) |
| x EAP | 0.013<br>(0.012) | 0.021*<br>(0.012) | 0.013<br>(0.012) | 0.021*<br>(0.012) |
| x LAC | 0.056***<br>(0.013) | 0.057***<br>(0.012) | 0.059***<br>(0.013) | 0.061***<br>(0.012) |
| Lagged difference | −0.000<br>(0.000) | −0.000<br>(0.000) | −0.000<br>(0.000) | −0.000<br>(0.000) |
| x EAP | | | 0.000<br>(0.000) | 0.000<br>(0.000) |
| x LAC | | | −0.003***<br>(0.001) | −0.003***<br>(0.001) |
| Constant | 0.017***<br>(0.000) | 0.017***<br>(0.000) | 0.017***<br>(0.000) | 0.017***<br>(0.000) |
| Observations | 592,480 | 592,480 | 592,480 | 592,480 |
| R-squared | 0.005 | 0.005 | 0.005 | 0.005 |

*Note:* In column (3), the sum (standard error) of the change and the interaction effect for EAP is 0.0787 (0.012) and for the differenced effect is 0.0003 (0.0003). For LAC, the sum (standard error) is 0.125 (0.013) and −0.0026 (0.0006). In column (4), the sums (standard errors) for EAP are 0.091 (0.012) and −0.0001 (0.0003). For LAC, the sums (standard errors) are 0.130 (0.012) and −0.0027 (0.0006). Standard errors in parentheses. *** $p < 0.01$, ** $p < 0.05$, * $p < 0.1$.

## Measure 3: Flows and barriers

The third measure appears often in the popular press as well as academic studies: flows and barriers. This literature commonly uses the term "de facto" to refer to the actual flows between countries, whether they are flows of goods, services, materials, capital, or labor. Flows are an important metric for measuring integration because they capture the intuition that, if there is much exchange between two regions, then the two regions are effectively integrated.

Flows are often reduced by barriers, and policy barriers are among the most debated. To refer to policy barriers, the term "de jure" is often used. Identifying de jure barriers is important because these are the ones that may be most directly affected by policy (by definition). Examples include migration restrictions, capital restrictions, and other regulations that directly affect flows. But they can be subtler as well, including standards, differential treatment, and institutional factors that are shaped by policy but may not be directed at international flows.

Both de facto and de jure measures can be subtle and heterogeneous. Migration policies, for example, may involve border enforcement or immigration status certification by employers. Capital market policies can be perhaps even more diverse. Almost equally diverse are the measures of de facto integration—especially when it comes to capital flows. Rojas-Suárez, Galindo, and Izquierdo (2010) cover both de facto and de jure measures of capital market integration. Their de facto measures include a range of different concepts, including, but not limited to, foreign direct investment (FDI), portfolio investment, access to loanable funds, savings rates abroad, mergers and acquisitions, and the presence of foreign banks in the region. Not all of these have comparable economic effects.

In the sections that follow we focus on both de jure and de facto measures of integration of both capital and labor markets. Using new benchmarking results, we evaluate the factors that contribute to each of these de facto measures of both labor and capital market integration. Both of these may contribute to the degree of integration we observe in the GDP per capita data.

## Labor market integration

Studies of labor market integration have applied several approaches. Many early studies focused on price convergence in the form of wage rate dispersion (for example, Rothenberg 1988) and wage convergence (for example, Allen 1990). Others focus on wage co-movements (for example, Rosenbloom 1990 and Robertson 2000). O'Rourke (1994) measures both the covariation of wages in different countries over time and the convergence of wage levels. Other studies focus on flows in the form of determinants of migration. All three approaches are applied in the following sections.

### Wage convergence (long run)

Earlier results suggested a lack of convergence of GDP per capita in both the world and in LAC. Differences in labor shares and demographics suggest that more accurate measures of wage convergence require microdata. LAC household surveys from 16 LAC countries serve this purpose.[4] Limiting the samples to the 2001–13 period, ages 18–65 years, and males with positive earnings helps increase the precision of the comparison. Figure 4.3 shows considerable differences in the age distribution across countries, which motivates matching comparable workers.

To compare wages across countries, it is useful to identify five age groups (18–26, 27–35, 37–45, 46–53, and 54–65) and five education groups based on years of education (1–5, 6–8, 12–15, and 16 years or more). Taking the mean of the PPP-adjusted 2005 dollar-value monthly earnings of each cell (using sample weights) generates a dataset that can be used to analyze wage convergence for comparable workers in each country pair.

FIGURE 4.3   **Age distribution by country**

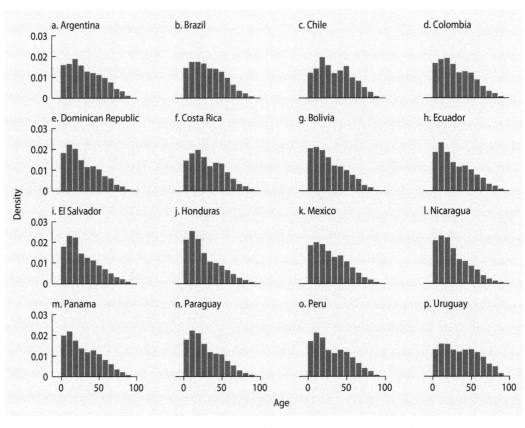

*Source:* World Bank calculations, using data from the Socio-Economic Dataset for Latin America and the Caribbean (SEDLAC).

FIGURE 4.4   **Comparing wages and GDP per capita**

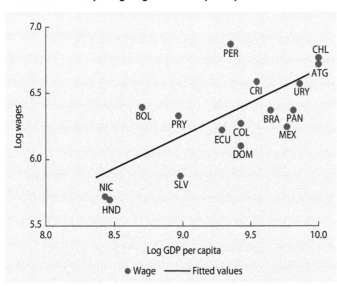

*Source:* World Bank calculations, using data from the Socio-Economic Dataset for Latin America and the Caribbean (SEDLAC) and the World Development Indicators.
*Note:* The adjusted R-squared from the simple fit line is 0.498, which suggests that GDP per capita explains about half of the wage variation across countries. See annex 3A, table 3A.2, for country acronyms.

As suggested by the differences in labor shares across countries, figure 4.4 shows that the mean wages calculated from the household surveys and the log GDP per capita for the 2009–13 period are not perfectly correlated; only about half of the variation in wages across countries is explained by GDP per capita.

Figure 4.5 contains the absolute value of the mean pairwise wage differentials and shows that the wage differentials across demographic groups are not constant. For example, the oldest workers also tend to have the highest differentials. Older workers are least likely to migrate. Using the matched pairs to formally compare the convergence or divergence of pairwise wage differentials generates the results shown in table 4.3. Table 4.3 contains the mean of the absolute value of the pairwise differential across all demographic groups for each country and

**FIGURE 4.5    Mean wage differentials by age and education**

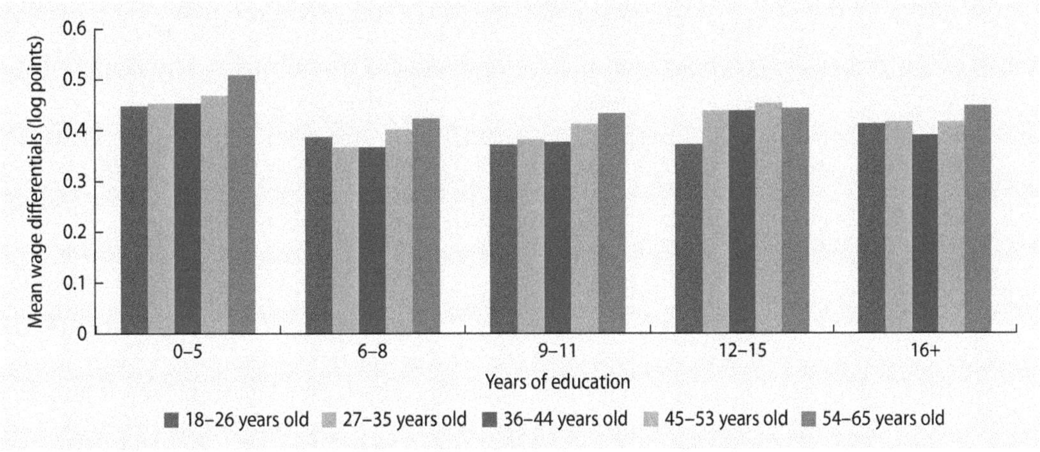

*Source:* World Bank calculations, based on data from the Socio-Economic Dataset for Latin America and the Caribbean (SEDLAC).

**TABLE 4.3    Mean wage differentials (standard deviations in parentheses)**

| Country | 2000–04 | 2005–08 | 2009–13 |
|---|---|---|---|
| Argentina | 0.390 (0.370) | 0.360 (0.295) | 0.360 (0.233) |
| Brazil | 0.464 (0.443) | 0.402 (0.313) | 0.346 (0.240) |
| Chile | 0.415 (0.413) | 0.360 (0.313) | 0.338 (0.226) |
| Colombia | 0.378 (0.347) | 0.297 (0.247) | 0.270 (0.181) |
| Dominican Republic | 0.416 (0.425) | 0.315 (0.266) | 0.308 (0.206) |
| Costa Rica | 0.581 (0.478) | 0.524 (0.342) | 0.424 (0.255) |
| Bolivia | 0.558 (0.329) | 0.376 (0.245) | 0.326 (0.220) |
| Ecuador | 0.521 (0.305) | 0.328 (0.244) | 0.298 (0.203) |
| El Salvador | 0.642 (0.288) | 0.424 (0.236) | 0.382 (0.226) |
| Honduras | 0.373 (0.380) | 0.402 (0.306) | 0.497 (0.326) |
| Mexico | 0.417 (0.402) | 0.314 (0.267) | 0.332 (0.218) |
| Nicaragua | 1.607 (0.313) | 1.098 (0.280) | 0.579 (0.264) |
| Panama | 0.377 (0.383) | 0.315 (0.263) | 0.300 (0.189) |

*(continued)*

**TABLE 4.3    Mean wage differentials (standard deviations in parentheses)** *(continued)*

| Country | 2000–04 | 2005–08 | 2009–13 |
|---|---|---|---|
| Paraguay | 0.366 (0.384) | 0.299 (0.258) | 0.275 (0.172) |
| Peru | 0.529 (0.465) | 0.504 (0.342) | 0.571 (0.290) |
| Uruguay | 0.400 (0.370) | 0.325 (0.261) | 0.311 (0.216) |

*Source:* World Bank calculations, based on data from the Socio-Economic Dataset for Latin America and the Caribbean (SEDLAC).

each of three periods (2000–04, 2005–08, and 2009–13). The falling mean wage differentials for all but four countries (some by more than 10 log points) suggest evidence of wage convergence. This result contrasts with the GDP results that generated little evidence of convergence. Estimating the time trend provides further support for wage convergence over time. The time trend results in table 4.4 suggest convergence over time of about 1.5 log points per year.

To put the LAC differentials in context, table 4.4 shows that the differentials across LAC countries are much larger than those within countries. The differentials between U.S. states are about half the size of those across LAC countries. Differentials between Mexican cities are somewhat larger than

TABLE 4.4  **Mean wage differentials over time**

| Year | United States | Mexico | LAC |
|------|------|------|------|
| 2000 | 0.204 | 0.250 | 0.467 |
| 2001 | 0.199 | 0.261 | 0.552 |
| 2002 | 0.196 | 0.269 | 0.524 |
| 2003 | 0.193 | 0.245 | 0.486 |
| 2004 | 0.195 | 0.223 | 0.454 |
| 2005 | 0.188 | 0.265 | 0.438 |
| 2006 | 0.194 | 0.253 | 0.417 |
| 2007 | 0.208 | 0.251 | 0.408 |
| 2008 | 0.207 | 0.237 | 0.359 |
| 2009 | 0.208 | 0.222 | 0.356 |
| 2010 | 0.209 | 0.220 | 0.364 |
| 2011 | 0.213 | 0.217 | 0.357 |
| 2012 | 0.205 | — | 0.372 |
| 2013 | 0.209 | — | 0.374 |
| Total | 0.202 | 0.243 | 0.422 |

*Note:* — = Not available. LAC = Latin America and the Caribbean. United States differentials represent the average absolute values of average wage differences across U.S. states. Mexico differentials represent the average absolute values of average wage differentials across Mexican cities. LAC differentials represent the average wage differentials across LAC countries. Data for each area come from household surveys and represent the averages across age-education cohorts. See annex 1A for a list of countries in LAC.

those across U.S. states, but are still much smaller than those found between LAC countries. Using the metric of wage differentials across countries, table 4.4 suggests that there may be efficiency gains from further LAC labor market integration. Table 4.5 compares these differentials over time and by age group; the results show evidence of convergence in wage levels within LAC.

## Responsiveness to shocks (short run)

To estimate the responsiveness to shocks across countries with the microdata requires a return to equation (4.6). These results, taken from Lederman and Robertson (2016), are shown in table 4.6. The results in column (1) show that shocks are strongly and positively correlated across countries for narrowly defined demographic groups. In addition, the lagged difference is negative and statistically significant, as expected. Boyer and Hatton (1994) suggest that the speed of convergence can be estimated as $(1-b)/b$. This implies that the speed of convergence would be very slow (taking more than

TABLE 4.5  **Wage differentials over time, levels, LAC, United States, and Mexico cities**

| Variables | (1) LAC: Levels | (2) LAC: Interactions | (3) United States | (4) Mexico cities |
|------|------|------|------|------|
| Year | −0.015*** (0.004) | −0.015*** (0.004) | 0.002*** (0.001) | −0.002 (0.001) |
| Education, 6–8 yrs | −0.077*** (0.013) | −0.087*** (0.016) | 0.015 (0.010) | −0.050*** (0.005) |
| Education, 9–11 yrs | −0.073*** (0.023) | −0.090*** (0.028) | −0.152*** (0.011) | −0.077*** (0.008) |
| Education, 12–15 yrs | −0.037 (0.037) | −0.059 (0.040) | −0.253*** (0.012) | −0.060*** (0.009) |
| Education, 16+ yrs | −0.049 (0.031) | −0.069* (0.033) | −0.191*** (0.013) | −0.061*** (0.011) |
| Border |  | −0.088 (0.067) |  |  |
| Education, 6–8 yrs x Border |  | 0.053* (0.029) |  |  |
| Education, 9–11 yrs x Border |  | 0.093 (0.053) |  |  |

*(continued)*

TABLE 4.5  **Wage differentials over time, levels, LAC, United States, and Mexico cities** *(continued)*

| Variables | (1)<br>LAC: Levels | (2)<br>LAC: Interactions | (3)<br>United States | (4)<br>Mexico cities |
|---|---|---|---|---|
| Education, 12–15 yrs x Border | | 0.119*<br>(0.056) | | |
| Education, 16+ yrs x Border | | 0.107*<br>(0.055) | | |
| Ages 27–35 | 0.012<br>(0.007) | 0.012<br>(0.007) | −0.026***<br>(0.004) | −0.009**<br>(0.003) |
| Ages 37–45 | 0.008<br>(0.010) | 0.008<br>(0.010) | 0.002<br>(0.005) | −0.001<br>(0.004) |
| Ages 46–53 | 0.032**<br>(0.014) | 0.032**<br>(0.014) | 0.019***<br>(0.004) | 0.005<br>(0.004) |
| Ages 54–65 | 0.053**<br>(0.019) | 0.053**<br>(0.019) | 0.043***<br>(0.006) | 0.039***<br>(0.007) |
| Constant | 30.162***<br>(8.044) | 30.162***<br>(8.044) | −3.669***<br>(1.028) | 4.195<br>(2.912) |
| Observations | 40,000 | 40,000 | 429,065 | 54,766 |
| R-squared | 0.031 | 0.034 | 0.181 | 0.027 |

*Note:* LAC = Latin America and the Caribbean. See annex 1A for a list of countries in LAC. Robust standard errors in parentheses. *** $p < 0.01$, ** $p < 0.05$, * $p < 0.1$.

53 years), which is consistent with the long-run convergence results above.

To put these results in context, columns (2) and (3) present the results from the same exercise for shocks within the United States[5] (2) and Mexico (3).[6] Columns (2) and (3) show that within-country convergence is much more rapid than convergence across countries, which is intuitive. Convergence to the equilibrium differential within Mexico takes considerably longer—about 7.6 years—than convergence in the United States, which would take about 4 months. For another comparison, Robertson (2000) finds that the speed of convergence to the equilibrium differential between the United States and the Mexican border city Tijuana is about 4 months. Convergence to equilibrium differentials between the United States and the interior of Mexico take longer. Chiquiar (2005) suggests that differentials between Mexico's northern border and southern regions grow over time, so the slow convergence estimated here is consistent with that result. Note, however, that the responsiveness of shocks is similar across the three columns,

TABLE 4.6  **Model of shocks in log wages, LAC, United States, and Mexico cities**

| Variables | (1)<br>LAC | (2)<br>United States | (3)<br>Mexico cities |
|---|---|---|---|
| Change in wage B | 0.372***<br>(0.006) | 0.389***<br>(0.012) | 0.335***<br>(0.004) |
| Lagged difference | −0.0188***<br>(0.002) | −0.324***<br>(0.015) | −0.0572***<br>(0.002) |
| Constant | −0.0859***<br>(0.001) | −0.112***<br>(0.005) | −0.0490***<br>(0.001) |
| Observations | 25,856 | 338,954 | 43,148 |
| R-squared | 0.114 | 0.196 | 0.135 |

*Source:* Based on results from Lederman and Robertson 2016.
*Notes:* LAC = Latin America and the Caribbean. See annex 1A for a list of countries in LAC. Standard errors in parentheses. *** $p < 0.01$, ** $p < 0.05$, * $p < 0.1$.

which may suggest that the three are subject to common external shocks.

The main message from the short-run analysis is that the labor markets in LAC are moderately integrated and that there is some evidence that integration with the North (for example, the relationship between Mexico and the United States) is especially strong. One obvious reason for the modest intraregional labor market integration and the stronger integration with the North may be migration flows, which is the topic of the next section.

## Flows: De facto and de jure measures of labor market integration

Abel and Sander (2014) and Bertoli and Mayda (2016) study LAC migration flows between 1960 and 2000. They show that the rate of emigration from LAC has increased considerably. Between 1960 and 2000, the total stock of emigrants from LAC increased from 3.7 to 24.9 million, which is an increase in the rate of emigration from 1.7 percent to 5.2 percent. The intraregional migration increased as well, but the numbers were far smaller. Over the 1960–2000 period, the intraregional migrant stock increased from 1.5 million to 3.7 million people. The share of intraregional migrants has fallen, from about 39 percent in 1960 to about 14 percent in 2000 (and fell to 12 percent in 2010).

Artuc, Kone, and Ozden (2016) analyze the patterns of migration in LAC. Their innovation is to apply a gravity model approach to migration destination choices by skill and gender. Using the global migration database for the years 2000 and 2010, they show that there is a great deal of heterogeneity in destination choices. That said, however, emigrants from LAC were the least likely to choose a country in their own region—when compared to emigrants from the European Union (EU), Europe and Central Asia (ECA), East Asia and Pacific (EAP), South Asia (SAR), LAC, Middle East and North Africa (MENA), and Sub-Saharan Africa (SSA)—in 2000. In 2010, however, the emigrants from South Asia were the least likely to stay in their own region (interestingly, in 2013, India and China surpassed Mexico as the main sources of U.S. immigrants). LAC emigrants, however, remained less likely to stay in their own region than emigrants from all other regions. Latin American females, however, remained at the top of the list of emigrant groups likely to leave their own region. These results are very similar to those of Bertoli and Mayda (2016); emigrants are much more likely to leave LAC than to find a destination within the region.

Table 4.7 shows that there are some exceptions, of course. In 2010, for example, Bolivians, Chileans, Paraguayans, and Uruguayans were more likely to migrate to Argentina than to either the United States or the other Organisation for Economic Co-operation and Development (OECD) countries. The lack of intraregional migration and the relatively high rate of emigration is the result of several factors. The United States is the most common destination for those from LAC, with Mexico leading as the source of most migrants. Other popular destinations for migrants, such as Spain and Italy, have relatively low migration costs for those from LAC. In particular, Bertoli, Fernàndez-Huertas Moraga, and Ortega (2011) and Bertoli and Fernàndez-Huertas Moraga (2013) show that migration costs in the form of visa policies significantly determine the destination of migrants. For example, nearly 500,000 Ecuadorans moved to Spain from 1998 until 2003, the year when the European Community introduced a new visa requirement. These countries (Italy, Spain, and the United States) generally offer higher wages, which, of course, is a principal driver of migration decisions.

One way to understand migration flows is through Gallup poll data about migration preferences. These preferences indicate where actual and potential migrants would like to move, if at all. Comparing these preferences with actual movements reveals important information about labor market integration, because differences between preferences and actual movements can reveal the presence of migration costs. Bertoli and Mayda (2016) and Docquier and Sekkat (2015) are examples of studies that have used these data to get a sense of migration costs and possible barriers to labor market integration.

One of the key results from Bertoli and Mayda (2016) is that there is a fairly large gap between LAC's migration preferences and actual migration. In fact, the number of Latin American immigrants living in other

**TABLE 4.7    Destinations of LAC emigrants in 2010**

| Country | United States | OECD | LAC | Top LAC destination |
|---|---|---|---|---|
| Antigua and Barbuda | 74.8% | 23.0% | 1.7% | Chile |
| Argentina | 21.7% | 56.2% | 21.5% | Paraguay |
| Aruba | 79.8% | 18.0% | 2.2% | Grenada |
| Bahamas, The | 88.2% | 11.6% | 0.1% | Trinidad and Tobago |
| Barbados | 58.4% | 40.1% | 1.4% | Trinidad and Tobago |
| Belize | 90.3% | 6.1% | 3.2% | Mexico |
| Bermuda | 66.4% | 32.5% | 0.1% | Trinidad and Tobago |
| Bolivia | 11.6% | 33.4% | 54.5% | Argentina |
| Brazil | 29.5% | 46.6% | 11.0% | Paraguay |
| Cayman Islands | 76.4% | 23.0% | 0.1% | Costa Rica |
| Chile | 18.8% | 39.5% | 41.5% | Argentina |
| Colombia | 45.3% | 40.7% | 13.9% | Ecuador |
| Costa Rica | 76.9% | 10.8% | 12.1% | Panama |
| Cuba | 82.5% | 13.0% | 4.4% | Puerto Rico |
| Dominica | 60.2% | 29.7% | 6.3% | Antigua and Barbuda |
| Dominican Republic | 76.4% | 16.3% | 7.2% | Puerto Rico |
| Ecuador | 43.6% | 52.9% | 3.3% | Chile |
| El Salvador | 92.0% | 6.0% | 1.9% | Costa Rica |
| Grenada | 51.5% | 34.6% | 13.5% | Trinidad and Tobago |
| Guatemala | 91.1% | 3.6% | 5.1% | Mexico |
| Guyana | 65.3% | 30.5% | 4.2% | Trinidad and Tobago |
| Haiti | 56.7% | 15.7% | 27.6% | Dominican Republic |
| Honduras | 86.4% | 7.2% | 6.2% | Mexico |
| Jamaica | 68.9% | 30.5% | 0.5% | Antigua and Barbuda |
| Mexico | 98.3% | 1.5% | 0.2% | Argentina |
| Nicaragua | 45.2% | 4.5% | 50.3% | Costa Rica |
| Panama | 84.6% | 5.3% | 10.0% | Costa Rica |
| Paraguay | 2.9% | 13.4% | 83.5% | Argentina |
| Peru | 38.2% | 32.2% | 26.2% | Argentina |
| Puerto Rico | 99.5% | 0.0% | 0.4% | Dominican Republic |
| St. Kitts and Nevis | 60.0% | 37.8% | 2.1% | Antigua and Barbuda |
| St. Lucia | 50.8% | 45.8% | 3.4% | Trinidad and Tobago |
| St. Vincent and the Grenadines | 45.2% | 41.3% | 13.5% | Trinidad and Tobago |
| Trinidad and Tobago | 70.0% | 29.3% | 0.6% | Grenada |
| Turks and Caicos Islands | 88.9% | 4.4% | 0.0% | Antigua and Barbuda |
| Uruguay | 15.6% | 38.6% | 45.6% | Argentina |
| Venezuela, RB | 36.4% | 49.5% | 14.0% | Colombia |

*Source:* Bertoli and Mayda 2016.
*Note:* LAC = Latin America and the Caribbean; OECD = Organisation for Economic Co-operation and Development. See annex 1A for a list of countries in LAC.

**FIGURE 4.6   Share of actual and intended intraregional emigration, 2010**

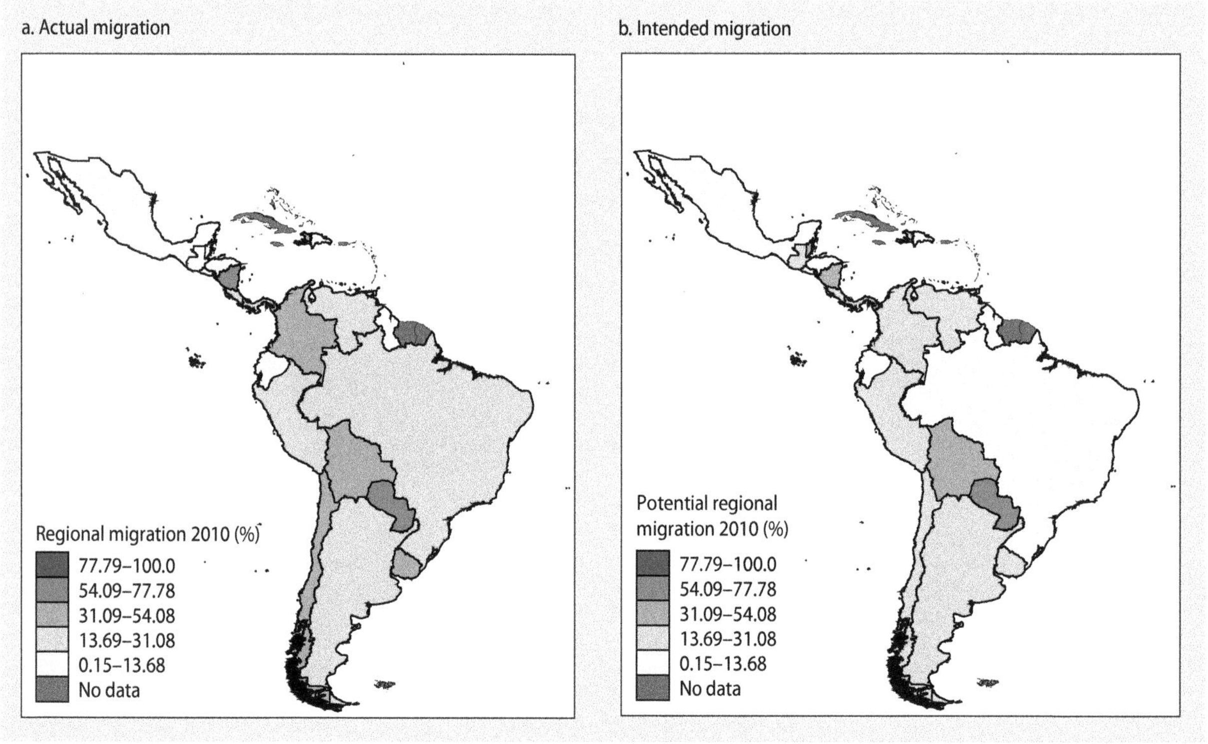

a. Actual migration

Regional migration 2010 (%)
- 77.79–100.0
- 54.09–77.78
- 31.09–54.08
- 13.69–31.08
- 0.15–13.68
- No data

b. Intended migration

Potential regional migration 2010 (%)
- 77.79–100.0
- 54.09–77.78
- 31.09–54.08
- 13.69–31.08
- 0.15–13.68
- No data

*Source:* Bertoli and Mayda 2016, from Gallup surveys on migration intentions.

countries of the region is larger than expected based on the data on migration preferences (figure 4.6). But the gap does not help explain the relatively low intraregional migration flows. On the contrary, their comparison between preferences and actual migration flows suggests that much of intraregional labor flows may be driven by the desire to migrate but the inability to migrate to their primary choice. The Gallup poll data suggest that most potential migrants would prefer to move outside the region but, for whatever reason, end up migrating within LAC instead. Abel and Sander (2014) find a similar result: intraregional flows within LAC are quite limited.

One reason intramigration flows may be so low is that government-imposed migration costs are high or destination country populations are not very welcoming to immigrants. To consider this possibility,

Bertoli and Mayda (2016) use the United Nations World Populations Policies Database to describe global immigration policies. In particular, these sources contain information about the perceptions government officials have about actual and desired migration policies. They show that for most of the Americas, including the United States, the predominant sense in 2011 was that current migration policies were designed to maintain the status quo—designed neither to lower nor to raise migration flows. Figure 4.7 shows that governments have relatively more agreement in LAC than in Asia (excluding the Gulf countries) and Europe. More see the current immigration levels as satisfactory, which coincides with the very low levels of immigration currently experienced by most LAC countries.

Government officials were also asked if they felt that the government's actual policies were, in fact, currently designed to raise, maintain, or lower current documented immigration levels. Figure 4.8 suggests that LAC government officials were the most likely to report that current government policies were designed to keep migration levels constant. Asian and European officials were more likely to report that migration policies are designed to reduce migration levels, which may be a response to higher migration flows.

The relatively comfortable government opinions about immigration are consistent with those expressed by citizens of LAC countries. Bertoli and Mayda (2016) show that LAC citizens have pro-immigration opinions that fare well compared to other countries in the world.[7] Together with the views of policy makers, these results suggest that LAC seems to be open to policies that might encourage additional intraregional migration.

This relatively pro-immigration sentiment notwithstanding, policy efforts to attract migrants to LAC may still be subject to difficulties if not managed carefully (see box 4.1 for a discussion of migration considerations in trade agreements). The views held by those in LAC about migrants may be a result of the relatively low levels of migration in the region. In fact, countries that have relatively high immigration rates have less positive attitudes toward migrants than those with low immigration rates (figure 4.9). Hence, policy efforts to foster immigration can end up affecting public opinion in a way that could reverse the pro-immigration attitudes displayed by those in LAC up to now. To be sure, migration attitudes appear to be affected by other policy-related factors. Research prepared for this study shows that positive attitudes toward migrants are more common among the more educated population. This highlights the fact that the effectiveness of LAC's integration agenda is tightly linked to the effectiveness of structural reforms in areas such as education; as the rate of accumulation of human capital in LAC advances, attitudes toward immigration might soften.[8]

**FIGURE 4.7    Government views on current documented immigration levels**

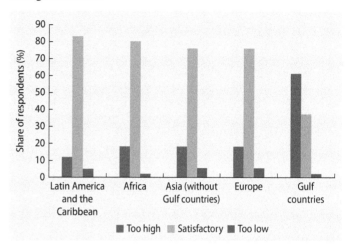

*Source:* Bertoli and Mayda 2016.
*Note:* Data include government's view on level of documented immigration, including work and family reunification, but not refugees or asylum.

**FIGURE 4.8    Government views on current immigration policies**

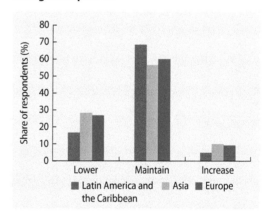

*Source:* Bertoli and Mayda 2016.
*Note:* See annex 1A for a list of countries in each region.

## Capital market integration

An extensive literature on CMI applies the three measures described above. Most of the current literature focuses on flows (the third measure described above) because most financial textbooks now present the idea of price equalization and responsiveness to shocks to be generally supported by empirical research. For example, Levi (2005)

### BOX 4.1    Labor mobility in trade agreements

Although trade agreements mainly focus on reducing barriers to the exchange of goods and services, some trade agreements also seek to facilitate migration. The European Union is perhaps the best-known example. Three of the largest regional agreements in LAC, however, also contain provisions to reduce barriers to migration. The Pacific Alliance explicitly states the goal of moving "progressively towards the free movement of goods, services, resources, and people." Mercosur provides citizens the legal right to obtain legal residence in other member countries and extends this right beyond full member countries

to include Bolivia, Chile, Peru, Colombia, and Ecuador. In 2001, the Andean Community implemented the Tarjeta Andina de Migracion, which was designed to harmonize migratory control documentation. In 2003 the Instrumento Andino de Migracion Laboral was approved with the goal of easing work-related migration. Additional measures were added to add portability to social security benefits. Preliminary estimates of a gravity-style migration model for this report suggest that trade agreements contributed positively to migration flows between countries in 2010, and less so in 2000.

---

**FIGURE 4.9    Anti-immigration views and immigration rates in selected LAC countries**

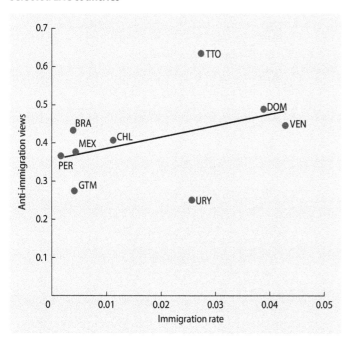

*Sources:* World Bank calculations from Bertoli and Mayda 2016 and from World Value Survey Data and World Development Indicators.
*Note:* The extent of anti-immigration views is captured by the share of the population that responds that its country should "prohibit people coming here from other countries" or that it should "place strict limits on the number of foreigners who can come here." See annex 3A, table 3A.2, for country acronyms.

has shifted toward describing the effects of CMI (that is, why CMI matters) and evaluating the flows.

## How integrated are LAC capital markets? Evidence from flows

LAC embarked on financial liberalization in the 1990s. Financial liberalization at that time was motivated by the Brady Plan, which started with Treasury Secretary Nicholas Brady of the George H.W. Bush administration in 1989. Rojas-Suárez, Galindo, and Izquierdo (2010) suggest that LAC was second only to the developed countries as the most financially open region in the world (see box 4.2). Chinn and Ito's (2006) index of financial openness, which is a de jure measure, is based on the IMF's *Annual Report on Exchange Arrangements and Exchange Restrictions* and shows that Argentina, Colombia, Honduras, and República Bolivariana de Venezuela were outliers among otherwise significantly liberalizing countries.

Unfortunately, the index of financial openness is not available after 2006. IMF (2016) reports alternative measures of CMI and finds very different results for recent years. IMF (2016) suggests that, rather than being quite liberalized, LAC financial markets are fragmented and often closed. One reason for the difference in

suggests that covered interest rate parity (CIRP) is generally supported and that deviations that occur as a result of crises or other macroeconomic phenomena are corrected relatively quickly. As a result, the literature

## BOX 4.2    The Pacific Alliance and MILA

The presidents of Chile, Colombia, Mexico, and Peru signed the Lima Agreement on April 28, 2011, to promote integration between the four countries. The agreement came into force July 20, 2015. This agreement took over the Integrated Securities Markets in the Latin America Integrated Market initiative (MILA) that was announced in September 2009 and launched in May 2011, and that was designed to unite the stock market exchanges of Colom-

bia, Chile, and Peru. Mexico joined in December 2014. Through 2015, the trading volume remained small relative to the Mexican and Brazilian stock exchanges, but the agreement is seen as a step toward deeper financial integration in LAC. See IMF (2016) for more details. Overall, MILA should be seen as an effort to improve the investment climate rather than as a way to replace investment from outside the region with investment within the region.

**FIGURE 4.10    Average number of bilateral investment treaties by region**

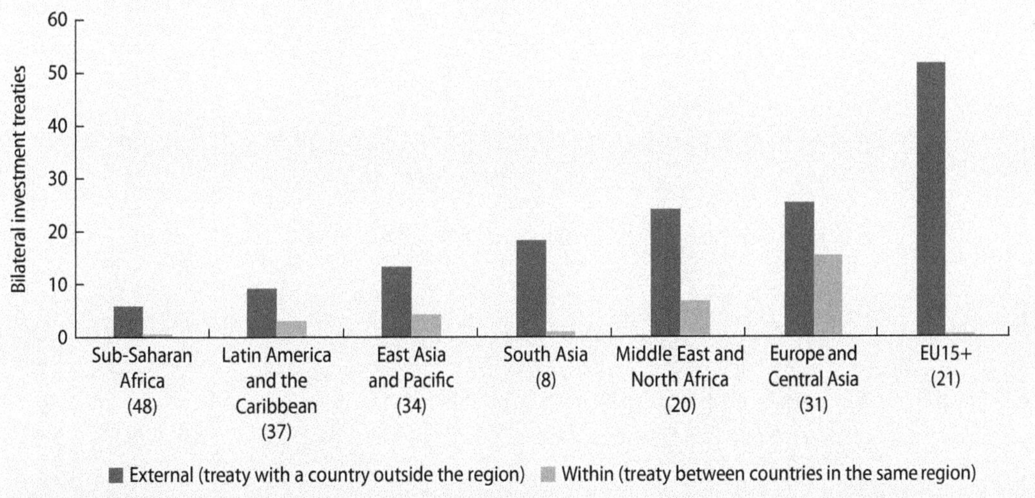

Source: World Bank calculations, based on data on international investment agreements from the United Nations Conference on Trade and Development (UNCTAD).
Note: "External" represents a bilateral investment treaty (BIT) with a country outside of the region. "Within" represents a BIT between countries in the same region. The numbers here represent averages for each region. See annex 1A for a list of countries in each region.

views is that the measures used to evaluate CMI are numerous and varied.

Rojas-Suárez, Galindo, and Izquierdo (2010) also describe the evolution of the de facto measures developed by Lane and Milesi-Ferretti (2008). One of these de facto measures is the sum of external asset stocks and external liabilities divided by GDP. This measure steadily increases from 1970 to 2007. When combined with Chin and Ito's de jure measure, this measure shows that LAC is one of the most

financially integrated regions of the world (again, second only to the developed countries). Further evidence of the de jure integration follows from the number of bilateral investment treaties (BITs) LAC countries have signed. Figure 4.10 shows that, although LAC has fewer BITs with partners outside the region than most other regions (on average), the average country in the region has a relatively large number of BITs with regional partners. Other measures, such as the participation of foreign banks in the economy, exhibit much more heterogeneity across LAC.

IMF (2016) argues that LAC's de facto financial integration remains quite low. Using international investment positions (IIP), one common indicator of de facto financial market integration, they show that assets plus liabilities as a share of GDP have not increased over the last decade. In addition, LAC has gained only a relatively small 3–5 percent of cross-border claims held by Bank for International Settlements (BIS) banks. FDI data also show that LAC country participation is relatively low. The low levels of financial integration showcased in IMF (2016) are robust to controlling for the level of development, trade openness, and the quality of the institutional framework.

The differences in measures of CMI suggest that additional research is needed. The next section presents some new research on CMI in LAC.

## New evidence of CMI in LAC

UNCTAD (2016) suggests that financial flows to most developing countries have been increasing but that flows to LAC have remained relatively flat. Didier, Llovet-Montanes, and Schmukler (2016) extend the analysis of de la Torre et al. (2015) and suggest that, although integration remains low,

**FIGURE 4.11   LAC investments to and from the rest of the world**

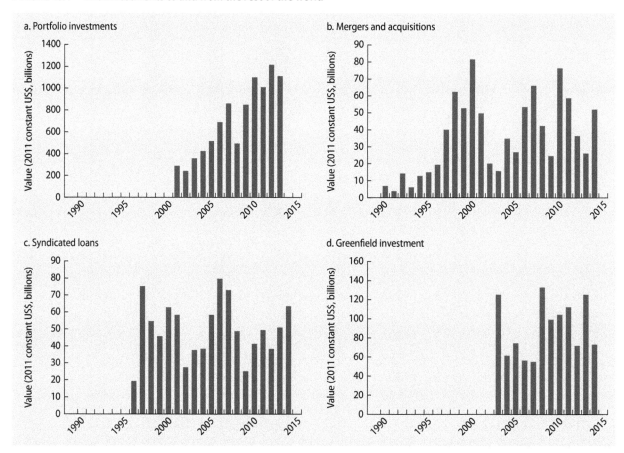

*Source:* Didier, Llovet-Montanes, and Schmukler 2016.
*Note:* See annex 1A for a list of countries in this region.

levels are increasing. Figure 4.11 shows that portfolio investment has been increasing for most of the 2000s. Average greenfield investment levels were higher in the 2008–14 period than in the 2002–07 period. Mergers and acquisitions and syndicated loans exhibit more procyclical patterns.

Perhaps the main finding from Didier, Llovet-Montanes, and Schmukler (2016) is that the measures of financial integration indicate much stronger integration, at least in terms of flows, with the North (the developed countries) than within LAC. Furthermore, perhaps consistent with the differences in development status, LAC tends to have positive net inflows, especially

from the North, as shown in figure 4.12. Figure 4.13 shows that LAC countries send less in investments than do EAP countries. LAC countries also have fewer intraregional investments than other major regions, especially EAP countries. Figure 4.14 compares the intraregional investments (measured as intraregional investments over the region's GDP). Aside from the North, which remains highest in all categories except greenfield investment, EAP and MENA countries tend to have the highest rates when compared to ECA, SAR, and SSA.

Figure 4.15 shows that the LAC countries are much more engaged with the North and much less with their own region than

**FIGURE 4.12    LAC net investments**

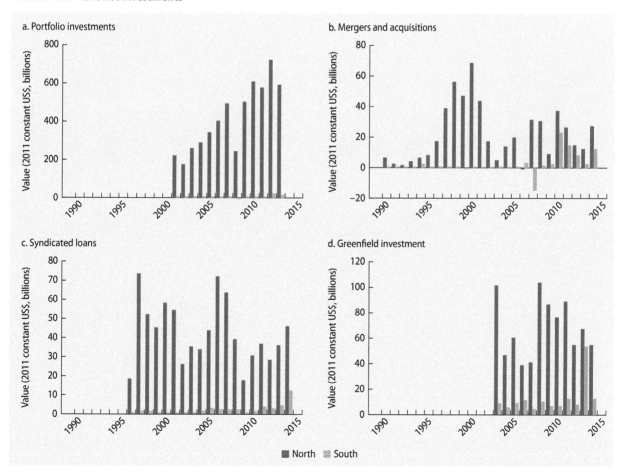

*Source:* Didier, Llovet-Montanes, and Schmukler 2016.
*Note:* See annex 1A for a list of countries in this region.

**FIGURE 4.13   Investments to the rest of the world over regions' GDP**

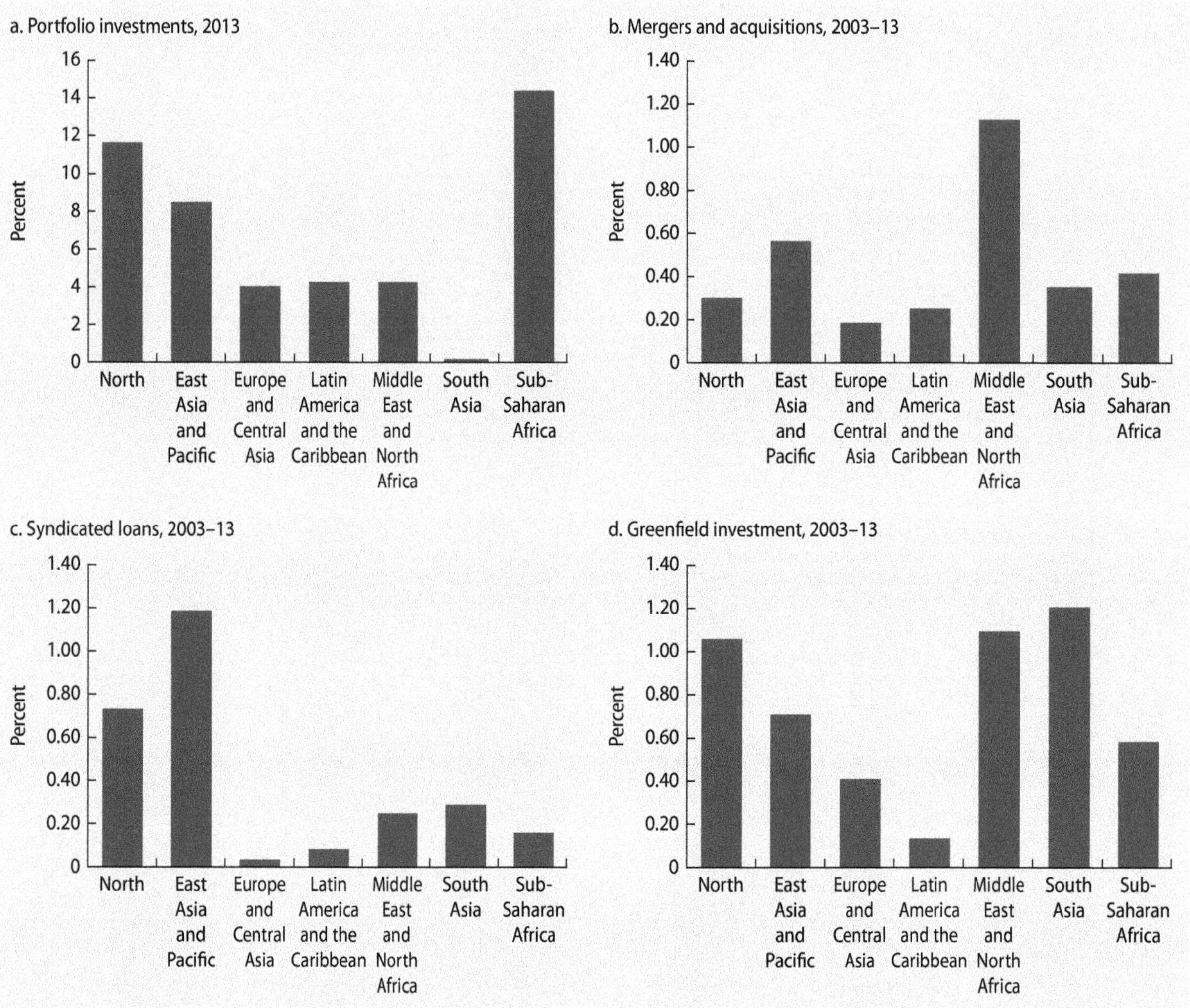

a. Portfolio investments, 2013

b. Mergers and acquisitions, 2003–13

c. Syndicated loans, 2003–13

d. Greenfield investment, 2003–13

*Source:* Didier, Llovet-Montanes, and Schmukler 2016.
*Note:* North = developed countries. See annex 1A for a list of countries in each region.

with other parts of the world. In particular, over 90 percent of LAC's syndicated loans are with the North. Other regions (EAP and MENA) have about two-thirds of that value, with the other third made of loans from within the region.

Although levels are low, the trends of intraregional investments seem to be increasing. This is especially true of portfolio investments and syndicated loans. Interregional investments seem to be increasing on the extensive margin for portfolio investments, mergers and acquisitions (M&A), syndicated

loans, and greenfield investments. De la Torre et al. (2015) show that LAC countries are also increasing their connections with the global South (developing countries). Across all four measures listed above, there is a greater connectivity to the South on the extensive margin (more countries with cross-border investments).

What drives these trends? To formally identify the contribution of different driving forces, a gravity model is often used. In this estimation, the flows of the variable described above are estimated as functions of the usual

**FIGURE 4.14    Intraregional investments over regions' GDP**

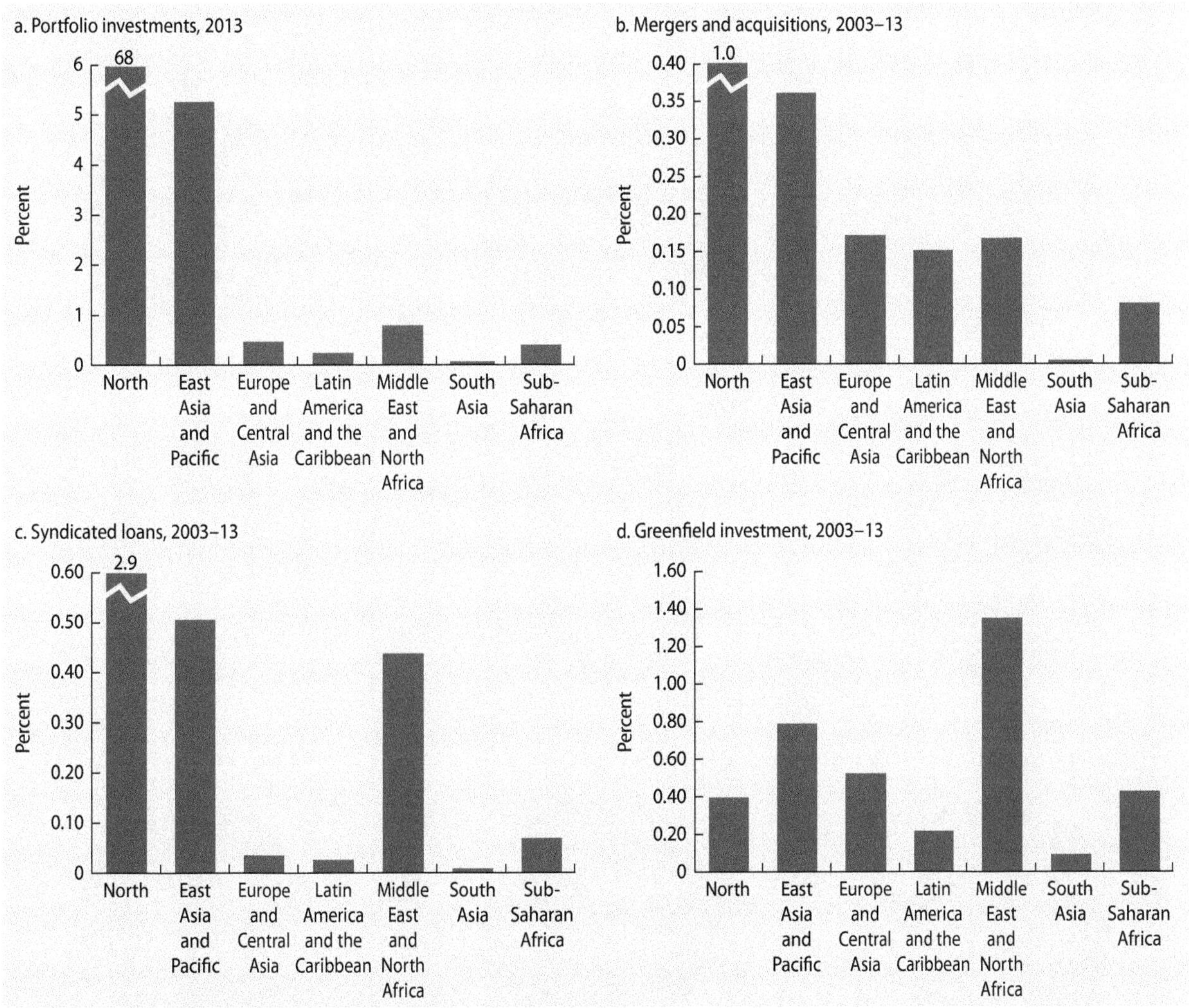

a. Portfolio investments, 2013

b. Mergers and acquisitions, 2003–13

c. Syndicated loans, 2003–13

d. Greenfield investment, 2003–13

*Source:* Didier, Llovet-Montanes, and Schmukler 2016.
*Note:* North = developed countries. See annex 1A for a list of countries in each region.

control variables found in gravity models, such as distance, time, language, common currency, and legal origins. Data representing the stock of portfolio assets at the bilateral level come from the IMF's Coordinated Portfolio Investment Survey (CPIS).[9] These data cover 2001–13 for 72 source countries and include information for more than 200 receiving countries. The data also include public and private sector holders of debt and equity. The data for transaction-level M&A and the flow of FDI come from SDC Platinum

and cover the 1990–2014 period for more than 130 source countries and more than 160 receiving countries.[10] Data for greenfield investment are transaction-level announced greenfield FDI from the *Financial Times'* FDiMarkets.[11] These data cover 2003–14 for more than 150 source countries and more than 190 receiving countries. The transaction-level syndicated loan data, from SDC Platinum, cover 1996–2014 for over 110 source countries and more than 180 receiving countries. For this analysis, all

**FIGURE 4.15    LAC's financial engagement with other regions**

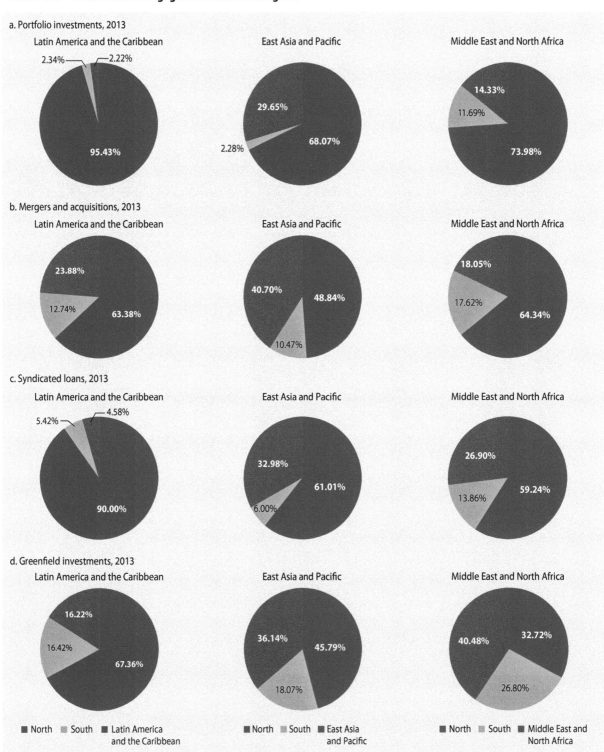

a. Portfolio investments, 2013

b. Mergers and acquisitions, 2013

c. Syndicated loans, 2013

d. Greenfield investments, 2013

*Source:* Didier, Llovet-Montanes, and Schmukler 2016.
*Note:* North and South refer to developed and developing countries, respectively. See annex 1A for a list of countries in each region.

transaction-level data are aggregated to the country level. The values of the dependent variables are the pairwise flow or stock in millions of 2011 U.S. dollars.

The empirical approach starts with the familiar gravity equation from the international trade literature. The base model of the levels of flows $x_{k,t}^{ij}$ is:

$$x_{k,t}^{ij} = exp\left(c_{k,t}^{i} + d_{k,t}^{j} + B_{k,t}b^{ij}\right) + e_{t}^{ij}. \quad (4.7)$$

In this specification, $c_{k,t}^{i}$ is an origin fixed effect (the push variable) for county $i$ and flow-type $k$ at time $t$, $d_{k,t}^{j}$ is the destination fixed effect (the pull variable) for country $j$ and flow-type $k$ at time $t$, $b^{ij}$ is a vector of bilateral variables between $i$ and $j$ (listed below), $B_{k,t}$ is the (transposed) coefficient vector, and $e_{t}^{ij}$ is the regression residual. As in the standard gravity equation, we include the standard bilateral variables: distance (measured as the logarithm of the distance between origin and destination), language (a binary variable equal to 1 if origin and destination share the same language, and 0 otherwise), and colonial link (a binary variable equal to 1 if origin and destination share a colonial link, 0 otherwise). The model is estimated using the Poisson Pseudo-Maximum Likelihood (PPML) estimator to estimate the differences of within-region flows across regions.[12] That is, the first estimates are the within-region effect (holding other variables constant), and the within-region effects across regions are estimated next. The regions follow the description above. The main results, therefore, start with the specification in (4.7), but add seven same-region dummy variables.

Figure 4.16 shows the estimates of the distance elasticity from annual regressions for each of the four capital flow categories. The coefficients are negative, which suggests that distance discourages financial flows. Some of the estimates seem to vary a great deal in the earlier years, but all four series seem to converge in the later years. The main point of figure 4.16, perhaps, is that the distance estimates are largely stable, which implies that there is little, if any,

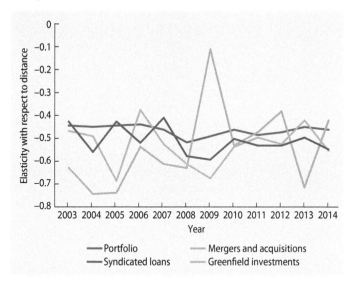

**FIGURE 4.16**   **PPML estimates of the effect of distance in financial flows, 2003–14**

*Source:* World Bank calculations, from Didier, Llovet-Montanes, and Schmukler 2016.
*Note:* PPML = Poisson Pseudo-Maximum Likelihood (estimator).

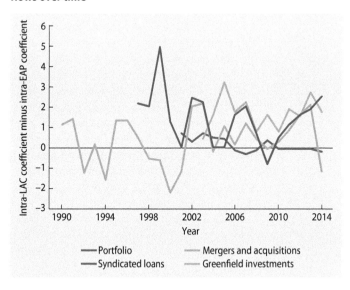

**FIGURE 4.17**   **The difference between intra-LAC and intra-EAP flows over time**

*Source:* World Bank calculations, from Didier, Llovet-Montanes, and Schmukler 2016.
*Note:* EAP = East Asia and Pacific; LAC = Latin America and the Caribbean. See annex 1A for a list of countries in each region.

change in the role of distance over time. In other words, the financial world does not appear to be shrinking over this period.

The main messages of the PPML estimations are summarized in figure 4.17.

It contains the estimated differences between the intra-LAC coefficient (which measures the relative importance of intra-LAC capital flows relative to flows out of LAC) and the intra-EAP coefficient for each of the four financial flow variables. Negative values (below zero on the vertical axis) are those in which intraregional exchange is more important in EAP, whereas positive values suggest that intraregional exchange is more important in LAC. There are several key lessons. The first is that intraregional exchange of portfolio investments is much larger in EAP, but intraregional exchange of greenfield and syndicated loans is more prominent in LAC. LAC, in contrast, gets much more portfolio investment from the North than from the rest of the LAC region. The second is that there seems to be little change over time. The differences in the estimated role of intraregional flows within the regions seem largely stable (with the possible exception of portfolio investment since the financial crisis).

The extensive margin analysis, which is based on probit estimations of whether or not a country has an active relationship with another country, suggests that in most regions intraregional relationships are usually more important than interregional relationships. Not for LAC, however. All four measures of capital flows suggest that intraregional relationships are fewer than interregional relationships. Trend analysis shows no clear pattern of catching up. The intraregional relationships are also relatively limited and are highly concentrated in Brazil, Mexico, and Chile. These three make up nearly 50 percent of the value of flows (intensive margin) for all four variables considered. They make up about 25–35 percent of the relationships on the extensive margin. These numbers might actually be considered small when one realizes that these three countries make up nearly 75 percent of the region's GDP.

## Implications of CMI

A relatively large literature examines the effects of financial liberalization and integration on other economic variables. A subset of this literature seeks to evaluate the balance between the benefits and costs of integration to estimate a net impact. For example, Rojas-Suárez, Galindo, and Izquierdo (2010) find that CMI is associated with real credit growth—even in the face of adverse economic shocks. Interest rates are also negatively associated with CMI, representing another benefit for consumers. The presence of foreign banks, however, seems to propagate foreign shocks (Rojas-Suárez, Galindo, and Izquierdo 2010), although the country of origin of the foreign banks seems to matter in the behavior of banks.

Others evaluate the effects on wage growth. For example, Chari, Henry, and Sasson (2012) and Henry and Sasson (2008) find that capital account liberalization leads to real wage growth. Clearly, capital and labor markets are linked, and capital market integration (CMI) can contribute to labor market integration. These effects, as well as the effects of migration, trade, and other forces, are either implicitly or explicitly the focus of studies and measures of labor market integration.

Finally, an extensive literature assesses the impact of FDI and multinational corporations (MNCs) on a country's growth. The broad argument is that FDI and MNCs can affect a country's growth by generating knowledge spillovers to local firms through a number of mechanisms. In particular, the literature has highlighted backward links (Javorcik 2004 and Rodriguez-Clare 1996), imitation by local firms, and worker turnover (Poole 2013) as some of the mechanisms through which MNCs can lead to productivity gains in local firms. These gains, however, may depend on the home country of the MNC. The literature emphasizes that knowledge diffusion and spillovers are more likely between countries that are close, both in level of development and geographically (Bravo-Ortega, Cusolito, and Lederman 2016; Kokko, Zejan, and Tansini 2001). Hence, FDI and MNCs from nearby countries and countries with similar levels of development are expected to lead to larger spillovers. In the specific case of LAC, the benefits of proximity may be dampened by the fact that MNCs from the region underperform relative to those from high-income countries. They invest less in R&D and have worse managerial practices relative to their peers from other regions, thus limiting the scope for spillovers and knowledge diffusion. This, in turn, implies that, for LAC to fully accrue the benefits from regional CMI, the region needs to solve structural factors such as the relatively low productivity and investment in innovation observed in firms in LAC, even MNCs.

Regional agreements can yield efficiency gains in other dimensions and, if enacted jointly, can magnify the growth and stability benefits from global capital integration. For example, the Mercado Integrado Latinoamericano (MILA) provides a unified set of norms and reduces transaction costs for investors seeking opportunities in countries of the Pacific Alliance, thus making it a more appealing investment option. Similarly, regional agreements can facilitate coordination in the provision of incentives to foreign capital among countries in the region and avoid a race to the bottom where countries sacrifice revenue as they compete for FDI. As a result, such coordination has the potential to maximize the positive impact of foreign capital across the region. The bottom line is that initiatives such as MILA should be seen as efforts to improve the collective investment climate, rather than as efforts to increase intraregional capital flows at the expense of foreign investment from the rest of the world.

## Conclusions

International factor market integration is important because it has the potential to affect growth and volatility. In the case of LAC, the results from the literature and from original analyses suggest that factor market integration within LAC is modest. Labor and capital markets are much more focused toward the North than within LAC, which sets LAC apart from other regions of the world.

It is very possible that the pattern of factor market integration—that is, the overall focus on the North—observed in LAC bodes very well for long-run growth. Rodrik (2011) evaluates the rate of convergence in particular between developed and developing countries. One of the key messages is that growth in developing countries does not necessarily depend on the growth of developed countries, but rather on the differences in productivity between the two. While Rodrik does not believe that such convergence is automatic—he advocates activist industrial policies—his analysis has implications for integration. If the goal is to close the productivity gap, then it seems that the kind of integration regions pursue would potentially affect their ability to close this productivity gap. Integration with the North may contain higher potential for the positive benefits of international integration and bring long-run benefits to regional growth.

That said, however, the results presented in this chapter suggest that there are still significant gains to be made from fostering LAC factor market (especially labor market) integration. The mean differentials across countries are much larger than those found within countries, and the rate of convergence to the equilibrium differentials is much slower than observed within countries. One possible reason for this might be the relatively small amount of intraregional immigration. Fostering further labor market integration may be another opportunity to promote growth and efficiency. Current agreements have taken important steps to facilitate labor market integration, and continuing in this direction seems to offer the promise of additional gains.

Moreover, the positive benefits from integrating with the North may depend on regional agreements. For example, deeper regional labor market integration could make investment in LAC countries more attractive because foreign firms could tap into a larger pool of talent. Similarly, as argued above, investment agreements that harmonize the rules and procedures governing investments in the region can make LAC as a whole a more attractive destination for foreign investors.

## Notes

1. Annex 1A presents detailed explanation of the regional classifications used throughout the report, along with the list of countries included in each region.
2. The data are PPP-valued GDP per capita in constant (2011) dollars from the World Development Indicators.
3. There may be too many papers to list here, but some examples include Broda and Weinstein (2006); Engel and Rogers (1996); and Robertson, Kumar, and Dutkowsky (2009).
4. Argentina, Bolivia, Brazil, Chile, Colombia, Costa Rica, Dominican Republic, Ecuador, El Salvador, Honduras, Mexico, Nicaragua, Panama, Paraguay, Peru, and Uruguay.
5. U.S. results are based on monthly data from the Monthly Outgoing Rotation Groups (MORG) of the Current Population Surveys.
6. Mexican results are based on quarterly household surveys from the national employment and occupation surveys (ENOE for its Spanish acronym).
7. Data on attitudes toward immigrants come from the World Value Surveys.
8. Between 2000 and 2014, the tertiary school enrollment rate in LAC increased from 20 to 40 percent. See Ferreyra et al. (forthcoming) for an analysis of the challenges facing university education in the region.
9. For more information on CPIS, see http://data.imf.org/?sk=B981B4E3-4E58-467E-9B90-9DE0C3367363.
10. For more information on SDC Platinum, see the Thomson Reuters website at http://financial.thomsonreuters.com/en/products/data-analytics/market-data/sdc-platinum-financial-securities.html.
11. FDiMarkets provides cross-border investment data. See https://www.fdimarkets.com.
12. Gourieroux, Monfort, and Trognon (1984) and Santos Silva and Tenreyro (2010) illustrate the development and application of the PPML estimator.

## References

Abel, G. J., and N. Sander. 2014. "Quantifying Global International Migration Flows." *Science* 343 (6178): 1520–22.

Acemoglu, D., and F. Zilibotti, 1997. "Was Prometheus Unbound by Chance? Risk, Diversification, and Growth." *Journal of Political Economy* 105 (4): 709–51.

Allen, Robert C. 1990. "Real Incomes in the English Speaking World, 1879–1913." In *Labour Market Evolution*, edited by G. Grantham and M. McKinnon, 107–38. London: Routledge.

Artuc, E., Z. L. Kone, and C. Ozden. 2016. "Regional Migration Patterns in Latin America." Background paper prepared for this report.

Baltagi, B., P. Demitriades, and S. Law. 2009. "Financial Development and Openness: Evidence from Panel Data." *Journal of Development Economics* 89 (2): 285–96.

Bonfiglioli, A. 2008. "Financial Integration, Productivity and Capital Accumulation." *Journal of International Economics* 76 (2): 337–55.

Ben-David, Dan. 1993. "Equalizing Exchange: Trade Liberalization and Income Convergence." *The Quarterly Journal of Economics* 108 (3): 653–79.

Berkowitz, Daniel, and David N. DeJong. 2003. "Regional Integration: An Empirical Assessment of Russia." *Journal of Urban Economics* 53 (3): 541–59.

Bertoli, Simone, Jesús Fernandez-Huertas Moraga, and F. Ortega. 2011. "Immigration Policies and the Ecuadorian Exodus." *World Bank Economic Review* 25 (1): 57–76.

Bertoli, Simone, and Jesús Fernandez-Huertas Moraga. 2013. "Multilateral Resistance to Migration." *Journal of Development Economics* 102: 79–100.

Bertoli, Simone, and Anna Maria Mayda. 2016. "Intra-regional Migration in Latin America and The Carribean." Background paper prepared for this report.

Bloom, David E., and Waseem Noor. 1995. "Is an Integrated Regional Labour Market Emerging in East and Southeast Asia?" Department of Economics, Columbia University, New York.

Boyer, G. R. and T. J. Hatton. 1994. "Regional Labour Market Integration in England and Wales, 1850–1913." In *Labor Market Evolution: The Economic History of Market Integration, Wage Flexibility and the Employment Relation*, edited by George Grantham and Mary MacKinnon, 84–106. London: Routledge.

Bravo-Ortega, C., A. P. Cusolito, and D. Lederman. 2016. "Faraway or Nearby? Domestic and International Spillovers in Patenting and Product Innovation." Policy Research Working Paper 7828, World Bank, Washington, DC.

Broda, Christian, and David E. Weinstein. 2006. "Globalization and the Gains from Variety." *Quarterly Journal of Economics* 121 (2): 541–85.

Chari, Anusha, Peter Blair Henry, and Diego Sasson. 2012. "Capital Market Integration and Wages." *American Economic Journal: Macroeconomics, American Economic Association* 4 (2): 102–32.

Chiquiar, D. 2005. "Why Mexico's Regional Income Convergence Broke Down." *Journal of Development Economics* 77 (1): 257–75.

Chinn, M., and D. Ito. 2006. "What Matters for Financial Development? Capital Controls, Institutions, and Interactions." *Journal of Development Economics* 81 (1): 163–92.

Dawson, P. J., and P. K. Dey. 2002. "Testing for the Law of One Price: Rice Market Integration in Bangladesh." *Journal of International Development* 14 (4): 473–84.

De la Torre, Augusto, Tatiana Didier, Alain Iza, Daniel Lederman, and Sergio Schmukler. 2015. *Latin America and the Rising South: Changing World, Changing Priorities.* Washington, DC: World Bank.

Didier, T., R. Llovet-Montanes, and S. Schmukler. 2016. "Benchmarking Intra-Regional Financial Flows in Latin America." Background paper prepared for this report.

Docquier, F., J. Machado, and K. Sekkat. 2015. "Efficiency Gains from Liberalizing Labor Mobility." *The Scandinavian Journal of Economics* 117 (2): 303–46.

Eichengreen, B., and M. Mussa. 1998. "Capital Account Liberalization: Theoretical and Practical Aspects." IMF Occasional Paper 172, International Monetary Fund, Washington, DC.

Engel, Charles, and John H. Rogers. 1996. "How Wide Is the Border?" *American Economic Review* 86: 1112–25.

Ferreyra, M.M., C. Avitale, C., J. Botero, F. Haimovich Paz, and S. Urzua. Forthcoming. *At a Crossroad: Higher Education in Latin America and the Caribbean.* World Bank: Washington, D.C.

Frankel, Jeffrey A., and David Romer. 1999. "Does Trade Cause Growth?" *American Economic Review* 89 (3): 379–99.

Galindo, A., A. Micco, and A. Powell. 2004. "Loyal Lenders or Fickle Financiers: Foreign Banks in Latin America." Research Department Working Paper Series 529, Inter-American Development Bank, Washington, DC.

Ghosh, Madhusudan. 2003. "Spatial Integration of Wheat Markets in India: Evidence from Cointegration Tests." *Oxford Development Studies* 31 (2): 159–71.

Gourieroux, C., A. Monfort, and A. Trognon. 1984 "Pseudo Maximum Likelihood Methods: Applications to Poisson Models." *Econometrica* 52 (3): 701–20.

Gourinchas, P. O., and O. Jeanne. 2009. "Capital Mobility and Reform." *2009 Meeting Papers* 107, Society for Economic Dynamics.

Guerriero, Marta. 2012. "Labour Share of Income Around the World: Evidence from a Panel Dataset." IDPM Development Economics and Public Policy Working Paper Series 32/2012, Institute for Development Policy and Management, University of Manchester, U.K.

Hendry, D. F., and N. R. Ericsson. 1991. "Modeling the Demand for Narrow Money in the United Kingdom and the United States." *European Economic Review* 35 (4): 833–81.

Henry, P. B., and D. Sasson. 2008. "Capital Account Liberalization, Real Wages, and Productivity," NBER Working Paper 13880, National Bureau of Economic Research, Cambridge, MA.

IMF (International Monetary Fund). 2016. "Financial Integration in Latin America." IMF Policy Paper, IMF, Washington, DC, March.

Javorcik, B. S. 2004. "Does Foreign Investment Increase the Productivity of Domestic Firms? In Search of Spillovers through Backward Linkages." *American Economic Review* 94 (3): 131–54.

Knetter, Michael M., and Matthew J. Slaughter. 2001. "Measuring Product-Market Integration." In *Topics in Empirical International Economics: A Festschrift in Honor of Robert E. Lipsey,* edited by Magnus Blomstrom and Linda S. Goldberg, 15–46. University of Chicago Press.

Kokko, A., M. Zejan, and R. Tansini. 2001. "Trade Regimes and Spillover Effects of FDI: Evidence from Uruguay." *Weltwirtschaftliches Archiv* 137 (1): 124–49.

Kose, A., E. Prasad, K. Rogoff, and S. Wei. 2009. "Financial Globalization: A Reappraisal." *IMF Staff Papers* 56 (1): 8–62.

Lane, P., and G. M. Milesi-Ferretti. 2008. "International Investment Patterns." *Review of Economics and Statistics* 90 (3): 538–49.

Lederman, Daniel, and Raymond Robertson. 2016. "Economic and Wage Convergence across Latin America 1990–2013." Policy Research Working Paper 7847, World Bank: Washington, DC.

Levi, Maurice D. 2005. *International Finance*, 4th Edition. New York: Routledge.

Levine, R. 1996. "Foreign Banks, Financial Development, and Economic Growth." *In International Financial Markets*. Washington, DC: American Enterprise Institute.

Levine, R., and S. Zervos. 1998. "Capital Control Liberalization and Stock Market Development." *World Development* 26 (7): 1169–83.

McCallum, John. 1995. "National Borders Matter: Canada-U.S. Regional Trade Patterns." *The American Economic Review* 85: 615–23.

Michaels, Guy. 2008. "The Effect of Trade on the Demand for Skill: Evidence from the Interstate Highway System." *The Review of Economics and Statistics* 90 (4): 683–701.

Mohanty, Samarendu, and Suchada Langley. 2003. "The Effects of Various Policy Regimes in the Integration of North American Grain Markets." *Canadian Journal of Agricultural Economics/Revue canadienne d'agroeconomie* 51 (1): 109–20.

Mohanty, Samarendu, E. Peterson, and Damell B. Smith. 1996. "Relationships between US and Canadian Wheat Prices: Cointegration and Error Correction Approach." *Canadian Journal of Agricultural Economics/Revue canadienne d'agroeconomie* 44 (3): 265–76.

Morgan, D. P., and P. E. Strahan. 2003. "Foreign Bank Entry and Business Volatility: Evidence from U.S. States and other Countries." NBER Working Paper 9710, National Bureau of Economic Research, Cambridge, MA.

Noguer, M., and M. Siscart. 2005. "Trade Raises Income: A Precise and Robust Result." *Journal of International Economics* 65 (2): 447–60.

O'Rourke, Kevin. 1994. "Did Labour Flow Uphill? International Migration and Wage Rates in Twentieth Century Ireland." In *Labour Market Evolution*, edited by G. Grantham and M. McKinnon, 139–60. London: Routledge.

Paul, Rodney J, Dragan Miljkovic, and Viju Ipe. 2001. "Market Integration in US Gasoline Markets." *Applied Economics* 33 (10), 1335–40.

Poole, J. 2013. "Knowledge Transfers from Multinational to Domestic Firms: Evidence from Worker Mobility." *Review of Economics and Statistics* 95 (2): 393–406.

Robertson, Raymond. 2000. "Wage Shocks and North American Labor-Market Integration." *American Economic Review* 90 (4): 742–64.

Robertson, Raymond, Anil Kumar, and Donald Dutkowsky. 2009. "Purchasing Power Parity and Aggregation Bias in a Developing Country: The Case of Mexico." *Journal of Development Economics* 90 (2): 237–43.

Rodriguez-Clare, A. 1996. "Multinationals, Linkages, and Economic Development." *American Economic Review* 86 (4): 852–73.

Rodrik, Dani. 2011. "The Future of Economic Convergence." NBER Working Paper 17400, National Bureau of Economic Research, Cambridge, MA, September.

Rojas-Suárez, Liliana, Arturo J. Galindo, and Alejandro Izquierdo. 2010. "Financial Integration and Foreign Banks in Latin America: Do They Amplify External Financial Shocks?" Center for Global Development Working Paper 203, Center for Global Development, Washington, DC.

Rosenbloom, Joshua L. 1990. "One Market or Many? Labor Market Integration in the Late Nineteenth-Century United States." *The Journal of Economic History* 50 (01): 85–107.

Rothenberg, Winifred B. 1988. "The Emergence of Farm Labor Markets and the Transformation of the Rural Economy: Massachusetts, 1750–1855." *The Journal of Economic History* 48 (3): 537–66.

Santos Silva, J. M. C., and S. Tenreyro. 2010. "On the Existence of the Maximum Likelihood Estimates in Poisson Regression." *Economics Letters* 107 (2): 310–12.

Schäfer, Andreas, and Thomas Steger. 2014. "Journey into the Unknown? Economic Consequences of Factor Market Integration under Increasing Returns to Scale." *Review of International Economics* 22 (4): 783–807.

UNCTAD (United Nations Conference on Trade and Development). 2016. *World Investment Report 2016—Investor Nationality: Policy Challenges*. Geneva: UNCTAD.